COME AND HEAR

ADAM KIRSCH

Come and Hear

What I saw in my seven-and-a-half-year journey through the Talmud

Brandeis University Press / Waltham, Massachusetts

Brandeis University Press
© 2021 by Adam Kirsch
Manufactured in the United States of America
Designed and composed in Arno Pro and
    Source Sans Variable by Mindy Basinger Hill

For permission to reproduce any of the material in this book,
contact Brandeis University Press, 415 South Street,
Waltham MA 02453, or visit brandeisuniversitypress.com

Library of Congress Cataloging-in-Publication Data

Names: Kirsch, Adam, 1976– author.
Title: Come and hear : what I saw in my seven-and-a-half-year journey
    through the Talmud / Adam Kirsch.
Description: First edition. | Waltham : Brandeis University Press, 2021. |
    Includes index. | Summary: "Mainly intended for readers who have little
    sense of what the Talmud actually is, Kirsch explores the Talmud as a critic
    and journalist. Maybe the best way to describe this book is as a kind of
    travelogue—a report on what Kirsch saw during his seven-and-a-half-year
    journey through the Talmud"—Provided by publisher.
Identifiers: LCCN 2021027680 (print)
    LCCN 2021027681 (ebook)
    ISBN 9781684580675 (cloth)
    ISBN 9781684580682 (ebook)
Subjects: LCSH: Talmud—Study and teaching.
Classification: LCC BM504 .K47 2021 (print)
    LCC BM504 (ebook)
    DDC 296.1/206—dc23

LC record available at https://lccn.loc.gov/2021027680
LC ebook record available at https://lccn.loc.gov/2021027681

5   4   3   2   1

CONTENTS

II SEDER NASHIM
Marriage and Divorce

INTRODUCTION

In August 2012, I read about an extraordinary event that took place at New Jersey's MetLife Stadium. Where crowds usually gather to watch the Jets and Giants play football, some eighty thousand Orthodox Jews filled the seats to celebrate a religious and intellectual milestone. The Siyum HaShas, "the completion of the Talmud," marked the conclusion of the cycle of Daf Yomi, "daily page"—a study program in which Jews around the world read one page of Talmud every day for 2,711 days, about seven and a half years.

I knew about Daf Yomi, but I hadn't realized what a major phenomenon it had become. And the Siyum itself, with its wonderful incongruity—a scholarly achievement celebrated like the Super Bowl—was a striking demonstration of the dynamism and possibility of American Jewish life. Where else in Jewish history could so many Jews have come together so openly to celebrate the Talmud? I decided that when the next Siyum rolled around, in January 2020, I wanted to be part of it.

Most people who do Daf Yomi are Orthodox Jews, for whom it is both a learning opportunity and a devotional exercise. I lead a secular life, and my interest in the Talmud had a different source: as a student of Jewish literature and history, I came to realize that I couldn't fully explore these subjects without some knowledge of the Talmud. After all, for 1,500 years the Talmud shaped the way Jews thought and what they thought about. Talmud study was the most prestigious activity in Jewish society, a key to social advancement as well as a rigorous training in how to think, analyze, and argue. It was also reserved for men, as it still is in the ultra-Orthodox world; only in recent decades have other denominations encouraged women to study Talmud.

The amazing continuity of Judaism across time and space is owed in large part to the Talmud. Rabbi Akiva, who was martyred by the Romans in the second century CE, pondered some of the same halakhic issues that occupied Maimonides, who lived in Egypt in the twelfth century. In the twenty-first century, yeshiva students in Lakewood, New Jersey, are analyzing the very same problems, in part by consulting the words of Akiva and Maimonides.

The difference is that, in American Judaism today, those Talmud students are the exception rather than the rule. For the 90 percent of American Jews who are not Orthodox, the Talmud plays little or no role in their Jewish education. I grew up in a Conservative synagogue and attended many years of Hebrew school, and while I learned a good deal, I never encountered a page of Talmud. In a way this makes sense, because what differentiates Orthodox from non-Orthodox Judaism is their attitudes toward halakha or Jewish law, and the Talmud is the foundation of halakha. There's not much reason to spend years studying the Talmudic tractates on Shabbat observance or marriage and divorce if you don't believe that these laws are divinely inspired or personally binding.

I'm sure that if I had been exposed to Talmud study as a teenager, I would have had no patience for it. But as an adult I was more curious and less defensive—free to learn without feeling obligated to argue. Daf Yomi was a chance to fill the Talmud-sized gap in my understanding of Judaism. As a literary critic, I'm accustomed to grappling with difficult texts by writing about them, so I was delighted when the online magazine *Tablet* agreed to have me write a column about my Daf Yomi experience. I started right away, in the first week of August 2012, and kept writing on an almost weekly basis until the end of the thirteenth Daf Yomi cycle in January 2020.

When I was thinking about embarking on this long journey, I asked a Jewishly learned friend for advice. He said I should go ahead, as long as I kept in mind the difference between what I was doing and actual Talmud study. I knew the differences were profound. Daf Yomi sounds like, and is, a major commitment, but it was invented in 1923 as a popularizing method, a way of making Talmud study accessible to lay people. You can read a page of Talmud in an hour before or after work and get the gist. But yeshiva students pore over the Talmud ten hours a day; great scholars study it their whole lives.

What's more, I was reading the Talmud in English translation, rather than in the original Hebrew and Aramaic, and I was doing it alone, rather than with a teacher or study partner. Such an undertaking would hardly have been possible even a generation ago. But in the twenty-first century, the appetite for Talmud study—and the need for English-language help, even among religious students—has grown to the point that there are now two complete English translations of the Babylonian Talmud in print, as well as a free digital version available at Sefaria, the online Jewish library. Since I started Daf Yomi in 2012, there has been an explosion of digital resources for learners—calendars, summaries, discussion groups, audio and video lectures.

For my study, I used the Noe Edition of the Babylonian Talmud published by Koren, which is based on the modern Hebrew edition of the Talmud by the great Israeli scholar Rabbi Adin Steinsaltz. This version includes the original Hebrew and Aramaic text along with an English translation that clarifies its terse, ambiguous language. It also includes footnotes, diagrams, and illustrations, while omitting the many commentaries that appear on a traditional Talmud page, which turn it into a forum of voices from across the centuries.

Early in the Daf Yomi cycle, I had a chance to study a page with my cousin, who is much more observant than I am. As we read together on a bench in Central Park, it occurred to me that no one in our family had studied Talmud for a least a century, since our great-grandparents came to America. But here we were, taking it up again after what turned out to be a long interruption, rather than a permanent parting. I was learning Talmud in a very different spirit than Jews in the past, or devout Jews today; but I was still learning.

This book is mainly intended for readers who are in a similar position. I've found that introductory books about the Talmud, some of which I've benefited from greatly, generally fall into two categories. Academic studies like *The Talmud: A Biography* by Barry Scott Wimpfheimer and *Halakhah: The Rabbinic Idea of Law* by Chaim Saiman, both published in 2018, focus on the Talmud's historical development and its role in Judaism. On the other hand, works by rabbis, such as Abraham Cohen's *Everyman's Talmud*—first published in 1932 and still in print—draw on the Talmud to synthesize general statements of Jewish belief.

Both approaches illuminate why the Talmud matters, but they give little sense of what the Talmud actually *is*—how the text moves and what it thinks about, its preoccupations and insights, its moments of strangeness and profundity. That's what I hope to do in this book. I am no kind of expert on the Talmud, neither religious nor academic. But as a critic, I have some experience in exploring difficult texts and discussing what I found there, and why it matters. In fact, maybe the best way to describe this book is as a kind of travel writing—a report on what I saw during my seven-and-a-half-year journey through the Talmud.

The Talmud is full of verbal formulas—words and phrases that are used repeatedly in certain situations. One of them is "ta shma," Aramaic for "come and hear," which is used when a rabbi quotes an earlier authority to settle a dispute about the law. Beyond its technical meaning, however, "come and hear" captures something important about the ethos of the Talmud, which always wants to widen the circle of discussion rather than close it off. That's what I hope this book will do: help readers to come closer to the Talmud and hear some of the wise, complicated, and challenging things it has to say.

The Talmud is difficult to describe in a way that's both brief and meaningful. Usually we approach unfamiliar books by likening them to ones we already know, but there is no book that resembles the Talmud—it is its own genre. Almost anything you could say about it requires qualification. It's the most important Jewish text next to the Bible, but it's nothing like the Bible; it's the source of Jewish law, but it's not a law code. Jewish tradition gestures at the Talmud's amorphousness and scale by comparing it to a sea. You can't grasp the whole thing at once; you have to dive in and start swimming.

Still, it helps to start with a map. The Talmud is made up of two layers: the Mishna, which was written in Hebrew around the year 200 CE, and the Gemara, a commentary on the Mishna that was composed in Aramaic over the following three hundred years. On a standard Talmud page, the Hebrew text of the Mishna and the Aramaic text of the Gemara sit at the center. Each unit of the Mishna, referred to as "a mishna," is followed by a corresponding unit of Gemara that comments on it, known as a sugya. Often a few sentences of Mishna can give rise to many pages of Gemara. The standard pagination of the Talmud was established in the first printed edition, in the 1520s; a page number is followed by "a" or "b," to signify the front or back of the folio page. (A daf is made up of both sides of a page.)

The key to understanding the Talmud's unique structure is that both the Mishna and the Gemara were originally oral traditions, not written documents like the Torah. The Mishna was a collection of laws that had been passed down from teacher to student for generations; according to the traditional understanding, they were given to Moses on Mount Sinai at the same as the written Torah.

These laws were finally written down in the second century CE, at a time when Jewish society in the land of Israel was in ruins. The Jewish revolt against the Romans in 66–70 CE had ended in the destruction of the Temple, the ancient center of Jewish worship. A second revolt in 132–135 CE had also been crushed, resulting in the death and deportation of hundreds of thousands of Jews and the erasure of the name Judea from the map of the Roman Empire.

These catastrophes were comparable to the Holocaust in their political and religious consequences. Fearing that the chain of transmission of the oral Torah would be broken, the rabbis of the second century began to collect and systematize its laws. This process culminated in the redaction of the Mishna by Yehuda HaNasi—"Judah the Prince," the leading rabbi of his generation—who arranged the laws by subject matter into six large divisions called orders, subdivided into sixty-three tractates. The Mishna is the foundation of Jewish law to this day, though much of it deals with subjects that had no practical application after the destruction of the Temple, such as the laws of animal sacrifice.

The structure of the Mishna reflects its oral origins. Rather than simply stating the law, it records the teachings of various rabbinic authorities, known as tannaim, even when they conflict with one another. The view that has the force of law is usually stated first without attribution, or attributed to "the rabbis," while a dissenting view is attributed to the tanna who holds it. For instance, the Mishna records many disagreements between the school of Hillel and the school of Shammai, rival sages of the first century BCE. As a rule, the law follows the opinion of Hillel, but the opinion of Shammai is always recorded too. As the Mishna says, their disagreements were "for the sake of Heaven," so both views are sacred and deserving of study.

In other ways, too, the Mishna is more like the record of a discussion among experts than a law code. It doesn't state abstract principles in a systematic fashion; rather, principles emerge from the analysis of concrete problems. Thus tractate Shabbat doesn't begin by stating that it is prohibited to transfer items between a public domain and a private domain on Shabbat.

Rather, it imagines a situation in which someone in a public domain hands an item to someone in a private domain, or vice versa, and asks which of them is guilty of violating Shabbat.

These features of the Mishna—the plurality of opinions and the focus on concrete problems—invite further analysis and discussion. What are the general principles that govern the Mishna's rulings, and how could they be applied to new situations that the Mishna didn't anticipate? Can the opinions of different tannaim be harmonized? Can one area of law yield insights into an apparently unrelated area?

These kinds of questions were discussed in rabbinic academies for three centuries following the redaction of the Mishna. The record of these discussions is the Gemara, the second layer of the Talmud, which was organized and written down in the sixth century CE. Unlike the Mishna, the Gemara is written in Aramaic, the language actually spoken by Jews (and other peoples) in the Middle East at that time. By the third century, the center of Jewish life had shifted from Roman Palestine to Babylonia (present-day Iraq), which was part of the Persian Empire and enjoyed greater prosperity and stability. Both countries produced a Gemara to accompany the Mishna, but the Babylonian Talmud (the Bavli) is richer and more authoritative than the Palestinian Talmud (the Yerushalmi). When people refer simply to the Talmud, they mean the Babylonian Talmud.

In the Talmud there is Gemara on thirty-seven of the sixty-three Mishnaic tractates, including all the ones that deal with issues of continuing relevance—holidays, marriage and divorce, civil and criminal law, kashrut. The rabbis of the Gemara, known as amoraim, take the oral and plural qualities of the Mishna to a new level. They engage in vigorous debates—positing, refuting, citing proofs, bursting out with insults. They use thought experiments, sometimes bizarre ones, to test the limits of concepts—for instance, asking if it's permitted to build a sukka using a live elephant as one of the walls. They closely analyze the Torah, reading it against the grain to find support for their position. There were eight generations of amoraim and many names are cited in the Gemara, though a few predominate, including rival pairs such as Rav and Shmuel or Rava and Abaye.

As with any conversation, the tannaim and amoraim often digress from the main subject. When a sage is cited on one issue, the Talmud might take the opportunity to list his teachings on other matters, or tell stories about his life. Sometimes a rule that takes a certain grammatical form will lead to a discussion of unrelated rules that follow the same pattern. This means that while each tractate is nominally devoted to a certain subject, their names aren't always a guide to their actual contents (for instance, to find the laws of circumcision, you have to look in tractate Shabbat.) This unpredictability is one of the things that makes the Talmud so difficult to master; simply knowing where to find the subject you're interested in requires a feat of memory.

Most of the rabbis' discussion is about halakha or law, but sometimes it swerves into aggada or storytelling. This category includes all kinds of non-legal talk: anecdotes about the personal habits of famous sages, miracle tales, speculations about the nature of the cosmos, ethical maxims, Biblical homilies. Only about ten percent of the Talmud is devoted to aggada, but it's the source of the best-known Talmudic sayings, and it's where the rabbis express their ethical and spiritual ideas most directly.

This heterogeneity means that the Talmud is a difficult text to pin down. A discussion doesn't always end in a clear statement of what the law actually is. Questions are often raised but not conclusively answered; sometimes the rabbis adjourn a debate with the formula "let it stand," meaning that they can't reach a decision. This complexity and ambiguity makes it difficult to be sure "what the Talmud says" about a given issue.

Still less can one assume that what the Talmud says is what Judaism says, since the process of halakhic interpretation didn't end in the sixth century. The Talmud, like the Bible, permits polygamy; according to tractate Ye-vamot, a man can have up to four wives, the most he can expect to satisfy sexually. Islam also permitted polygamy, and Jews living under Islamic rule continued the practice. But Ashkenazi Jews, living in Christian Europe where monogamy was the norm, gave up polygamy around the year 1000 by rabbinic edict. Slavery, too, was common when the Talmud was composed but later disappeared from Judaism.

To know the halakha on a particular subject, then, Jews today don't consult the Talmud but the Shulchan Aruch, a practical and systematic digest written in the sixteenth century. Still, codifications like the Shulchan Aruch and Maimonides's earlier Mishneh Torah have never stopped Jews from going back to the Talmud, because in Judaism, Talmud study isn't a goal-oriented activity; it's an end in itself, a sacred practice. According to

Rabbi Meir, one of the most important tannaim, anyone who engages in study for its own sake is "exalted above all of creation."

This identification of the sacred with the intellectual is what makes rabbinic Judaism so distinctive. For Judaism, learning and thinking are forms of worship—an idea that continues to shape Jewish culture today, even among Jews who have no interest in the Talmud. In fact, Talmud study isn't only or even mostly about what we now think of as religious matters, like morality or spirituality. Halakha governs every part of human life, and the Talmud is interested in all of it—Shabbat observance and kosher slaughter, inheritance and real estate, marriage and divorce, personal injury and capital punishment, the size of the universe and the nature of the afterlife, how to deliver a baby and how to bury a corpse, semen and menstrual blood, good table manners and the inscrutability of divine justice. As one sage says, "Turn it and turn it, for everything is in it."

In *Come and Hear*, I hope to give some sense of the Talmud's richness. The book follows the order of the tractates in the Daf Yomi cycle, but makes no attempt to be comprehensive. Instead, I pay attention to particular arguments, episodes, and themes, to illuminate what the Talmud thinks about and how. Modern readers will find many things to object to in the logic and values of the Talmud—how could it be otherwise, with a text written more than 1,500 years ago? But my purpose here isn't to register objections, even when I share them. It's to enter into the Talmud's world, with all its difference and difficulty, and share some of what I found there in the seven and half years of my Daf Yomi journey.

Tractate Berachot
and Seder Moed

Prayers, Shabbat,
and Holidays

Berachot On how to pray, whose prayers are granted, and the perils of snubbing a rabbi's wife.

Two thousand years ago, when the Temple stood and the earliest sages quoted in the Talmud were teaching, Jews recited the same major berachot or prayers that they do today. This remarkable continuity makes tractate Berachot one of the most directly relevant sections of the Talmud, and a good place to begin the Daf Yomi cycle. In the twenty-first century, Jews no longer need to know how to sacrifice a lamb, or what denomination of copper coin to use in betrothing a wife, or how many times an ox has to gore someone before its owner becomes liable for the damage. These areas of law and many others addressed in the Talmud can be fascinating to study, and the principles behind them inform the way halakha deals with contemporary dilemmas. But when the sages discuss when to recite the Shema, or what form of grace after meals is required when three people dine together, they are giving information needed by every observant Jew.

Even with these familiar subjects, however, the way the Talmud imparts its knowledge can be disorienting. Take the first words of the Mishna in Berachot 2a: "From when does one recite the Shema in the evenings?" What the Shema prayer is, and the fact that it must be recited in the evening, are taken for granted; these are things we are expected to know already, from a lifetime of Jewish practice. The discussion starts with a concrete problem: For purposes of prayer, how is the evening defined?

The question is simple, but the answer isn't: "From the time when the priests enter to partake of their teruma until the end of the first watch. That is the statement of Rabbi Eliezer. The Rabbis say: until midnight. Rabban Gamliel says: until dawn." Already, two challenging features of Talmudic discourse are evident. First, different areas of Jewish law are interconnected, so that to understand one you have to understand them all. In this case, the time for prayer is defined by the operations of the Temple in Jerusalem, so to know when to pray you have to know when the priests ate teruma, the tithe of produce reserved for them, and how the Temple's night watches were measured. Berachot may be the first volume of the Talmud, because printed texts have to have some kind of order, but it isn't the beginning in any logical sense.

Then there's the fact that the Mishna doesn't give an answer to its own question; instead, it gives three answers. When multiple opinions are stated in the Mishna, the one attributed to "the rabbis"—that is, the majority of the rabbis, the consensus—is the one that determines the law. In this passage, the rabbis say that the Shema can be recited until midnight. So why do we need to know what Rabbi Eliezer and Rabban Gamliel think?

By including minority opinions, the Talmud shows that it isn't simply a compendium of rules issued by a central authority, like the Code Napoleon or the Federal Register. It's a record of teachings handed down over centuries by many different sages who sometimes disagreed. All of these traditions are important and sacred, and the Talmud doesn't want to discard any of them. In fact, in addition to the Mishna there is another collection of laws called the Tosefta, "additions"; often the Talmud will quote a baraita, one of these extra-Mishnaic opinions, as evidence in a dispute. This eagerness to put different views in dialogue with one another is key to the Talmudic ethos of pluralism, which continues to inform modern Judaism.

Another function of the Gemara is to make explicit what the Mishna takes for granted. In this case, the Gemara begins by asking: "On the basis of what does the tanna [the Mishnaic source] ask: From when?" In other words, how do we know that we are supposed to recite the Shema in the evening in the first place? The answer comes in the form of a quotation from Deuteronomy 6:7: "You will talk of them when you sit in your home and when you walk along the way, when you lie down and when you arise." Actually, the Gemara only quotes the most relevant words, "when you lie down and when you arise," which shows that the Shema must be recited morning and night; and it doesn't give chapter and verse, since those divisions hadn't been invented yet. The Talmud assumes that we can recognize any Biblical passage from just a few words.

As for when the priests entered the Temple to eat teruma, the Gemara explains that this happened "from the time of the emergence of the stars." So the original question is finally answered: You can start saying the evening Shema as soon as stars are visible in the sky. As for how late you can say it, the Gemara examines each of the three proposed answers. When

Rabbi Eliezer says "until the end of the first watch," how does he define a watch? Is the night made up of four three-hour watches or three four-hour watches? The answer comes from a baraita that says you can identify the watches according to signs. At the first watch, donkeys bray; at the second, dogs howl; at the third, infants wake up to suckle and women begin to talk to their husbands.

But this statement raises new questions in turn. Do these signs mark the beginning of the watch or the end? Either way, the Gemara points out, there is a logical objection. If the signs happen at the start of a watch, we don't need to be told the first sign, since night obviously begins when the sun sets. Likewise, if they mark the end of a watch, we don't need to know the third sign, since night ends when the sun rises. So why does the baraita include all three?

One possible answer is that the baraita was carelessly phrased or logically inconsistent. But the Talmud rarely entertains this kind of explanation: a central principle of Talmudic interpretation is that every word is there for a good reason. The interpreter's job isn't to criticize the text but to figure out what information it's trying to convey. In this case, the Gemara decides that the signs mark the end of the watches—but this doesn't mean that the signs of the third watch are superfluous. Rather, they are stated so that if you wake up in a room with no windows, you will have a way to tell if it's time to say the morning Shema. If your wife is talking to you or your child is suckling, it must be daytime. (As always, the Talmud's implied addressee is a man.) These concrete examples bring Jewish life in the Talmudic era close to us: infants still wake up early to nurse, just as they did in Babylonia.

Berachot also deals with more intimate kinds of problems related to prayer. What should you do, for instance, if you pass gas while praying? The Talmud discusses this issue without embarrassment; its treatment of the body's subversive agendas is always matter-of-fact. Rather than thinking of flatulence as a shameful interruption of prayer, the rabbis simply turn it into an occasion for more prayer, offering a formula to recite (24b): "Master of the Universe, you formed us with openings upon openings and cavities upon cavities. It is revealed and known before you, our shame and humiliation during our lives, and at our end, worms and maggots await us." Embodiment and mortality are part of the human condition, but since God created us that way, there is no need to try to hide our frailties from him.

Indeed, the Gemara says that even Yehuda HaNasi, the compiler of the Mishna, would belch, yawn, sneeze, and spit while praying. This presents a problem, however, because according to a baraita, those actions are forbidden during prayer. The Talmud is caught between two impossibilities: The baraita can't be wrong, yet Yehuda HaNasi would never commit a sin. How can the two statements be interpreted in such a way that neither has to be rejected? The Gemara announces its solution using the formula "lo kashya," "this is not difficult," which means the opposite of what it says—there is a difficulty, but the rabbis have found a way to overcome it. In this case, what the law means is that it's forbidden to yawn or belch deliberately during prayer. Yehuda HaNasi did these things unintentionally, so he isn't guilty of any sin.

This doesn't fully solve the problem, however. The distinction between intentional and unintentional actions may work for yawns and belches, but sneezes are always unintentional, yet they are still prohibited during prayer. Doesn't this suggest that intention is irrelevant? Once again the Gemara responds with "lo kashya": what Yehuda HaNasi did was an ordinary sneeze, and what the law means to forbid is a sneeze "from below"—that is, deliberately passing gas.

The particular prayers mentioned in Berachot are still recited today—the Shema, the Amida, the Birkat Hamazon. Yet there are profound theological gulfs between today's Judaism and the Talmud's. Modern Judaism insists that there are no such things as demons; the God of monotheism leaves no room in the universe for other supernatural powers. And it goes without saying that the Jewish God is transcendent and does not exist in space, much less in the form of a human body. These ways of thinking about the divine are supposed to mark Judaism's advance over paganism.

But in Berachot 6a, the sages take for granted that demons and magic are a real part of God's creation. According to Abba Benjamin, "If the eye would be granted permission to see, no creature would be able to stand in the face of the demons that surround it." Abaye says, "They are more numerous than us, and they stand about us like a ditch around a mound." And according to Rav Huna, "Each one of us has a thousand to his left and ten thousand to his right."

Fortunately, these demons seem more like naughty sprites than devils. When your knees become tired, when your clothes wear out, when you feel squeezed in a crowd—according to Rava, this is all the work of demons. And there are magical ways of making demons show themselves. All you have to do is find a black female cat who is the firstborn daughter of a firstborn mother, burn her placenta, grind the ashes, and put some in your eye. Be sure, however, to place the remainder of the ashes in a sealed iron tube, so the demons can't steal it.

The Talmud doesn't explain how these demons fit into a world where God is the source of all law and power. Did he create them, and if so, why? But things get still stranger when we learn that God wears tefillin. The rabbis base this idea on Isaiah 62:8: "The Lord has sworn by His right hand, and by the arm of His strength." If God has an arm, it stands to reason that he would wrap tefillin on it, though his are slightly different from ours. The tefillin worn by human beings contain a scroll with the words of the Shema: "Hear, O Israel, the Lord is our God, the Lord is one." Conversely, God's tefillin are inscribed with the words of 2 Samuel 7:23: "And who is like Your people Israel, one nation in the land."

In fact, a High Priest called Yishmael once saw God in the Temple on Yom Kippur, sitting on a throne in the Holy of Holies. God asked Yishmael to pray for him, and when he heard the prayer, Yishmael says, "He nodded to me with his head." This is a beautiful idea, capturing the mutuality of the covenant between God and his people. But can we really imagine God with an arm and a head? Later Jewish thinkers like Saadia Gaon and Maimonides, who strongly rejected the idea that God has a body, struggled to find ways around the anthropomorphizing language of the Bible and the Talmud. Saadia proposed that Yishmael couldn't have seen God in human form, but only as a great light.

This kind of revisionist interpretation is Judaism's favorite technique for concealing its own theological evolution. Rather than admit that Jewish beliefs change over time, later readers reinterpret earlier texts to reflect their own ideas and values. The Talmud engages in this process all the time. At the end of 2 Samuel, for instance, there is a roster of King David's warriors that sounds like it could come from the Iliad. Josheb-Basshebeth killed eight hundred enemy warriors in one battle; Shammah son of Agee singlehandedly defeated a Philistine army in a battle in a lentil field. Then there is Benaiah son of Jehoiada, whose deeds include killing the two sons of Ariel of Moab and fighting a lion in a pit on a cold winter day.

According to Berachot 8a, however, Benaiah wasn't the Homeric hero this description suggests. For the rabbis, feats of physical strength meant nothing; only feats of Torah scholarship mattered. It stands to reason, then, that the Bible's description of Benaiah is an allegorical way of saying that "he increased and garnered achievements for Torah." When we read that Benaiah struck down two men, it actually means that "he did not leave anyone comparable to himself in scholarship, neither in the period of the First Temple nor in the period of the Second Temple." When we read that he killed a lion in a pit on a winter day, this means that he immersed in a freezing pool to purify himself before studying Torah. Another sage suggests that he studied an entire treatise on the Book of Leviticus on a single freezing day.

This remarkable transformation of Benaiah from a fighter into a scholar reflects a dramatic change in the Jewish ethos between Biblical and Talmudic times. The rabbis' elevation of spiritual and intellectual strength over physical strength would continue to shape Judaism for two thousand years. Not until the creation of the state of Israel in the twentieth century would Jews once again have military heroes to put beside Benaiah.

The sages may have scorned the idea of winning fame on the battlefield, but that doesn't mean they were uninterested in prestige. On the contrary, the Talmud shows they could be as touchy about status as any courtier at Versailles. In the absence of a royal court, an army, or a functioning priesthood, the rabbis created a new kind of hierarchy, based less on birth or wealth than on piety and learning. The Bible tells us how many enemies a warrior killed, but Berachot remembers rabbis for the spirit in which they prayed. Rabbi Elazar prayed hopefully, asking for love and brotherhood, a large number of students, and a portion in the Garden of Eden. Rabbi Yochanan prayed darkly, asking God to "gaze upon our shame and behold our evil plight." Rabbi Hiyya prayed simply: "May it be Your will, Lord our God, that Your Torah should be our vocation" (16b).

And the greatest sages could compel God to grant their prayers. Once, when Rabban Gamliel's son fell ill, he sent two of his students to Rabbi Chanina, asking him to pray for the patient. "As soon as [Chanina] saw them," the Gemara relates, "he went up to his attic and sought mercy for him. On coming down he said to them: Go back to Rabban Gamliel, for the fever has left him." The students wondered how Chanina could be so sure about the immediate power of his prayer: "They asked him, are you then a prophet?" Chanina admitted, "I am neither a prophet nor the son of a prophet," but he was nonetheless certain: "I have a tradition that if my prayer is fluent in my mouth then I know that it has been well received. But if not, then I know that my prayer has been rejected" (34b). When the students returned to Rabban Gamliel, they found that his son had recovered just at the moment when Chanina said his prayer.

Does God really play favorites in this way, answering one person's prayer and ignoring another's? The cosmic unfairness of Chanina's gift clearly troubles the rabbis, since they go on to tell another story about him. Just like Rabban Gamliel, Yochanan ben Zakkai once had a son who fell ill, and he too asked Chanina to intercede with prayer; Chanina "lay his head between his knees and sought mercy for him and he lived." Yochanan ben Zakkai observed, perhaps a little resentfully, "Had ben Zakkai stuck his head between his knees all day long, they would not have paid any attention to him in the heavenly court."

"Is Chanina then greater than you?" asked his wife. After all, Yochanan ben Zakkai was the leader of his generation, credited with saving Judaism from oblivion after the destruction of the Temple. "No," he replied, "rather, Chanina is like a servant before the King, while I am like a minister before the King." That is, Chanina had the right to enter into God's presence at any time and ask for favors, while Yochanan was God's official representative and had to maintain a dignified distance.

These aristocrats of Torah looked down on Jews whose knowledge and observance didn't meet their standards. Berachot 47b discusses the "am haaretz," literally a "person of the land," which is how the Talmud refers to an uneducated Jew who is lax about observance. There are several ways of identifying an am haaretz: "anyone who does not recite the Shema in the evening and the morning," "anyone who does not wear tefillin," "anyone who does not have a mezuza on his home's entrance." By the strictest definition, "even if one read scripture and studied Mishna, but did not serve Torah scholars"—that is, did not study in a rabbinic academy—"he is an am haaretz."

The voices of these ordinary Jews, who must have been the majority, are missing from the Talmud—as are the voices of women, who could not study Torah or become rabbis. Yet occasionally the Talmud does record a protest against the rabbinic elite. Berachot 51b relates that the sage Ulla once dined at the house of Rabbi Nachman. After the wine was blessed, Nachman wanted to send the cup to his wife, Yalta. (Naturally, Yalta would not have eaten at the same table with a male guest.) But Ulla forbade this, on the grounds that "the fruits of the woman's body are blessed only through the fruits of the husband's body." In other words, it was enough for the husband to drink, since the blessing would trickle down to his wife.

Yalta overheard Ulla's words and, to put it mildly, she did not agree: "She stood up in anger and went up to the wine-storage room, where she broke four hundred barrels of wine." This was enough to change Ulla's mind and he sent her a cup of wine, but she replied with an insult: "From itinerant peddlers come idle words, and from old rags come lice." On this occasion, at least, patriarchal beliefs were no match for a woman's passion for respect.

Shabbat On forbidden labors, set-aside items, and learning the Torah while standing on one leg.

The basis of Jewish law is the mitzvot, the commandments God gave to Moses in the Torah. If Jews have the Torah, then, why do we also need the Talmud? Doesn't the Torah tell us everything we need to know about God's will? That was the argument made by the Sadducees in the Second Temple period and the Karaites in the Middle Ages—sects that hoped to cut back the teeming growth of halakha and go back to basics. In a sense, modern Reform Judaism is another such movement, except that it rejects most of the mitzvot, too, seeing the ethical spirit of the Torah as the essence of Judaism. Those first two movements failed, however (on the third, the jury is still out). The Sadducees disappeared with the Temple, while their rivals, the Pharisees, created the rabbinic tradition that is codified in the Mishna. There is still a small population of Karaites today, but Orthodox Judaism is the Judaism of the Talmud.

The rabbis didn't see themselves as adding to the Torah, as if human beings shared God's power to issue commandments. Rather, they believed they were preserving the oral Torah, a set of instructions God gave to the Israelites at the same time that he gave them the written Torah. The idea that there were two revelations on Sinai, one recorded in the Five Books of Moses while the other goes unmentioned, might seem historically dubious, but it is central to Judaism. In the twelfth century CE, Maimonides began the Mishneh Torah, his codification of Jewish law, with a statement of this belief: "All of the commandments which were given to Moses on Sinai were given together with their oral explanation."

Explanation may be the best way to think about the relationship between the Torah and the Talmud: the Talmud explains how the laws of the Torah can be put into practice. For as a guide to actually living a Jewish life, the Torah turns out to be radically inadequate. Take Shabbat observance, which isn't just a mitzva but one of the Ten Commandments: "Remember the Sabbath day by keeping it holy. Six days you shall labor and do all your work, but the seventh day is a sabbath to the Lord your God. On it you shall not do any work" (Exodus 20:8–10).

The principle is clear, but how do we know what qualifies as work? Does it mean strenuous physical labor, or do household tasks count? Multiply such questions by all the mitzvot in the Torah and it becomes clear that, to paraphrase Voltaire, if the oral Torah didn't exist, it would be necessary to invent it. Surely God wouldn't have given the Jewish people commandments without explaining how to carry them out.

Tractate Shabbat, the second-longest in the Talmud, takes 157 folio pages to explicate those three verses in Exodus. Like Berachot, it begins by analyzing a small, concrete problem. Say that a homeowner is standing in his doorway facing a poor man who is standing in the street. The economic status of the two men isn't important: this is just the Talmud's way of distinguishing between the one who is in a private domain and the one in a public domain. On Shabbat, it's prohibited to transfer an object between these domains. So if something is transferred between the man in the house and the man in the street, which of them is guilty of violating Shabbat?

The Mishna explains that there are eight possible ways such a transfer could take place. If the poor man "extended his hand inside the house and placed an object in the homeowner's hand," the poor man is guilty and the homeowner is exempt from punishment. The same is true if the poor man reaches into the house and takes an object from the homeowner's hand. Conversely, if the homeowner reaches out into the street and takes something from the poor man's hand, or places something there, the homeowner is guilty and the poor man is exempt. In these four cases, assigning responsibility is straightforward because the same person initiates the transfer, by reaching into the other man's domain, and completes it, by taking or giving an item.

But there are also four possible cases in which one of the parties initiates the transfer but the other completes it. If the poor man extends his hand into the house and the homeowner takes an item from his hand or places one into it, or the homeowner extends his hand outside the house and the poor man takes or places an item, which party is responsible for violating Shabbat? According to the Mishna, neither is guilty, since neither man performed the entire transfer himself.

This seems problematic, since it allows two people to get away with doing something that neither of them is permitted to do individually. The Gemara raises this objection: "Are they both exempt? Wasn't a prohibited labor performed between them?" But laws apply to actions, not outcomes. The law doesn't say that it's forbidden for an object to be transferred on Shabbat; what's forbidden is for a person to transfer it. Since transferring involves taking the object out of one domain and placing it in another, a person who performs just one of these elements hasn't accomplished a transfer.

This may sound like leniency, but the Talmud is very strict when it comes to actions it considers true violations. One of the key principles of Talmudic jurisprudence is stated in Pirkei Avot, a section of the Mishna that is a collection of rabbinic maxims: "Be cautious in judgment, raise many disciples and make a fence round the Torah." For the rabbis, making a fence around the Torah isn't just a metaphor, it has a technical meaning: instituting new prohibitions to discourage people from violating Torah laws.

The Talmud frequently distinguishes between Torah laws, which come directly from God, and rabbinic laws, which were implemented by the sages as a "fence." For instance, it is forbidden by Torah law to light a fire on Shabbat, which includes relighting an oil lamp by tilting it to wet the wick. To ward off the temptation to tilt a lamp, rabbinic law prohibits doing various things by lamplight on Shabbat, including reading. One might think that rabbinic laws are only guidelines: if the point is not to tilt the lamp, what does it matter if you read a book, as long as you make sure not to tilt the lamp? But rabbinic laws are fully binding, and for good reason. Rabbi Yishmael ben Elisha once thought he could get away with reading by lamplight if he made a firm promise not to tilt the lamp; but then he reached out to tilt it by instinct, barely stopping himself in time. "How great are the words of the sages," he reflected, "for they said, 'One may not read by lamplight'" (12b).

Another activity that is prohibited by lamplight on Shabbat is searching your clothes for lice, a common problem in the ancient world. But if lice appear in your clothes on Shabbat, is it permitted to kill them? This was a subject of dispute between Beit Shammai and Beit Hillel, two schools whose clashes are recorded throughout the Talmud. Usually Beit Shammai takes a stricter line and Beit Hillel a more lenient one, and so it is here: Shammai forbids killing lice on Shabbat, while Hillel allows it. As a general rule, the law follows the opinion of Hillel, and the Talmud says that some rabbis gleefully took advantage of the right to kill lice on Shabbat. "Rabba would kill them. And Rav Sheishet would kill them. Rava would throw them into a bucket of water." Toughest of all was Rav Nachman, who "said to his daughters: Kill the lice and let me hear the sound of my enemies as they die."

The prohibition on transferring items from the public to the private domain, or vice versa, means that it's forbidden to carry things around on Shabbat. Animals are included in this rule: they can't carry burdens on Shabbat, though they are permitted to wear standard equipment like collars and halters. In discussing this issue, the Mishna mentions that "the cow of Elazar ben Azarya used to go out with a strap between her horns, against the will of the Sages" (54b). It's a minor point, but to the Gemara, there is something strange about it. Elazar ben Azarya was an enormously wealthy man who "used to tithe twelve thousand calves from his herd every year"—so why does the Mishna refer to "the cow of Elazar ben Azarya," as if he only had one?

A casual reader might assume that there was no special intention behind the use of the definite article, but rabbis draw a moral from it. The cow that went out with a strap on Shabbat didn't actually belong to Elazar ben Azarya at all, the Gemara says. It belonged to his neighbor, "but because he did not protest against her, it was called his cow." This shows that we are responsible not only for our own transgressions, but for other people's transgressions that we failed to prevent. "Whoever has the ability to protest against the members of his household but does not protest is punished for the transgressions of the members of his household," the Gemara says, and goes on to expand the principle from one's household to the entire world.

By this standard, just about everyone is guilty of some kind of sin of commission or omission. For the Talmud, this explains why every human being is destined to die, since as Rav Ami puts it, "There is no death without transgression, and there is no suffering without sin" (55a). The idea that suffering is always merited comes up a number of times in the Talmud, but it is usually challenged, since the world gives so many examples of innocent people who suffer for no reason. The Talmud finds examples in the Bible itself: didn't Moses observe all the commandments? No, the Gemara responds; in Numbers 20, he sinned by striking a rock in order to make it produce water, instead of trusting God to provide it. The Talmud imagines

God telling Moses, "Had you believed in me, your time to depart from the world would not have arrived."

But while the rabbis are ready to believe that Moses's ambiguous action was punishable by death, they argue that Biblical figures who were much greater sinners were actually innocent of the transgressions ascribed to them. According to Genesis 35:22, "While Israel stayed in the land, Reuben went and lay with Bilhah, his father's concubine, and Israel found out." Reuben is punished for this quasi-incest in Israel's deathbed speech, where he tells his son: "Unstable as water, you shall excel no longer; / For when you mounted your father's bed / You brought disgrace" (Genesis 49:4).

This seems very clear, but according to Rabbi Shmuel bar Nachman, "Whoever says that Reuben sinned is simply mistaken." After all, in Genesis 35:22, immediately after describing Reuben's sin, the verse continues: "Now the sons of Jacob were twelve in number," which means that Reuben was equal to his brothers, including morally. When the Torah says "Reuben went and lay with Bilhah," the Gemara argues, it really means that "Reuben disturbed his father's bed" by moving it out of Bilhah's tent and into Leah's. But he did this for a noble reason: he wanted to defend the rights of Leah, his mother, against Bilhah, the concubine given to Jacob by Rachel, his second wife. For the rabbis, it's better to read the Torah against its plain meaning than to think that a figure as venerable as Reuben was capable of sinning.

It's not until Shabbat 73a, about halfway through the tractate, that we find an explanation of exactly what types of work are forbidden on Shabbat. "The primary labors are forty minus one," the Mishna says, and they are divided into several categories. First come the kinds of work necessary to make bread, from sowing seeds and plowing a field to sifting flour, kneading dough, and baking. Then come the labors involved in making clothing, from shearing wool to weaving threads, tying knots, and sewing stitches. Next are the labors involved in preparing hides—trapping a deer, slaughtering it, skinning it—and writing a document, which includes erasing. Last are the six most general categories: building and demolishing, kindling and extinguishing, "striking the final blow"—that is, putting the finishing touch on any piece of work—and "taking from one domain to another domain"—transferring an object from a private area such as a house to a public one such as a street or vice versa, as discussed at the beginning of the tractate.

Earlier, in Shabbat 49b, the rabbis explain that these thirty-nine categories are derived from the types of work performed by the Israelites when they built the Tabernacle, the portable dwelling-place of God they carried with them in the desert. "One is only liable for a labor the likes of which was performed in the Tabernacle. They planted, and you shall not plant; they reaped, and you shall not reap; they lifted the boards from the ground onto the wagon, and you shall not bring articles in from the public domain to the private domain," and so on.

That last example suggests that, for the rabbis, the actions involved in building the Tabernacle are representatives of larger, more abstract categories. On a narrow interpretation, one might think that lifting a board onto a wagon is prohibited on Shabbat, but not lifting a bundle of wheat onto a wagon, since the builders of the Tabernacle didn't handle wheat. But the Talmud says that corollaries of the original actions are also forbidden.

Connecting the forbidden labors to the building of the Tabernacle is a way of bringing some conceptual unity to what might seem like a random collection of tasks. It's also a way of giving Jews in every era an imaginative connection with Moses. For the Talmud, reasoning about Shabbat means recreating every detail of the Tabernacle: How wide were the boards used to build its walls? How many boards made up each wall? Did they taper at the top or were they rectangular? And what about the tapestry that was draped over the walls and ceiling—how long was it, and how much material hung down on each side, and how much of the bottom of the wall was exposed?

The thirty-nine categories include almost anything a Jew might think of doing on Shabbat, except quiet activities like reading, eating, and sleeping. But the core prohibitions are further fenced around by the rabbinic concept of muktzeh, which literally means "set aside." On Shabbat, it's only permitted to handle items that have been prepared for use on the day; everything else is muktzeh and can't be touched. Because this status is determined by human intention, it gives rise to some interesting dilemmas. For example, lighting a fire is prohibited on Shabbat, so firewood is presumptively muktzeh. But can you sit on a stack of firewood, or does its muktzeh status rule out using it even for a permitted action?

The Talmud decides that sitting is only permitted if the owner of wood intended to use it as a seat before Shabbat began. Rabba bar bar Chana says that tying the wood into bundles is required as a concrete sign of this intention, but Rabbi Chanina ben Akiva holds that thought alone is enough. On one occasion, he "went to a certain place and found branches of a date palm that were harvested for the sake of firewood, and he said to his students, 'Go out and intend, so that we may sit on them tomorrow'" (50a).

To clarify the limits of muktzeh, the rabbis employ a striking thought experiment. A corpse is always muktzeh, since there's no possible use for it. It follows that if someone dies on Shabbat, you can't move the body—which could lead to some unpleasant consequences, especially on a summer day in Babylonia. Is there any legal method for moving a corpse out of the sun on Shabbat? The Talmud offers several possible solutions. Two men could sit next to the corpse and an awning could be placed over all of them; this would be permitted because the awning would technically be for the sake of the living men, who are not muktzeh. More startlingly, Rav suggests, "One could place a loaf of bread or an infant on the corpse and then move it" (43b). In that case, the legal presumption is that the bread or the infant is what you intend to move, while the corpse is just along for the ride.

Throughout the discussion, the rabbis assume that a Jew would only break Shabbat in a "lapse of awareness," inadvertently. This is a key part of how the Talmud thinks about law breaking and law enforcement. Tractates Sanhedrin and Makkot discuss serious crimes like incest and murder that are punishable by flogging or execution. But the Talmud acknowledges that Jewish courts rarely enforced such penalties, out of principled aversion to violence or simple lack of authority. In effect, halakha is sanctioned not by the threat of force, as in secular legal systems, but by fear and love of God, who punishes sins in this world or the next. As a rule, the Talmud assumes that Jews don't commit sins intentionally.

But what would it mean to violate Shabbat unintentionally? The Talmud imagines three ways this might happen. First, a person might "forget the essence of the Sabbath"—that is, he might not know that it is a holy day on which work is forbidden. The rabbis found it impossible to imagine that anyone raised in a Jewish community could be so ignorant, however. Only "a child who was captured and raised among gentiles" (68a) might grow up not knowing what Shabbat is.

Second, a person might lose track of the calendar and not realize what day it is—for instance, "if someone was walking on the way or in the desert, and he does not know when it is the Sabbath." In that case, Rav Huna advises, he should count six days and then observe the seventh as Shabbat, so he will at least be preserving the principle of a day of rest. Hiyya bar Rav, on the other hand, says that the man should observe Shabbat immediately and treat the next six days as weekdays.

Finally, there is the third kind of sinner—one who knows what Shabbat means and when it is, but doesn't know the rules about the thirty-nine categories of forbidden labor. Such a person is liable to sacrifice an animal as a "sin offering." But he is obligated to bring one offering for every category of labor he performed, not for each individual violation: If he planted three times and wrote four times, he would only have to bring two offerings, not seven. Violating Shabbat intentionally carries a much more severe punishment; according to Exodus 35:2, "On six days work may be done, but on the seventh day you shall have a Sabbath of complete rest, holy to the Lord; whoever does any work on it shall be put to death."

In fact, the rabbis sometimes preferred to let people go on violating Shabbat unwittingly, rather than reminding them of rules they might end up violating deliberately. It's forbidden by rabbinic law to clap your hands and dance on Shabbat, since it might lead to repairing a musical instrument, a prohibited labor. Yet as Rava bar Rav Chanan points out in Shabbat 148b, "We see that people do these things, and we do not say anything to stop them." The Gemara concludes that sometimes discretion is the better part of valor: "Leave the Jewish people alone, and do not rebuke them. It is better that they be unwitting in their halakhic violations and that they not be intentional sinners, for if they are told about these prohibitions they may not listen anyway."

Followed to its logical conclusion, this reasoning would make nonsense of halakha: Simply keep the Jewish people ignorant of all the laws, and they can do whatever they like. A cynic might say that this is close to describing the state of American Jewish observance today. Perhaps that's why modern Jews frequently quote a Talmudic anecdote which seems to imply that obedience to the law is of no real importance. This is the famous story, in Shabbat 31a, about the gentile who told Hillel and Shammai that he would convert to Judaism if they could teach him the entire Torah while he stood on one foot.

The sages' answers reveal their different personalities. The stern Shammai impatiently "pushed him away with the ruler he was holding in his hand," rejecting the question as mockery. But the mild Hillel gave an answer that has become proverbial: "That which is hateful to you, do not do to another; this is the entire Torah, all the rest is an elaboration. Now go and learn it." "The sternness of Shammai sought to banish us from the world," says a group of proselytes later in the chapter, "but the humble manner of Hillel brought us under the wings of the divine presence."

Hillel's words are often taken to imply that we can be good Jews simply by being good people, whether or not we observe Jewish law. It's certainly true that the Talmud believes observance of the laws means nothing without piety and goodness. But if we are to be true to the moral of the story, we can't forget the last part of Hillel's message: "Now go and learn it." For rabbinic Judaism, learning Torah is the necessary expression and natural result of piety. As Rabba bar Rav Huna says, "Any person who has acquired Torah, but has not acquired the fear of Heaven, is comparable to a treasurer to whom they gave keys to the inner door of the treasury but not the outer door." In other words, piety is important because it leads to Torah study, not the other way around.

In Shabbat 63a, the rabbis offer a series of aphorisms about the virtues of Torah study, emphasizing that it must be undertaken in the proper spirit. The blessings of Torah knowledge are forfeited if the scholar is arrogant, or if he studies for an ulterior motive like personal advancement. Still, Reish Lakish says, "Even if a Torah scholar exacts revenge and bears a grudge like a serpent, gird him to your loins; even if an am haaretz is pious, do not dwell in his neighborhood." Despite his personal faults, the scholar is able to teach Jews how they are supposed to live, which is what really matters; an ignorant man might lead people astray despite his virtues.

The tension in Talmudic thinking between strictness and leniency is dramatically expressed in the legend of Rabbi Shimon bar Yochai, who lived in Palestine in the second century CE, when Roman persecution was at its worst. Once, when he heard a Jew praising the Romans' achievements in building marketplaces, bridges, and bathhouses, Shimon replied angrily: "Everything that they established, they established only for their own purposes. They established marketplaces to place prostitutes in them; bathhouses to pamper themselves; and bridges to collect taxes from all who pass over them." These words were reported to the authorities and Shimon was sentenced to death, whereupon he and his son Rabbi Elazar fled and hid in a cave. For twelve years, they stood buried up to their necks in sand, sustained by a magic carob tree, while they did nothing but study Torah.

Finally, the prophet Elijah came and informed them that Caesar had died and the death sentence had been lifted. When the father and son left the cave, they saw ordinary Jews going about their business, plowing and sowing. "These people," Shimon complained, "are forsaking the life of the World to Come and occupying themselves with the transitory life!" So holy and enraged were Shimon and Elazar that everyone they looked at was incinerated. Finally, "a heavenly voice rang out and proclaimed to them: 'Have you emerged from seclusion in order to destroy my world? Return to your cave!'"

This tale expresses a certain wisdom about religious zeal. God doesn't expect every Jew to be as holy as Shimon and Elazar, and he doesn't punish people for being spiritually average. Finally, after another year in their cave, the sages emerged chastened: "My son," Shimon says, "the world has enough devotees of Torah study in you and me alone."

Shimon's story also offers an interesting perspective on how the rabbis measure Torah knowledge. Before he entered the cave, the Gemara explains, Shimon would pose a legal question and Rabbi Pinchas would respond with twelve possible solutions. But after his years of isolated study, Shimon was able to provide twenty-four possible answers to every question of Pinchas's. Unlike scientific knowledge, which seeks one correct answer for every question, Torah knowledge is measured by the power to multiply possibilities, to see more facets of a problem. This is what comes from viewing Torah study not as a means to an end but an end in itself.

The Talmud places a high value on the intellectual aspects of Judaism, but it doesn't ignore spirit and emotion. Shabbat the tractate is full of difficult problems and minute distinctions, but Shabbat the day is meant to be celebrated with joy. According to Rabbi Yosei, "Anyone who delights in Shabbat, God gives him a boundless portion," and Rav Nachman bar Yitzchak says that "One who delights in Shabbat is rescued from the oppression of exile" (118b). The Talmud is especially impressed by the way the sages set aside their usual dignity to prepare for Shabbat. Rava salted fish, Rav Safra cooked, and Rav Huna lit the lamps in his house—tasks that would ordinarily have been done by servants. This humility was a way of acknowledging the greatness of Shabbat.

Shabbat can even bring magical good luck to those who love it. The Talmud tells a story about an ordinary man, not a rabbi, who was known as "Yosef who cherishes Shabbat." One day, a man crossing a river by ferry dropped a valuable pearl in the water, which was then swallowed by a fish, which was caught by a fisherman. Knowing Yosef's habit of buying delicacies for Shabbat, the fisherman sold him the fish, and when Yosef cut it open he found the pearl and sold it for thirteen jars full of gold coins. Folktales like this are found in many cultures, but only in the Talmud's version does it become a parable about the rewards of celebrating Shabbat.

And the Talmud is proud of the fact that Shabbat's pleasures are known only to Jews. Once a Roman emperor asked Rabbi Yehoshua ben Chanania why the dishes the Jews prepared for Shabbat smelled so good. "We have a certain spice called dill," the rabbi explained, "which we place in the cooked dishes, and its fragrance diffuses." But when the emperor demanded some of the spice for himself, Yehoshua replied, "For anyone who observes Shabbat the spice is effective, and for one who does not observe Shabbat, it is not effective." The emperor of Rome could have anything in the world, except for the joy of Shabbat.

Eruvin On boundaries, interpreting the Torah, and why the Messiah will come on a weekday.

In addition to work, Jewish law prohibits walking more than a certain distance on Shabbat, in accordance with Exodus 16:29: "Let every man abide in his place; let no man go out of his place on the seventh day." The boundary is two thousand cubits, measured from your location when Shabbat begins. A cubit is about twenty inches, so this equals about two-thirds of a mile. Objects can be carried freely inside a private domain like a house, but in a public domain like a street it's forbidden to carry something more than four cubits, about seven feet.

When the Israelites received these laws they were living in the desert in tents, so it would have been easy to stay put on Shabbat—there was no reason to leave the boundary of the camp. But by the Talmudic era, many Jews in the Roman and Persian empires lived in cities and towns, where the two-thousand-cubit limit was more of an impediment. Indeed, their urban lifestyle was probably closer to that of Jews in New York or Tel Aviv today than to the nomadic shepherds of Genesis and Exodus.

Tractate Eruvin is devoted to the legal strategies Judaism developed to make these aspects of Shabbat observance easier. An eruv is a "merger" of different spaces for the purposes of Shabbat, designed to extend the range for walking and carrying. This can involve joining adjacent courtyards into a single domain, or depositing food at a distant location to establish a fictional Shabbat residence, allowing you to measure the two-thousand-cubit boundary from there.

Just as the Torah forbids work on Shabbat without defining work, it also says "abide in your place" without defining a place. "These two thousand cubits, where are they written?" the Gemara asks. How does the Mishna arrive at this figure for the Shabbat boundary when it is never mentioned in the Torah? The answer demonstrates the complicated and counter-intuitive ways that the rabbis read the written Torah in order to find an anchorage for concepts in the oral Torah.

The instruction to "abide in your place" was God's way of rebuking the Israelites for violating Shabbat in order to gather manna, the miraculous food that fell from the sky. The people were instructed not to store it but to gather their daily ration every morning. Since no manna would fall on Shabbat, they were supposed to gather a double measure on the sixth day.

As frequently happens in the Torah, however, the Israelites ignored God's instructions and went out on Shabbat expecting to find manna. Instead, they got a reprimand: "And the Lord said unto Moses: 'How long do you refuse to keep My commandments and My laws? See that the Lord has given you the Sabbath; therefore He gives you on the sixth day the bread of two days. Let every man abide in his place; let no man go out of his place on the seventh day.'"

The two different Hebrew words translated here as "place," the Gemara explains in Eruvin 51a, refer to the two kinds of Shabbat restriction. "Let no man leave his place" refers to the two-thousand-cubit boundary that defines a person's place on Shabbat, while "sit each man in his place" refers to the rule that, if you find yourself outside the Shabbat boundary for any reason, you should move no more than four cubits in any direction.

But how does this solve the problem, when the verse doesn't mention the figure two thousand cubits? To answer this question, the rabbis engage in a remarkable relay-race of interpretation, using a technique of verbal analogy called gezeira shava. With this tool, they can connect any appearance of a word in the Torah with any other appearance—a kind of pre-Internet hyperlinking.

In this case, the Gemara performs five consecutive linkages. The word "place" in Exodus 16:29 connects with the word "place" in Exodus 21:13, where it appears near the word "flee." This connects with another use of "flee" in Numbers 35:26, which also contains the word "border." The following verse in Numbers uses the word "border" near the word "outside," which connects to Numbers 35:5: "And you shall measure from outside the city on the east side, two thousand cubits." Thus the rabbis conclude that "place" is equivalent to two thousand cubits.

Clearly, if you didn't know the two-thousand-cubit rule and were searching the Torah to find out how far you can walk on Shabbat, you would never find the answer this way. But the rabbis aren't trying to discover the rule; they are looking for support in the written Torah for a practice already established by the oral Torah. And they know the support must be there, because the Torah was written by God. Human beings may write by picking the first words that come to hand, but every word God uses, like everything he does, has a purpose. Once this idea is accepted, gezeira shava becomes not just rational but necessary.

For the sages, coming up with ingenious interpretations was a competitive sport. In the Bible, the Israelites brag about how many warriors their kings have killed: "Saul has slain his thousands, and David his tens of thousands." The Talmud, by contrast, brags about how many interpretations a rabbi can make: Sumakhos could give forty-eight reasons why any item should be considered ritually pure or impure, while another, unnamed student could give a hundred and fifty reasons.

Yet it's possible for a sage to be too clever. Rabbi Meir is one of the most frequently quoted authorities in the Mishna, and the Talmud says "there was none in the generation of Rabbi Meir like him." But often his colleagues "did not fix the halakha in accordance with his view," because they "could not fathom the depths of his reasoning." They were disconcerted by the way he could argue both sides of a question: "He would assert that something impure was pure and make it seem plausible, and that something impure was pure and make it seem plausible" (13b).

Some disputes between sages were so fierce that God himself had to intervene. Beit Hillel and Beit Shammai debated each other for three years until "a heavenly voice went forth and declared: 'Both these and those are the words of the living God, but the law follows Beit Hillel.'" This famous sentence is often used to illustrate the Talmud's intellectual pluralism: even when they disagree, Beit Hillel and Beit Shammai both serve God by helping to illuminate the Torah. So why does Hillel's interpretation of the law prevail over Shammai's, in all but a few cases? The reason doesn't have to do with intellectual acuity, but with humility. Beit Hillel "would study their own opinion and the opinion of Beit Shammai. Not only that, but they would mention the matters of Beit Shammai before their own."

One of the most momentous of these debates concerned nothing less than the value of human existence. "For two and a half years, Beit Shammai and Beit Hillel disagreed. The former said: It would have been preferable had man not been created than to have been created. And the latter said: It

is preferable for man to have been created than had he not been created."
In the end, the majority of sages sided with Beit Shammai's pessimistic
view. But, they say, "now that he has been created, let him examine his
actions" and avoid sin. No matter how hard life is, there is no excuse for
not following God's law.

Indeed, the Talmud's mission is to bring the entire world under the rule of
law—not just human beings, but nature too. Rainwater has the legal status
of an ownerless object, which means that anyone who collects it can carry
it within his own two-thousand-cubit boundary. But the Gemara raises a
problem based on the water cycle. After all, rainwater originally comes from
the ocean, where it evaporates to form a cloud: as Rabbi Eliezer states, "The
entire world drinks the waters of the ocean" (45b).

If rain was in the ocean when Shabbat began, shouldn't the ocean be
considered its residence for the purpose of calculating its boundary? By
evaporating and raining down on land, the water already traveled past its
two-thousand-cubit limit, so by the time a person collects it, the water
should only be able to move four cubits. Alternatively, if the rain was in
a cloud at the beginning of Shabbat, why doesn't it establish its residence
there? And how can we know where any given drop of water came from in
the first place? Such questions might seem insoluble, but the rabbis don't
give up. They decide that when water is in the ocean or in a cloud, it's constantly in motion, so it doesn't establish a Shabbat residence until it comes
to a halt by falling to the ground as rain.

Anyone who finds himself outside his Shabbat boundary is restricted
to a domain of four cubits—about three square feet, just enough to sit
down in. But for Shabbat purposes, any enclosed space, including a house,
a corral, or even a city, qualifies as a personal domain. That's why Orthodox
Jews living in cities build an eruv out of wires strung from post to post; this
notional boundary is enough to define the city as a single domain, making
it possible to carry items and push strollers on Shabbat.

What if the place you find yourself in on Shabbat is itself in motion? In
Eruvin 41b the Mishna tells a story about four sages who were traveling by
ship from "Prandisin" (probably Brindisi, a city in southern Italy). When
Shabbat began the ship was in port, so their legal residence was established
in the city. But then it put out to sea, carrying them more than two thousand

cubits away. Were the rabbis required to stay within their four-cubit personal zone, since they had gone past their Shabbat boundary? Or were they free to move around the ship, on the theory that it constituted a single domain?

The sages were divided: Rabban Gamliel and Elazar moved around the ship, while Yehoshua and Akiva "wished to be strict with themselves" and didn't move. But the Gemara holds that the law follows the more lenient interpretation of Gamliel and Elazar, for two reasons. First, since the passengers were already on board when Shabbat began, the ship rather than the city should be considered their Shabbat residence, leaving them free to move around inside it. Alternatively, one could say that since a ship is constantly in motion, there's simply no way to remain stationary within a four-cubit area.

Another factor is the height of the boat, since according to some authorities the Shabbat boundary only applies up to ten handbreadths from the ground. Since a ship is more than ten handbreadths (two and a half feet) above the seabed, it could be that a passenger is free to move around because he is floating above the boundary. Other authorities, however, believe that the boundary continues upward indefinitely in an imaginary line. This might seem like a purely hypothetical issue, since anyone walking on the ground would come in contact with the barrier even if it is only two feet high. Only someone who can fly through the air would have to worry about whether the boundary applies higher up; and in an age before airplanes, no one could get that high.

Except one person: the Messiah, who the rabbis believed would one day come down from heaven.

And it turns out that whether the Shabbat boundary applies in the upper atmosphere has important consequences for when the Messiah might arrive. If he is descending from heaven, the rabbis reason, he would have to travel more than two thousand cubits; and since the Messiah would never violate his boundary, it follows he won't arrive on Shabbat. Thus, the Gemara says, if a man swears an oath that he won't drink wine once the Messiah comes, he can safely drink on Shabbat, since the Messiah won't come that day.

But what if the boundary doesn't extend into the sky? In that case, the Messiah could come on Shabbat as easily as on any other day. So why is Jewish tradition certain that the Messiah won't arrive on Shabbat? The rabbis explain that it's because the Messiah will be heralded the day before his arrival by the prophet Elijah. And if Elijah arrived the day before Shabbat, the ensuing uproar would make it impossible for Jews to prepare for Shabbat properly. To preserve the sanctity of Shabbat, then, the Messiah will make sure to arrive during the week.

If you were looking for a discussion that qualifies as "Talmudic" in the pejorative sense—unnecessarily complicated and irrelevant to real life— you couldn't do better than this one. Yet it also demonstrates one of the distinctive strengths of rabbinic thinking—the way it weaves together the messianic and the pragmatic, this world and the World to Come. The rabbis aren't dazzled by the presence of the Messiah in their argument, because they don't see him as a legend or symbol; he is just another part of reality, a variable they must take into account in order to solve a problem. Of course, if the Messiah did come, the rabbis would have greeted him in ecstasy. But even in the messianic age, we'll still need to know how far we can walk on Shabbat.

Pesachim   On searching for chametz, the Passover sacrifice, and the size of the universe.

On the night before Passover, Jews traditionally search their homes for crumbs of chametz, the leavened bread that is prohibited on the holiday. Today, just about all of those homes are full of light bulbs; yet the search still takes place by candlelight, in accordance with the first mishna in tractate Pesachim: "The night of the 14th of Nisan we search for chametz by the light of a candle."

Is it important that we use a candle, or are we free to substitute modern tools that are better suited for the purpose, like a flashlight? This is a more complex question than it might seem, since in Jewish law actions aren't always judged by their results. Some things must be done a certain way simply because that's how God wants them done. It can even be dangerous to start looking for pragmatic justifications for mitzvot, since you might end up deciding you can achieve God's goal more effectively by disregarding the letter of the law. The sound of a trumpet carries further than the sound of a shofar, and a printed book is easier to read from than a Torah scroll; if results are all that matter, why do we keep using those ancient technologies?

Is using a candle to search for chametz a mitzva of that kind? Candles aren't actually mentioned in the commandment in Exodus 12:19, which simply says, "For a seven-day period leaven shall not be found in your homes." Accordingly, the Talmud rules that a candle isn't necessary when searching in areas that are brightly lit by a skylight, only in the dim corners of a room. A candle is preferable to a torch for practical reasons: it's less dangerous and can be used to search small holes.

The rabbis also try to anchor this rule in the Torah by using the technique of gezeira shava. As Rav Chisda points out, the word "found," used in Exodus 12:19, also appears in Genesis 44:12, when Joseph's steward searches for a missing silver cup: "Then the steward proceeded to search, beginning with the oldest and ending with the youngest. And the cup was found in

Benjamin's sack." The word "search" in this verse connects to Zephaniah 1:12: "At that time I will search Jerusalem with candles." In this way, the To-rah teaches that finding requires searching and searching requires candles. Clearly, the Talmud prefers not to think of any Jewish practice as merely instrumental. One way or another, custom has to be rooted in Torah.

Is it enough to search your house for chametz once, or do you have to worry that a crumb might enter the house after it's been cleared? The Mishna in Pesachim 9a tries to make matters simple: "We are not concerned that a weasel may have dragged chametz from house to house or from place to place." After all, if you had to keep checking and rechecking for chametz, "there would be no end to the matter."

But that isn't the end of the discussion. Say that you had nine piles of matza and one pile of chametz, and a mouse came and took a piece from one of the piles and carried it into a house, but you weren't sure which pile it was. Do you have to worry that the mouse picked up chametz, which would require the house to be searched again? In a math class, this would be an easy problem: there's a ten percent chance that the mouse took cha-metz and a ninety percent chance that it took matza. But the Talmud thinks differently about probability. Instead of counting the number of piles, it counts the number of alternatives, which in this case is two—chametz or matza. By this reckoning, there is a fifty-fifty chance that the mouse took chametz into the house, so it must be searched again—a way of calculating that enforces extra stringency.

But this principle doesn't hold in every case. What if a mouse carried some chametz into one of two houses, but we aren't sure which one? Would both houses have to be searched again? Here the odds really are fifty-fifty, but the answer in Pesachim 10a is surprising. If the owner of each house comes to a rabbi separately and asks if he must search his house again, the rabbi can tell each of them no, since he can assume the mouse went into the other house. But if the two owners come at the same time the rabbi must tell them both to search again, since at least one of the houses must be contaminated.

This is one of those Talmudic debates that can seem absurd if taken literally, but it's fascinating if viewed as a thought experiment, a way of testing the limits of a concept. It even bears an unlikely resemblance to a famous scientific thought experiment from the twentieth century, invented by the Austrian physicist Erwin Schrödinger as a way of dramatizing the strangeness of quantum physics.

In the Schrödinger's Cat scenario, a cat is locked in a box with a decaying radioactive element and a bottle of cyanide. The box is constructed so that when the radioactive material emits a particle, the bottle is shattered and the cat dies. The problem is that as long as the box remains closed, the laws of quantum physics make it impossible to say for sure whether or not a particle has been emitted. As a result, we're forced to say that the cat is both alive and dead at the same time. Similarly, in Pesachim, the mouse is considered to be in neither house until the owners ask at the same time, at which point the uncertainty collapses and it has to be located in real space.

For all its foretastes of the future, however, the Talmud thinks about material objects the way Aristotle did, as metaphysically distinct units of substance, rather than as arrangements of matter in space, the way we do today. In Pesachim 33b, for instance, the rabbis ask: Is a grape's juice part of the grape, or is it another entity contained within the grape?

This isn't a purely semantic question, since it has implications for the laws of ritual purity. This area of halakha has largely lapsed in the modern world, but in the Talmud the rabbis often discuss what makes food items tahor—pure, and therefore fit to be consumed by a priest—or tamei, impure. Like a virus, ritual impurity or tumah is an invisible contamination that is communicated by touch. It originates from taboo substances—including dead bodies, certain animals, semen, and menstrual blood—and can be passed on to other objects, including food.

If you squeeze grapes that are ritually impure, does the juice that comes out share the impurity? According to Rabbi Yochanan, juice and grapes are separate entities, so the juice is pure while it's inside the grape. It only becomes impure once it's squeezed out, by coming into contact with the grape's skin. But this can be avoided by squeezing the grapes one at a time, since the rule is that a piece of food smaller than an egg can't communicate impurity.

Some of the Passover observances discussed in Pesachim are the same today as they were two thousand years ago, but the languages spoken by Jews have changed many times since then. Linguistic change is already visible in the Talmud itself, since the Hebrew vocabulary used in the Mishna is sometimes opaque to the Aramaic-speaking rabbis of the Gemara. In Pesachim 39a, the Mishna lists the vegetables that count as maror, the bitter herbs eaten on Passover: hazeret, tamcha, harhavina, ulshin. To make sense of this list, the Gemara has to find the Aramaic equivalents: chasa, hindvei, tamachta. And the chain of translation doesn't end there. Rashi, the great medieval commentator on the Torah and Talmud, was uncertain what species were being referred to in the Gemara, and speculated about their French equivalents: hindvei, he suggested, was the same thing as krespelah. A thousand years later, krespelah is obscure, and scholars wonder if it means endive or escarole.

So while Jews still eat maror on Passover, it's likely that what we're eating—horseradish, at most American Seders—is quite different from what our ancestors put on their Seder plates. Fortunately, the Talmud defines maror primarily by taste: "Whatever has retained the taste of maror, we may fulfill our obligation with it; and whatever has not retained the taste of maror, we do not fulfill our obligation with it."

Another ingredient of the ancient Passover feast is missing today: the Pesach offering, the lamb that was sacrificed and eaten on the first night of the holiday. In Exodus 12:8, as God prepares to smite the Egyptians' first-born and finally release the children of Israel from slavery, he commands the people to prepare a lamb or kid for slaughter: "They shall eat the flesh that same night; they shall eat it roasted over the fire, with unleavened bread and with bitter herbs. Do not eat any of it raw, or cooked in any way with water, but roasted—head, legs, and entrails—over the fire."

This was the first Passover sacrifice, and it served as a prototype for those offered in the Temple for centuries afterward. But the Talmud wonders about details that the Torah doesn't address. Ordinarily, you would roast a lamb on a metal spit; but as the Gemara points out in Pesachim 74a, "With regard to a metal utensil, once part of it is hot, it is all hot, and the meat is roasted due to the heat of the spit. And the Merciful One states in the Torah that the lamb must be roasted in fire and not roasted through something else." To avoid this, Rabbi Akiva says the innards should be extracted and roasted separately: "One suspends the legs and entrails from the spit above the animal's head outside it."

While the Temple stood, the Passover sacrifice could only be offered there, and Jews came to Jerusalem for the holiday in large numbers. But many people lived too far away to make the pilgrimage; were they allowed to roast a lamb at home? Rabbi Yehuda says no: "It is forbidden for a person to say 'this meat is for Pesach,' because he appears as one who consecrates his animal and eats consecrated meat outside of Jerusalem" (53a). Some Jewish communities decided not to eat any roast meat on Passover rather than encourage such a mistake.

But Todos of Rome had a different view. Todos (the Talmud's rendering of Thaddeus) is an unusual figure: he wasn't a rabbi, like almost everyone quoted in the Talmud, and he didn't live in Palestine or Babylonia, the main rabbinic centers. But apparently he had authority over the Jews of Rome, decreeing that on Passover they should eat goats roasted in the same way as in the Temple—on a spit with the entrails removed. The rabbis were none too pleased with this, but apparently they felt unable to challenge it: "If you were not Todos we would decree excommunication upon you, for you are causing Jews to eat sacrificial meat outside Jerusalem," they said. Once the Temple was destroyed, all Jews had to do without the Pesach sacrifice; at today's Seders, it is represented symbolically by a shank bone.

A whole lamb is too much for one person to eat, and the custom was for groups of pilgrims to register to share a sacrifice. This could lead to complications: you could end up sharing your meal with someone who had "fine hands," a Talmudic euphemism for a glutton who takes more than his share of food. Even the sages weren't immune to this vice, as Rav Huna discovered when he agreed to "mix his bread together" with Ravina, only to find that "by the time Rav Huna ate one slice, Ravina ate eight" (89b). If such a person is sharing your Passover meal, can you tell him "Take your portion and leave," or could he reply "You accepted me" in the group without preconditions?

The Gemara approaches the problem by making an analogy. If one member of a registered group invites a new person to join without consulting the other members, that person isn't entitled to his own share of the meat; instead, he's considered a guest of the person who invited him, and they share a single portion. Similarly, a person with "fine hands" isn't entitled to eat for two; if he can't make do with his rightful share of the meat, he can be told to leave the group. But a registered group can't dismiss a member for no reason, leaving him unable to fulfill the mitzva of the Passover offering.

Anyone can join in a registered group, but it's forbidden to form a group of women and slaves without a free adult man present, because the Talmud believes they would engage in "frivolity"—that is, sexual misbehavior. Rabbi Yochanan adds that "We do not make a group that is entirely of converts," but the reason is not, as one might assume, that they would be ignorant of the right way to perform a sacrifice. On the contrary, "Perhaps they will be overly meticulous and cause [the animal] to be unnecessarily disqualified." Converts might find a blemish in a sacrifice where a native-born Jew would be more lenient.

In the course of this discussion the Gemara quotes a verse from Hosea, leading to a long digression about the prophet's life and message. Hosea, infuriated at the sins of his people, begged God to divorce the Jews and "exchange them for another nation." In response, God told Hosea to marry a prostitute, which he did, having three children with her. But when God instructed him to divorce her, Hosea refused: "Master of the Universe, I have children with her and I am unable to dismiss her or to divorce her." God replied that he felt the same way about the Jewish people: he could not dismiss them, even though they were steeped in sin. "Even at the time of the anger of the Holy One, Blessed be He, He remembers the attribute of compassion," says Rabbi Elazar.

In fact, even the exile of the Jews from their holy land is a sign of God's compassion, says Rabbi Oshaya. By scattering the Jewish people around the world, God made sure that their enemies couldn't exterminate them at one blow. Oshaya once argued this point with a Roman: If the Romans hadn't managed to annihilate the Jews after so many years, it wasn't for lack of trying, but "because you do not know how to do it." The Roman agreed: "I swear by Gappa, god of the Romans, with this we lie down and with this we rise up." The idea that the Jews should be grateful to God, not for saving them but for making it harder for their enemies to annihilate them, is a poignant example of how rabbinic Judaism turns suffering into a basis for faith.

Most Jews in the twenty-first century live in a very different world, and not just spiritually. Today we see Earth as just one of countless planets in the vastness of empty space. But ancient cosmology held that the Earth is at the center of the universe, surrounded by a series of concentric spheres, the outermost of which is studded with stars. Greeks and Jews had the same picture of the cosmos, though the Talmud says that they differed about one issue: "The Jewish sages say the celestial sphere is stationary, and the constellations revolve in their place within the sphere," while the gentile sages "say the entire celestial sphere revolves, and the constellations are stationary within the sphere" (94b).

This is one of the only moments in the Talmud where the rabbis take a respectful interest in what gentiles think; when it comes to astronomy, they recognized that the Greeks and Babylonians, who invented the subject, were worth listening to. The Talmud also recounts another debate among the sages about rotation of the sun. Ancient astronomers knew that the earth is round, but they believed that the sun moves around the earth, rather than vice versa. The Jewish sages believed that the earth is covered by a kind of opaque dome: during the day the sun is visible as it travels below the dome from east to west, and at night it returns from west to east by traveling above the dome, which is why we can't see it. This explains how the sun manages to return to the eastern horizon every morning.

The "sages of the nations of the world," however, had a different theory. They believed that at night the sun continues its rotation "beneath the earth," continuing to move in the same direction around the bottom of the globe so that it returns to the east at daybreak. Surprisingly, Yehuda HaNasi concedes that on this matter, "the statement of the sages of the nations of the world appears to be more accurate than our statement." The reason he gives is that subterranean springs stay warm at night, proving that they are warmed by the sun as it passes beneath the earth.

The Talmud usually doesn't engage in this kind of scientific speculation for its own sake, but to solve a concrete problem—in this case, who is allowed to participate in the "second Passover." According to Numbers 9:10, anyone who is unable to participate in the Passover sacrifice on the 14th of Nisan, because he is ritually impure or "on a journey far away," can make it up a month later, on the 14th of Iyyar. This raises the question of how to define "far away." The Talmud's rule is that a Jew is excused from coming to Jerusalem if he is "anywhere from the city of Modi'im and beyond," a distance of about ten miles.

After a complicated series of calculations about how long it takes to walk that distance and how far the sun travels in an equivalent period, Rava concludes that the size of the Earth is six thousand parasangs (a Persian unit of distance), or about twenty-one thousand miles. This is not too far from the correct figure for the circumference of the Earth, twenty-five thousand miles. Other sages believe the figure must be much larger, on the grounds that a given star is always in the same direction relative to the observer, no matter where he stands. This shows that the inhabited part of the world "rests under one star," and since there are thousands of stars in the sky, the whole globe must be thousands of times larger than the inhabited zone.

According to one estimate, "The size of Egypt was four hundred parasangs by four hundred parasangs, and Egypt is one-sixtieth of the size of Cush, and Cush is one-sixtieth of the world." By this reckoning, the surface of the Earth would be five hundred seventy-six million square parasangs, or about two billion square miles—ten times the correct figure. But the Talmud doesn't stop there. Earth is one-sixtieth of the size of the Garden of Eden, and the Garden of Eden is one-sixtieth of the size of Eden, and Eden is one-sixtieth of the size of Gehenna, the Jewish equivalent of Hell. Rava's sober attempt to figure out the size of the Earth has given way to cosmological fantasies.

Not until late in tractate Pesachim does its attention turn to what is now the heart of the holiday, the Seder. In some ways, the experience clearly hasn't changed much. The rabbis discuss ways to keep children awake and interested during the meal: They should be given "roasted grains and nuts . . . so that they will not fall asleep and also so they will ask the Four Questions" (109a). For the same reason, the Seder should start promptly at sundown. On most days Rabbi Akiba would keep his students at the study hall late into the night, but on Passover he sent them home early so their Seders could start on time.

Some of the familiar text of the Haggadah is taken directly from this tractate, such as the words of Rabban Gamliel in Pesachim 116b: "Anyone who did not explain these three matters on Passover has not fulfilled his obligation: Pesach, matza, and maror." As for the Four Questions, the Talmud's versions of the first, second, and fourth questions are the same ones we still recite today. But while our third question asks about why we recline on Passover, the Talmud's reads: "On all other nights we eat roasted, stewed, or cooked meat, but on this night only roasted." The new question was substituted by Maimonides in the twelfth century, since Seders hadn't included roasted meat for more than a thousand years.

In other ways, modern Seders differ from Talmudic ones. Take the rule that guests at a Seder are supposed to recline: This is the fourth of the Four Questions, yet today it's almost never observed. The reason is simple: In the ancient world wealthy people dined on couches, while today everyone sits on chairs at a table. Still, if we wanted to, we could surely find a way to recline, as Abaye did in a difficult situation: "When we were in the house of my teacher, there was not enough room for everyone to recline on Passover, so we reclined on each other's knees." Like everything in the Talmud, reclining must be done just so: "Lying on one's back is not called reclining," and "reclining to the right is not called reclining."

Then as now, Seders involved drinking four cups of wine. But in the Talmud this practice raises worries that seem strange today. Why do we drink four cups of wine when this is "a matter through which one will come to danger?" The danger doesn't have to do with drunkenness; rather, the rabbis believe that all actions performed in multiples of two expose one to witchcraft and demons. "A person should not eat pairs, and he should not drink pairs, and he should not wipe himself with pairs, and he should not attend to his sexual needs in pairs," the Gemara explains.

This idea doesn't have anything to do with Judaism, exactly; the rabbis don't trace it to any Torah verse. Rather, they seem to think of avoiding pairs as simple common sense, the way we might say "Always look both ways before crossing the street." Everyone just knows that demons are attracted by pairs. Indeed, Rav Pappa once heard it directly from Yosef the Demon, who explained that if a man drinks two cups of wine, the demons kill him, but if he drinks four cups they only injure him.

Fortunately, if a man happens to drink two cups of wine there's a way he can protect himself: "He should take his right thumb in his left hand, and his left thumb in his right hand, and say as follows: 'You, my thumbs, and I are three, which is not a pair.'" If a demon should overhear this and try to turn the tables by adding, "You and I are four," the man can do him one better by saying, "You and I are five," and so on indefinitely. Once, the Gemara relates, "there was an incident in which someone kept counting after the demon until he reached a hundred and one, and the demon burst in anger."

On another occasion, a man was tricked by his vengeful ex-wife into drinking an even number of cups of wine—after he drank sixteen cups he lost count, understandably—and a demon seized him. He escaped by hugging a palm tree, causing the demon to be transferred into the tree, which dried up and burst. According to Ameimar—who heard it from "the chief of witches"—if you are set upon by witches you can banish them with an incantation: "Hot dung in torn date baskets in your mouth, witches."

There are other ways besides pairs to attract the attention of demons. According to Reish Lakish, "There are four matters. The one who performs them, his blood is upon his own head, and he is held liable for his own life: One who relieves himself between a palm tree and a wall, one who passes between two palm trees, one who drinks borrowed water, and one who passes over spilled water." Just as the rabbis have precise rules about how tall an eruv has to be and when to say the Shema, so they have rules about urinating between a wall and a palm tree. This is dangerous "only when there are not four cubits of space between the two objects. However, if there are four cubits, we have no problem."

The tractate's last word on folk beliefs, however, is remarkably sensible. The rabbis observe that superstitions are relative: the Jews of Babylonia worried about pairs, but in Palestine they were indifferent. "The rule of the matter is that all who are particular about pairs, the demons are particular with him; and if one is not particular, they are not particular with him." In other words, the whole idea of pairs being dangerous is a self-fulfilling prophecy. If we suffer from performing even-numbered actions, it's because we expect to suffer. Of course, that doesn't mean the demons don't exist.

Shekalim   On money changers in the Temple, the appearance of impropriety, and what happened to the Ark of the Covenant.

The world's understanding of ancient Judaism has been profoundly shaped, and not for the better, by the New Testament story about Jesus throwing the money changers out of the Temple. "It is written, my house shall be called a house of prayer, but you have made it a den of thieves," Jesus says in Matthew 21:13. Apparently the Jews were so obsessed with money that they even allowed it to profane their holiest place. But what were those money changers doing in the Temple? Were they merely profiteers, or were they actually serving a sacred purpose themselves?

The answer can be found in tractate Shekalim, which deals with the tax paid by Jews in the ancient world for the upkeep of the Temple. (There is no Gemara on Shekalim in the Babylonian Talmud, so for this tractate the Daf Yomi cycle substitutes the Jerusalem Talmud.) This obligation originates in the Torah, where Moses levies a half-shekel tax on every adult male Israelite to pay for the construction of the Tabernacle. But things were much more logistically complicated in the days of the Second Temple, when many Jews lived far from Jerusalem. How could they make sure their contributions reached the priests? And what was the equivalent of the Biblical half-shekel in the many different currencies used in the Roman and Persian Empires?

That is where the money changers came in. "On the 15th of Adar," the date the half-shekel was due, "money changers would sit at tables set up in the rest of the country, outside the Temple, to handle the collection of shekels. On the 25th they would set up in the Temple." It's not certain exactly what services they provided—whether they collected coins, made change, or exchanged foreign coins into Judean ones. But it's clear that they weren't profiteers; they were functionaries who made it possible for Jews to discharge a religious obligation.

In the absence of a modern banking system, the tax could only be paid in cash, which meant that large quantities of coins had to be transported to Jerusalem. Jews would deposit their coins into "horns," chests with a small mouth and a wide base. If a community wanted to make things easier, they could exchange the collected half-shekels for large gold coins that weighed less.

These annual shipments must have been a tempting target for thieves, and the Talmud discusses what to do if the money is lost or stolen en route. Every year on a certain date, the Temple priests would make "the collection of the chamber," withdrawing all the funds necessary for the coming year's expenses. Before that date, the coins were technically still the property of their donors; after it, they become Temple property. As a result, if a shipment is lost before the collection of the chamber takes place, the community must replace them, but after that date the loss is born by the Temple treasury. But if the coins are lost and the donors replace them, and then the original shipment is found, they don't get their money back; both payments go to the Temple.

How could Jews using different currencies calculate the value of a Biblical half-shekel? Rabbi Yehuda observes that "for shekels there is no real fixed value" (2a). When the Temple was rebuilt after the Babylonian exile, the tithe was paid in darkonot, gold coins from Persia. Later, under Greek rule, Jews paid with a sela, a silver coin. Some Jews tried to use a dinar, but apparently this wasn't valuable enough and the priests "refused to accept it." The only constant is that everyone must pay the same amount, however it is denominated. The attempt to calculate the exact worth of a half-shekel even takes on a mystical dimension: Rabbi Meir says that when God originally instructed Moses about the tithe, he showed him "a kind of coin of fire" (4b)—the Platonic original of the half-shekel, showing its exact volume and weight.

The image expresses nostalgia for an era when God made his expectations of the Jewish people crystal clear. In the Talmud, by contrast, the sages are sometimes in the dark. For instance, the Mishna in Shekalim 5a offers a list of "the officials who served in the Temple": Yochanan ben Pinchas was in charge of the seals, Achiyya was in charge of the libations, Petachya was responsible for bird-offerings, and so on. But the Gemara doesn't know how to interpret this catalog. Why are these particular names recorded, when over the centuries many individuals must have served in those offices? Rabbi Shimon suggests that the men named were "the most fit ... from whatever generation"—the best ever to serve in each office. Others believe that the list is simply a snapshot of a moment in time: "The tanna who was in that generation enumerated those who served in his generation."

Traditions gathered around some of these officials. Ben Bevai was in charge of braiding the wicks used in the Temple's lamps—a menial job, so his willingness to perform it became an example of piety. When some Jews resisted serving as charity commissioners in the town of Kufra, Rabbi Yosei brought up Ben Bevai: "If this man, who was appointed to deal with the wicks, merited to be listed with the greatest of that generation, are you not all the more honored to deal with life-sustaining matters?" Hugras ben Levi was in charge of the Levites who sang Psalms in the Temple. Apparently he had a technique that involved "sticking his thumb in his mouth" in order to "produce several kinds of music" at the same time, which was so enchanting that when he sang "all of his fellow priests would lurch toward him at once."

The Talmud also makes clear that Temple service involved material and psychological temptations, which some priests were unable to resist. "There was great haughtiness among the high priests" when it came to building the ceremonial ramp used for the sacrifice of the red heifer. Each new holder of the office would build a ramp at great expense, even though the old one was still standing, to show off his wealth. Then there was the House of Garmu, a priestly family whose duty was to prepare the showbread, the sacred loaves perpetually on display in the Temple. The recipe was a trade secret and they refused to share it with anyone. To break their monopoly, the priests "brought in craftsmen from Alexandria" to bake the showbread, but they turned out to be "not as proficient as the house of Garmu" in taking the loaves out of the oven, and their bread kept getting spoiled. The Garmuites had to be hired back at twice the salary: "They had been receiving twelve maneh, and they gave them twenty-four."

Another family, the House of Avtinas, was in charge of making incense for the Temple, and the rabbis note that its female members never wore perfume, to avoid the suspicion that they were using Temple incense for their own benefit. This shows that public officials must avoid even the appearance of impropriety. According to Rabbi Yonatan, "A person must appear justified before people as he must appear justified before the Omnipresent."

The same principle applied to the priest in charge of withdrawing funds from the Temple treasury. To avoid suspicion that he was pocketing coins for himself, he couldn't wear cuffed sleeves, tefillin, or shoes. Other priests would publicly comb his hair to show that there were no coins hidden in it. According to one authority, the priest had to talk continuously while making the collection, to prove he wasn't hiding coins in his mouth.

From the details of coin collection, the Talmudic discussion drifts into speculation about other aspects of the Temple, including its physical dimensions. The rabbis had no first-hand witnesses to consult; all they had were oral traditions and Biblical descriptions, which were often contradictory and hard to interpret. They knew, for instance, that the Holy of Holies, the chamber at the heart of the Temple, once contained the Ark of the Covenant, in which Moses placed the tablets inscribed by God with the Ten Commandments.

The book of Exodus gives the measurements of the Ark as two and a half cubits high and one and a half cubits across. Using these measurements, the rabbis try to calculate how large the tablets must have been, since they had to fit inside. But there are a number of unknown variables. Did the Ark also contain the fragments of the original tablets that Moses smashed when he came down from Sinai and saw the Israelites worshiping the golden calf? At the end of Deuteronomy, Moses instructs the people to "take this book of the law and put it by the side of the Ark of the Covenant": does that mean the Ark also contained a complete Torah scroll?

The rabbis could only speculate, because the Ark disappeared in 586 BCE, when the Babylonians conquered Jerusalem and destroyed the First Temple. In the Second Temple, the Holy of Holies was empty. So where, the rabbis wonder in Shekalim 15b, did the Ark end up? According to Rabbi Elazar, it was one of "the vessels of the House of the Lord" plundered by the Babylonian king Nebuchadnezzar. But would God really allow such a holy object to vanish into the Babylonian treasure houses?

Reish Lakish argues that the Ark never left Jerusalem, but remained hidden inside the Holy of Holies. Others say that it was buried underneath the Temple and that the priests would genuflect in its honor. On one occasion, a priest saw an unusual paving stone and was about to start digging it up, when he was struck down and "his soul left him." This was proof that something supernatural was happening: "And they knew with certainty that the Ark was sequestered there."

If the Ark could be hidden, so could other magical relics mentioned in the Bible that later disappeared: a canister of manna, Aaron's rod, and the flask of oil used to anoint Judah's kings. In talking about the fate of these objects, the rabbis seem to be grappling with the gulf between Biblical times, when God regularly performed miracles, and the fallen present, when God's power must be taken on faith. But the rabbis believed that the Ark was only hidden, not destroyed—leaving open the possibility that one day the age of miracles would return.

Yoma On sacred choreography, the meaning of atonement, and the many uses of manna.

Today as in the days of the Second Temple, Jews observe Yom Kippur with penitence, prayer, and fasting. But the holiday is missing what used to be its most important element: the elaborate ritual performed by the high priest to obtain forgiveness for the sins of the Jewish people. Most of tractate Yoma, which is devoted to Yom Kippur, focuses on this ritual.

The preparations for Yom Kippur began seven days before the holiday, when the high priest moved from his house to a room in the Temple called the Chamber of Parhedrin (from a Greek word meaning "public official"). This was meant to keep him safe from ritual impurity—in particular, to ensure that he didn't have sex with his wife, in case she turned out to be menstruating. It's required that the high priest have a wife, since Leviticus 16:6 says that Yom Kippur atones "for him and for his house," meaning his wife and children.

But what would happen if the high priest's wife died in the seven days leading up to Yom Kippur, leaving him unable to perform the ceremony? According to Rabbi Yehuda, a substitute wife was designated for this contingency; but other rabbis are skeptical, since in that case "there is no end to the matter." If you have to worry about whether the high priest's wife might die, you would also have to worry about whether her substitute might die, and so on.

Sex isn't the only way to contract ritual impurity. Even when he's alone the high priest might experience a seminal emission, rendering him unfit for Temple service. But miraculously, "a seminal emission did not befall the high priest on Yom Kippur" in the whole history of the Temple (21a). This is one of ten miracles God performed to keep the Temple running. Even though animals were constantly being sacrificed there, "no fly was seen in the slaughterhouse" and "no woman miscarried from the aroma of the sacrificial meat." And while huge crowds visited the Temple on major holidays, there was always enough room for everyone to bow down to pray.

Even so, the high priest's purity wasn't left up to chance; he was forbidden to eat foods that might lead to sexual excitement. The rabbis disagree about exactly which foods fall into this category, but they mention several possibilities, including eggs, fatty meat, and white wine. Instead, they would deliberately feed the high priest food with a laxative effect, to empty his bowels so that he wouldn't need to defecate on Yom Kippur.

On the night before Yom Kippur, the high priest had to keep vigil in prayer and repentance. To keep him from falling asleep, "the young priests would snap the middle finger before him" and make him get out of bed to stand on the chilly stone floor. He was also kept awake by lectures and reading: "If he was a scholar, he would teach Torah. If he was not a scholar, Torah scholars would teach Torah before him. And if he was accustomed to read the Bible, he would read, and if not, they would read the Bible before him."

This passage opens up a surprising perspective on the priesthood: apparently it was possible to be appointed high priest without knowing anything about Torah. The Mishna even contemplates the possibility of a high priest who can't read. In that case, he wouldn't be able to read the description of his Yom Kippur duties, and a group of elders would have to instruct him. The Gemara marvels at this: "Is it conceivable that perhaps the high priest did not learn to read? Do we appoint a high priest of that sort?" Doesn't tradition say that the high priest must be preeminent "in strength, in beauty, in wisdom, and in wealth" (18a)?

During the days of the First Temple, the Gemara says, this was true. But the Second Temple was inferior to the first in every respect, including the quality of its priests. Indeed, the ancient Jewish historian Josephus writes that the high priesthood was a political appointment, used by kings to reward allies or solicit bribes. In the Gemara, Rav Asi mentions one such occasion, when "Marta, daughter of Baitos, brought a half-se'a of dinars to King Yannai"—Alexander Jannaeus, who ruled Judea in the early first century BCE—in exchange for appointing Yehoshua ben Gamla as high priest.

As if politics and money weren't bad enough, the high priesthood was also afflicted by religious sectarianism. The theological differences between Pharisees and Sadducees became symbolized in small ritual distinctions. The Pharisees believed that on Yom Kippur the high priest should light his pan of incense inside the Holy of Holies, while the Sadducees thought he should light it before entering. The Pharisees made each high priest vow that he would follow the official protocol and not engage in any Sadducee deviations. The necessity of this, the Gemara says, made the Pharisees themselves weep for shame.

Still, on one occasion a Sadducee high priest managed to light the incense outside the Holy of Holies. His punishment was immediate: "A type of sound was heard in the courtyard, as an angel came and struck him in the face." When examined, he was found to have "the likeness of the footprint of a calf between his shoulders" (19b)—proof of divine punishment, since angels had cowlike feet. Within a few days the Sadducee died "and was laid out in the garbage," denied a proper burial.

It's because Temple service is a life-and-death matter that the Talmud goes to such lengths to get it right. At one stage in the ceremony, the high priest has to offer incense in the Holy of Holies. In Yoma 47a, the Mishna says he would scoop incense out of a container with his bare hands and then transfer it to a spoon or ladle. He would take the spoon full of incense in his left hand and a pan of burning coals in his right hand and carry them into the Holy of Holies, which no one ever entered except for the high priest on this day. There he would put the incense on the pan to create fragrant smoke.

Detailed as it is, this account doesn't satisfy the Gemara, which raises a number of questions. Why does the high priest use a spoon to carry the incense, when the instructions in Leviticus 16:12 say that he should come to the altar with "his hands full of sweet incense"? And why does he carry the spoon in his left hand, when as a rule priests only used the right hand to perform sacred duties? The answer turns out to be pragmatic: It's not physically possible to carry a handful of incense and the coal pan at the same time, so a spoon is necessary. And since the coal pan is heavy and hot, the high priest needs to use his right hand to carry it, so the spoon has to go in his left hand.

But is it true, the Gemara wonders, that there is no way around using a spoon? Couldn't the high priest "take the coal pan in his teeth," freeing his hands to carry the incense? This method is ruled out as undignified: "Now, before a king of flesh and blood one would not do so. All the more so before the King of kings, the Holy One, Blessed be He."

There is another logistical problem. According to Leviticus, the incense must be put into the coal pan by hand, so the high priest can't simply pour it from the spoon. To transfer the incense from the spoon to his hands, he has to execute a complex maneuver. Holding the bowl of the spoon with his fingertips, he slowly pushes it backwards with his thumbs, so that the handle rests between his outstretched arms. Then he uses his elbows to turn the spoon over and pour the incense into his hands. This was so hard to do, the Gemara says, that offering incense was considered the most difficult of all the rites in the Temple service.

Every element of the Yom Kippur ritual is given a similar degree of scrutiny. After lighting the incense, the high priest sprinkled the blood of a bull and a goat in the Holy of Holies, and this too had to be done in a certain way. Dipping his fingers into the bowl of blood, the high priest flung the blood "like one who lashes with a whip" (53b). He sprinkled the blood upward once and then downward seven times, keeping track by counting out loud: "One; one and one; one and two; one and three," and so on.

The strangest part of the Yom Kippur ritual is the scapegoat. Following the procedure laid down in Leviticus 16, the high priest took two identical goats and cast lots, assigning one to be sacrificed in the Temple and the other to be led into the wilderness "for Azazel." Who or what Azazel is, the Talmud doesn't say; it sounds very much like the name of a demon, though some commentators believe it is a place name.

The high priest then placed both his hands on the sacrificial goat and recited a prayer asking God to forgive the people's sins: "Please God, Your people, the house of Israel, have sinned, and done wrong, and rebelled before you. Please God, grant atonement, please, for the sins, and for the wrongs, and for the rebellions" (66a). In this prayer the high priest didn't call God by a title like Adonai but used his full, proper name, which it is ordinarily forbidden to pronounce. This was the only time God's name could be heard publicly.

But what was that name? No one knows for sure, since it was never written down. Some commentators believe it was the name written in the Torah as YHWH, pronounced with the same vowels as in the word "Adonai." Others say it was an esoteric name forty-two letters long. Whatever the Jews heard, it was a sacred and emotionally overwhelming moment, as the Talmud explains: "When they would hear the name emerging from the mouth of the high priest, they would kneel and prostrate themselves and fall on their faces, and say: Blessed is the name of his glorious kingdom forever and ever."

After making his confession on behalf of the people, the high priest handed over the scapegoat to a specially chosen priest, who led it out of Jerusalem into the desert. The route from the Temple gates to the designated cliff had ten booths, at each of which the priest would be offered food and drink, though the Gemara says that "no man ever needed this." A crowd of people, including the most prominent citizens of Jerusalem, would escort the priest and the goat from booth to booth, until they reached the last one; then the priest would proceed alone to the cliffside.

There he performed the most overtly magical part of the ceremony. The priest would take a strip of crimson cloth and divide it in two, tying one half to the horns of the goat and the other to a rock. Then the goat was pushed over the cliff to its death: "it would not reach halfway down the mountain until it was torn limb from limb." At this point the crimson strip would announce, like a piece of litmus paper, whether the Jews' sacrifice had been accepted by God and their atonement granted. If the people's sins were forgiven, the crimson would turn white, following the words of the prophet Isaiah: "Though your sins be as scarlet, they will become white as snow." If not, the strip would remain red.

At first, the Gemara says, the strip was displayed at the entrance to the Temple. But the priests found that if the strip stayed crimson, the Jews would be so dejected that Yom Kippur was ruined. To avoid this, the strip was moved inside the Temple where only the priests could see it; but even then, the people would try to peek inside. Finally the priests decided to tie the strip to a rock in the wilderness, so that the Jerusalemites couldn't find out its message until the day after Yom Kippur.

Next came the public reading of the Torah, a practice instituted when the Second Temple was built. On that occasion, described in Nehemiah 9, the whole people of Israel listened to the Torah and pledged to follow its commandments. The Gemara in Yoma 69a expands on this story, adding that the people also asked God to take away the yetzer hara, the evil inclination that tempted them to commit idolatry in the past. God had given this temptation to the Jews so they could earn merit by overcoming it, but now they declared that they weren't up to the challenge: "We do not want it, and we do not want its reward."

Then a miracle occurred: "A tablet fell from the heavens upon which was written: Truth." This was a sign that God had granted the prayer, and after the people fasted for three days, God "delivered the evil inclination to them" in the form of "a fiery lion cub" that emerged from the Holy of Holies. The prophet Zechariah instructed the Israelites to "throw it into a container of lead and seal the opening with lead." As a result, they were freed once and for all from the temptation to commit idolatry—and indeed, the worship of foreign gods seems to have been much less of a problem in the Second Temple period than it was earlier in Jewish history.

But the story doesn't end there. Seeing that God was in a mood to answer their prayers, the Israelites asked to be delivered from sexual temptation as well. But when this was granted it turned out to be a mixed blessing, since every living creature lost the desire to procreate—even the chickens, so that not a single fresh egg could be found in the Land of Israel. Zechariah warned that without sexual desire the world would die out, so the Jews decided to set the evil inclination free. But first they gouged out its eyes, which is why, the Talmud explains, "A person is no longer aroused to commit incest with his relatives." The story expresses the rabbis' ambivalent feelings about sexuality: A world without sex would be a dead world, but the sexual impulse is dangerous and must be kept under tight control.

The high priest is the star of the Yom Kippur ceremony, but Yoma explains that on ordinary days, priests were assigned their roles in the Temple rituals by lottery. The priesthood was divided into watches or shifts, and every day the watch on duty would gather in the Chamber of Hewn Stone, a large basilica on the Temple grounds. There the priests were counted and one was chosen by lot for each duty.

As the Talmud observes, however, there is a problem with this account: "It is prohibited to count Jews, even for the purposes of a mitzva." In 2 Samuel 24, King David's insistence on taking a census of the fighting men in his kingdom is punished by God with a plague that kills seventy thousand people. But there were ways to get around this prohibition. King Saul counted men "by sheep": each man would add a sheep to the flock, and then the flock would be counted. Similarly, in the Temple, the priests would stick out their fingers and those would be counted—a thin legal fiction to avoid counting people.

Apparently priests would sometimes try to double their odds by sticking out a thumb as well as a finger, a form of cheating punishable by lashes. The necessity for this rule suggests that competition for certain duties was intense. Tradition had it that the priest who burned the incense would become rich, creating such high demand for the post that no priest was allowed to hold it twice. In fact, the lottery system was instituted because jockeying for the best jobs had gotten out of hand. Priests would race each other up the ramp to the altar for the chance to remove the ashes. On one occasion, the loser in the race took a knife and stabbed the winner in the heart—a sign, the Talmud says, of how "bloodshed had become trivialized" among the Jewish people (23a).

The low moral standard of the priesthood contrasts sharply with the virtue of great Torah scholars such as Hillel, whom the Talmud offers as a role model. Hillel started life as a day laborer, and he would save half of his meager earnings for admission to the study hall. One winter Friday, when he hadn't found work and couldn't afford to pay the entrance fee, he climbed up on the roof of the study hall to listen through the skylight. That evening, the heads of the academy noticed that the skylight was blocked; when they went to investigate, they found Hillel buried in snow "three cubits high." Even though it was Shabbat, they built a fire to warm him and save his life: "This man is worthy for us to desecrate Shabbat for him," they said (35b).

Hillel's story shows that being poor is no excuse for not studying Torah; Rabbi Elazar's shows that being rich is no excuse either. The Talmud says that Rabbi Elazar owned a thousand villages and a thousand ships, yet he spent his whole life traveling "from city to city and from state to state to study Torah" with various teachers. "In all his days, he never went and saw" his own properties; once his servants seized him and put him to forced labor, not recognizing the master they had never seen.

Not until the last chapter in Yoma does the focus shift from the role of the priests to the experience of the ordinary Jew on Yom Kippur. Six activities are forbidden on the day: "It is prohibited to engage in eating and in drinking, and in bathing, and in smearing oil on one's body, and in wearing shoes, and in conjugal relations" (73b). (Olive oil was commonly used for bathing in the ancient world.) The Biblical basis for these prohibitions is Leviticus 16:29: "You shall afflict your souls, and shall do no manner of work." But how do we know, the Gemara asks, that the words "afflict your souls" refer specifically to fasting? "I might have thought that one should sit in the sun or in the cold," or other ascetic acts. The rabbis find an answer in Deuteronomy 8:3, where the word "afflict" refers specifically to going hungry:

"And he afflicted you and caused you to hunger, and fed you with manna."

The mention of manna leads the Gemara to a long digression about this miracle food. According to Exodus 16, God fed the Israelites in the desert with manna, a white substance that fell like dew. This was a sign of his great care for the Jewish people, yet the rabbis note that the Torah describes manna in ambivalent terms. In Deuteronomy 8:16, why does Moses say that God fed the Israelites manna "in order to afflict you"? Wasn't manna supposed to be the cure for the affliction of hunger, rather than the affliction itself? According to Rabbi Ami, what the Torah means is that the Israelites suffered from anxiety about the manna. Since it spoiled quickly, they had to gather it every day and could never be sure there would be enough to eat tomorrow. "There is no comparison between one who has bread in his basket and one who does not have bread in his basket," Rabbi Ami observes.

The Gemara goes on to speculate about the taste, texture, and appearance of manna. According to Exodus 16:31, it was "white like coriander seed and tasted like wafers in honey." This is puzzling, because coriander seed is brown; but the rabbis suggest that the Torah means manna was "round like coriander seed but white like a pearl." Another explanation is based on a verbal similarity: in Hebrew coriander is called "gad," which sounds like "maggid," the word for telling, suggesting that manna could be used to tell the answers to problems.

That's because of another miraculous quality of manna: no matter how much or how little a family gathered, it always turned out to equal an omer (about three and a half pounds) per person. As the Talmud points out, this made it possible to use manna to count the number of people in a household. If a widow immediately remarried and got pregnant, she might be unsure which husband was the father. Manna held the answer: all she had to do was figure out whether the baby's ration showed up with her dead husband's family or her new husband's.

Similarly, in a divorce case, "Moses would say to [the husband and wife]: In the morning there will be a judgment. The following day, if her omer of manna was found in her husband's house, it would be clear that she sinned against him," since God still regarded her as part of her husband's family. On the other hand, if the manna "was found in her father's house, it would be clear that he sinned against her," since she would return to her father's house after the divorce. This way of thinking about manna captures the difference between the Torah and the Talmud: for the former it is a miracle of sustenance, for the latter a miracle of jurisprudence.

Fasting on Yom Kippur is required for all healthy adults, but children, pregnant women, and sick people are exempt. With pregnant women, in particular, the Talmud is very lenient when it comes to food. Even a pregnant woman's craving for pork should be satisfied—first, by tasting a bit of pork juice through a straw; then, if she's still craving it, by eating the meat itself. That's because the rabbis see a pregnant woman's appetites as a health matter, and "there is no halakha that stands in the way of saving a life" (82a). When a life is at stake, even on Shabbat or Yom Kippur, one must act immediately, without waiting to get a rabbi's permission. For instance, if a child is drowning in the sea you should cast a net to save him, even if in the process you end up catching some fish, which is forbidden on Shabbat. Even a child who gets stuck behind a locked door, but isn't in imminent danger, should be freed on Shabbat, since it's possible he will end up getting hurt.

There are only three sins that must be avoided even at the price of one's life: idol worship, forbidden sexual relations, and murder. Once a man came to Rava with a dilemma: "The master of the village where I live said to me: Kill so-and-so, and if you do not do so, I will kill you." Killing an attacker in self-defense is legally permitted, but in this case the man would be saving his own life by killing an innocent third party, and Rava rules that this is forbidden. "What did you see to make you think that your blood is redder than his?" Rava asks. No life is more valuable than another, even one's own.

Just as bad as murder is chillul Hashem, the desecration of God's name. "What are the circumstances that cause desecration of God's name?" the Gemara asks, and gives a few examples. If a Torah scholar takes meat from a butcher but doesn't pay for it right away, it is a descration of the name, because it might give people the impression that a pious Jew is acting unethically. Similarly, if a sage walks four cubits without wearing tefillin, he would be giving the impression that he treats God's laws lightly, even if he is legally excused from wearing them because of frailty.

Desecrating the name, in other words, is anything that brings disgrace on Jews and Judaism. A person who represents Judaism publicly must be unimpeachable in every area of life. "One who reads Torah, and learns Mishna, and serves Torah scholars, but his business practices are not done faithfully, and he does not speak pleasantly with other people, what do people say about him? Woe to so-and-so who studied Torah, woe to his father who taught him Torah . . . see how destructive are his deeds, and how ugly are his ways," the Gemara says (86a).

Chillul Hashem is such a serious sin that it's impossible to atone for. For minor sins, "repentance atones": if you are genuinely sorry, God will forgive you. For more serious sins, "repentance suspends punishment and Yom Kippur atones": being penitent will make God hold off punishing you until Yom Kippur, which absolves the sins of the Jewish people. For one who desecrates the name of God, however, only "death absolves him."

God forgives most sins on Yom Kippur, but that doesn't mean one can sin freely during the rest of the year. "With regard to one who says, I will sin and Yom Kippur will atone, Yom Kippur does not atone," the Talmud says. In particular, the sinner must gain forgiveness from the people he has injured: "for transgressions between one person and another, Yom Kippur does not atone until he appeases the other person." Even the greatest rabbis obeyed this rule. Once Rabbi Yirmeya insulted Rabbi Abba, so he "went and sat at the threshold" of Abba's house, seeking to apologize. While he was sitting there, Abba's maid accidentally poured a chamber pot onto Yirmeya's head. When Abba heard about this, he went and sought Yirmeya's forgiveness in turn. Neither rabbi wanted to be put in the wrong by refusing to apologize.

Indeed, it could be dangerous not to apologize to a Torah scholar. Once a butcher insulted Rav, who went to the butcher's shop to get an apology. But when he saw Rav he said, "Go, I have nothing to say to you"—whereupon one of the bones from the carcass he was cutting flew up and struck him in the throat, killing him. Sages are held to a high ethical standard, but they are also entitled to a high degree of respect, and Heaven makes sure that they get it.

Sukka On squaring the circle,
using an elephant as a wall,
and why the sages juggled torches.

In Leviticus 23:42, God institutes the holiday of Sukkot as a commemoration of the Israelites' years of wandering in the desert: "You shall dwell in booths [sukkot] seven days . . . that your generations shall know that I made the children of Israel to dwell in booths when I brought them out of the land of Egypt." But what exactly is a sukka? Clearly the Torah intends it to be different from an ordinary house. But does any temporary structure qualify, or does the sukka have to meet certain specifications about height, seating capacity, or building materials? These are the kinds of questions the Talmud asks in tractate Sukka, as it tries to translate the Torah's brief commandment into a detailed blueprint.

The Mishna begins by setting a height limit: "A sukka that is more than twenty cubits high is unfit." It's unlikely that anyone would want to build such a giant sukka—twenty cubits is about thirty feet—but the rule helps to express the Talmud's idea of what it means to celebrate a Jewish holiday. As Rabba explains, someone in a sukka should be able to tell at a glance that he's in a temporary structure covered by branches, not an ordinary house with a roof. If the sukka is more than twenty cubits high, someone sitting inside can't see the top without craning his neck.

If a sukka has a maximum height, it stands to reason that there must be a minimum height as well, which the Mishna fixes at ten handbreadths, about two and a half feet. Anything shorter than that belongs legally to the domain of the ground and doesn't count as a separate structure. The Gemara ingeniously deduces this rule from Psalm 115:16, "The heavens are the heavens of the Lord, and the Earth he gave to the children of man," which suggests that heaven and earth are separate, non-overlapping domains.

How do we know where to draw the line between them? The Gemara finds an answer in Exodus 25:22, where God promises to speak to Moses from the top of the Ark. Based on the Torah's detailed instructions for building the Ark, the rabbis deduce that the Ark with its cover was ten handbreadths tall. If God came no closer to the ground than that, it must be because ten handbreadths is the height at which the heavens stop and the earth begins.

The Talmud is adept at this kind of sacred geometry, but figuring out the dimensions of a valid sukka also requires the ordinary Euclidean kind. The minimum size of a square sukka is four cubits by four cubits, about forty-two square feet. If you wanted to build a circular sukka, what would its diameter have to be in order to have the same area? This question, in Sukka 8a, brings the rabbis up against the problem of "squaring the circle," one of the mysteries of ancient geometry. Because pi is an irrational number that extends to an infinite number of decimal places, it's impossible to draw a square with exactly the same area as a given circle—a fact that was already known to the ancient Greeks.

However, it's possible to find a rough-and-ready answer by using approximate values for irrational numbers. Defining pi as 3 (instead of 3.14159 ...) and the square root of 2 as 1.4 (instead of 1.414213 ...), the rabbis find that a 4-by-4-cubit square is about the same size as a circle with a circumference of 16.8 cubits. Assuming that each seat is two-thirds of a cubit wide, such a sukka could fit twenty-four people sitting with their backs to the walls. It sounds simple enough, but the actual Talmudic discussion is difficult to follow thanks to the terse language of the Gemara, which doesn't use numerals or diagrams. For generations of Talmud students, this tractate must have functioned as a demanding introduction to geometry.

Yet there are also fanciful moments. After establishing the dimensions of a valid sukka, the rabbis discuss what materials it can be made of. In Sukka 23a, the Gemara asks, could you build a sukka using an elephant as one of the walls? It's certainly tall enough; even if the elephant died and fell over, it would be more than ten handbreadths high. To make sure it didn't wander off, leaving the sukka open, it could be tied up. A wall isn't supposed to have gaps, which makes the big space between an elephant's legs a problem, but this opening could be filled up with leaves.

The image of celebrating Sukkot in the shade of an elephant is surreal, and surely no Jews in history have actually done it. So why do the rabbis bother worrying about it? That question can be asked about many of the unlikely scenarios in the Talmud, but it would be a mistake to take these problems literally. They can be compared to the thought experiments used in philosophy to clarify our beliefs, such as the famous "trolley problem" devised by the British philosopher Phillipa Foot. In this scenario, a trolley speeding down a track is about to strike five people, unless the driver steers it onto a different track where it will kill one person.

Probably no trolley driver has ever been in this situation, but the point of the problem is to make us think about how intention and consequences figure into our moral judgment. Similarly, the Talmud isn't trying to solve a real dilemma, but to define exactly what makes a wall qualify as a wall. The elephant shares some of a wall's qualities, like height and solidity, but not others, like immobility. Maybe there's an element of whimsy here as well. Why shouldn't the rabbis occasionally let their imaginations loose?

Certainly they had a great deal of historical imagination; they had to, since the Talmud often deals with practices that ceased with the destruction of the Temple. One of the most joyous Temple festivities was the Celebration of the Drawing of the Water, described in Sukka 51a. A priest would fill a golden jug with water from the pool of Siloam, bring it into the Temple to the accompaniment of shofar blasts, and pour it into silver basins.

This was accompanied by rejoicing and celebration in the Temple court-yard, which was lit up by tall golden candelabras. Boys in training for the priesthood would climb up ladders to light them, using wicks made from worn-out priestly garments. This created a radiance so bright that "there was not a courtyard in Jerusalem that was not illuminated." Musicians stood on the Temple steps and played "lyres, harps, cymbals, and trumpets, and countless musical instruments." Even the greatest Torah scholars took part in the fun: "It is said of Rabban Shimon ben Gamliel that when he would rejoice at the Celebration ... he would take eight flaming torches and toss one and catch another, and they would not touch each other."

Bright as those Sukkot nights must have been, they were even brighter in the Talmud's recollection: "One who did not see the Celebration of the Drawing of the Water never saw celebration in his days. One who did not see Jerusalem in its glory never saw a beautiful city. One who did not see the Temple in its constructed state never saw a magnificent structure." For the rabbis, as for generations of Jews after them, the bitterness of what they've lost is sweetened only by the certainty that it will be restored when the Messiah comes.

In fact, the Messiah could come at any moment, which is one reason why the Talmud is so concerned with getting the details of the Temple services right—it might be necessary to start them up again at any time. For instance, the Gemara asks in Sukka 41a, what would happen if the Temple was miraculously rebuilt on the 16th of Nisan, the second day of Passover? That's the date when the priests began to offer the omer sacrifice, to show that it was permitted to start eating produce from the new year's harvest. While the Temple stood, Jews had to wait to eat the harvest until the afternoon of the 16th, when they could be sure the sacrifice was complete. After the Temple was destroyed, however, the omer could no longer be offered, so people began to eat the new year's harvest at dawn on the 16th.

In response, Rabbi Yochanan ben Zakkai ruled that the new crop shouldn't be eaten until the next day, 17th of Nisan. After all, when the Temple is rebuilt, the sacrifice will resume and Jews will once again have to wait for the afternoon of the 16th to eat the new harvest. If they get used to eating it at dawn on the 16th, they might end up sinning. Better to accustom people to waiting an extra day, so they will be ready to return to the Temple's calendar when necessary. As the twentieth-century German-Jewish thinker Walter Benjamin observed, for Judaism "every second of time was the strait gate through which Messiah might enter."

Beitza On newly laid eggs, good table manners, and why the Jewish people need a fiery law.

Most of the tractates in Seder Moed, whose name means "festival," are devoted to special days in the Jewish calendar: Shabbat, Pesach, Yom Kippur, Sukkot. But beitza is the Hebrew word for egg—what sort of holiday is that? In fact, tractate Beitza discusses rules that apply to all holidays, but it's named after the first word in the Hebrew text: "About an egg that was laid on a festival, Beit Shammai say: It may be eaten even on that day, and Beit Hillel say: It may not be eaten."

The dispute has to do with muktzeh, a concept dealt with extensively in tractate Shabbat. Something that is muktzeh, "set aside," can't be touched on Shabbat or a holiday unless it was specifically designated for use in advance. The disagreement between Shammai and Hillel has to do with a particular type of muktzeh referred to as "just born"—an item that comes into existence on the holiday itself, such as a newly laid egg. Since it didn't exist before the holiday, the egg couldn't have been designated for use in advance.

Does that mean it's automatically off-limits? In disagreements between the school of Shammai and the school of Hillel, usually the former is more stringent. But in this case they change places, and the Gemara speculates about Hillel's reasoning. After all, if a chicken is designated as food, then the same designation should apply to its egg, which is legally considered a part of the chicken that happened to be separated. In that case, the egg isn't muktzeh and can be eaten on the holiday. It follows that Hillel's prohibition must apply only to a chicken that is designated for laying eggs; since the owner never intended to eat it, he can't change his mind on the holiday and treat the egg as food. The paradoxical result is that if you were expecting an egg to be laid, you can't eat it on a holiday, but if you weren't expecting it, you can.

Fewer people raise chickens today, so this particular dispute isn't very relevant to modern Jewish life. But another rule discussed in Beitza 4b is central to American Judaism. In the twenty-first century as in the second, Jewish communities outside the land of Israel observe holidays for an extra day—two days instead of one for Rosh Hashana, eight days instead of seven for Passover. This practice was originally introduced because of a sectarian dispute between Jews and Samaritans, who in the Talmud are known as Cutheans.

The Samaritans, like the Sadducees and Karaites, rejected the oral Torah and based their practice solely on the written Torah, leading rabbinic Judaism to view them with mistrust. In the Talmud's view, the Samaritans weren't Jews at all, but descendants of foreigners who settled in the Land of Israel after the Ten Lost Tribes were exiled by the Assyrians. This is the background to the famous parable of the good Samaritan told by Jesus in the Gospels, in which a priest and a Levite ignore a Jew in need, while a Samaritan stops to help him. The message would have been clear to Jesus's original Jewish listeners: Moral behavior is what matters, not halakhic orthodoxy.

For the Talmud, however, the two cannot be separated. Ethical commandments and ritual commandments both come from God and require equally strict obedience. That's why holidays must start on the exact dates mentioned in the Torah, not a day earlier or later. The Jewish calendar is based on lunar cycles, and while the Temple stood, the official beginning of the month was established by the priests based on the sighting of the new moon. To spread the news beyond Jerusalem, the priests originally used a relay of signal torches.

But the Samaritans, who had their own methods of determining the calendar, began to interfere with the torches, deliberately lighting them at the wrong time. This forced the priests to switch to a messenger system. Since a messenger couldn't reach distant areas as quickly, Diaspora communities were ordered to start observing holidays for two days, to make sure that at least one of them would be calendrically correct. By the time of the amoraim, Jews were relying on astronomy to calculate the calendar in advance, making the two-day rule unnecessary. Yet the Talmud insists that it's still legally binding: "Be careful to observe the custom of your fathers that you have received," warns Beitza 4b, because one day "the monarchy may issue decrees" prohibiting Torah study, as in the days of the Romans.

The rabbis' main concern in the Talmud is halakha, but from time to time they also discuss the rules of polite conduct, which they refer to as derekh eretz, "the way of the land." The rabbis were the elite of Jewish society, and they expected their students to become gentlemen as well as scholars. In Beitza 25a, for instance, in the course of a discussion about the rules for slaughtering animals on a holiday, the Gemara says that one shouldn't hover over the slaughterer and take a piece of meat as soon as it's cut, but wait until the butchering is finished. The Gemara goes on to list other types of greediness that should be avoided. Don't devour a bulb of garlic or an onion by the roots; instead, peel it and eat it slowly. Don't drain your cup of wine in one gulp. On the other hand, it wouldn't do to seem excessively dainty by taking many small sips; the correct number of sips per cup is two.

Another piece of advice is more cryptic: On the Day of Judgment, "the sea squill will cut off the feet of the wicked." In Babylonia it was customary to mark the boundaries of a piece of land by planting sea squills, which produce large, leathery green leaves, so this is a dramatic way of saying "Don't trespass." In a sense, the Talmud itself can be thought of as a vast maze of sea squills, marking off the permitted areas of life from those where Jews are not allowed to tread.

But any reader of the Bible knows that the Jewish people don't always follow the laws God gave them. That is the message behind another cryptic warning: "the lupine will cut off the feet of the enemies of the Jewish people." Whenever the Talmud has to speak harshly about the Jews, it employs this euphemism, saying "the enemies of the Jewish people" when it actually means the Jewish people themselves. Why is the lupine, a spiky flowering plant, mentioned in this connection? Rabbi Elazar explains: "The Holy One, Blessed be He, said: My children did not treat me even like this lupine, which must be boiled seven times and then one eats it as a dessert." The lupine's seeds are bitter and inedible until they are patiently prepared. The implication seems to be that the Israelites didn't have the patience to accustom themselves to God's commandments, which are difficult to obey at first but become sweet over time.

According to the Gemara, that's why the Israelites received the Torah in the first place: they needed to learn obedience. "For what reason was the Torah given to the Jewish people? Because they are impudent . . . they are fit to be given a fiery law," strict enough to bring them into line. "There are three impudent ones," Reish Lakish elaborates: "The Jewish people among the nations, the dog among the animals, and the rooster among birds."

Perhaps this critical view of Jewish character was informed by the rabbis' experience as community leaders. But there's also a certain wistful pride here. If the Torah alone keeps the Jews in check, imagine what they would be capable of without it! "Were it not for the fact that the Torah was given to the Jewish people, no nation or tongue could withstand them," the Talmud says.

Sometimes the Jewish people were too much for the rabbis themselves to cope with. If one has to do work on a holiday, we learn in Beitza 29b, it should be done in an unusual manner, marking the difference from a regular work day. "One who brings wine jugs from one place to another place may not bring them in a basket or a tub," as he ordinarily would, but should carry them "in front of himself," even though this is more unwieldy. These modifications are mainly symbolic, however, and the Gemara says "if it is impossible to modify, it is permitted."

But Rav Chanan bar Rava notes that many people don't even try to change the way they work on a holiday. "The Sages said: As much as it is possible to modify the workday manner, one should modify on a festival. But don't those women fill their jugs with water on a festival without modifying, and we say nothing to them?" Rav Ashi replies that in this case, there's no good way to modify the work. Women could carry small jugs instead of the large ones, but then they would have to make extra trips to the well, which would defeat the purpose. They could spread a scarf over the jug, but it might fall in and they would have to wring it out, which is forbidden on holidays.

Another sage points out that this isn't the only rule Jewish women fail to obey. "We learned that one may not clap, nor strike a hand on his thigh, nor dance on a festival . . . But nowadays we see that women do so and yet we do not say anything to them." Likewise, one isn't supposed to sit at the entrance to an alleyway on Shabbat. "But don't these women take their jugs, and go, and sit at the entrance to an alleyway, and we do not say anything to them?" And on the day before Yom Kippur, "people eat and drink until darkness falls and we do not say anything to them," despite the rabbinic rule that the fast should start before sundown.

In such cases, the rabbis decide, there's no point in trying to enforce laws that no one will obey. "Better that they be unwitting sinners and not be intentional sinners," the Gemara says. If people aren't told that a certain practice is a sin, at least they won't be committing the additional sin of conscious disobedience. This principle shows that the Talmud's extensive system of laws wasn't necessarily a description of Jewish reality.

Rosh Hashana On the date of Creation, hearing the shofar, and how to trick death.

When does the Jewish year begin? The question seems unnecessary: obviously it begins on Rosh Hashana, which literally means "head of the year." Yet in Exodus 12:1, on the eve of the departure from Egypt, God tells Moses and Aaron, "This month shall mark for you the beginning of the months; it shall be the first of the months of the year for you." This suggests that the calendar should begin with the spring month of Nisan, when Passover takes place. So why is Rosh Hashana celebrated in the autumn month of Tishrei?

In fact, tractate Rosh Hashana explains, things are even more complicated than that. There are multiple new year's days in the Jewish calendar, each for a different purpose. The 1st of Nisan is what the Talmud calls "the New Year for kings." In the ancient world, official documents were dated by the regnal year of the king, and that year is calculated from the 1st of Nisan. Thus if a king takes the throne one day before the 1st of Nisan, the second day of his reign would mark the beginning of the second year of his reign.

The 1st of Elul is the New Year for animal tithes; animals born after that date must be tithed within the next twelve months. For fruit tithes, the year is calculated from the 15th of Shevat. Today there are no more tithes, but the 15th is still celebrated as Tu B'Shevat, a kind of Jewish Arbor Day that now carries environmentalist overtones.

And then there is the first of Tishrei, when Rosh Hashana is celebrated. According to the Mishna, this date is "the New Year for counting years"— but what does that mean in practice? The Gemara isn't completely certain. According to Rav Pappa, it means that legal documents are dated according to the year that begins in Tishrei. But this contradicts what was said earlier about dating them according to kings' reigns, which are measured from the 1st of Nisan. Characteristically, the Gemara offers a solution that allows both statements to be true: The reigns of Jewish kings are dated from Nisan, but those of gentile kings are dated from Tishrei.

More is at stake than dating documents. Judaism believes that God created the world on the first day of the year—but which first day was it? Rabbi Yehoshua believes that it was Nisan while Rabbi Eliezer opts for Tishrei, and each supports his position with a reading of the Torah's creation story. According to Genesis 1:11, on the third day of creation God said, "Let the earth sprout vegetation: seed-bearing plants, fruit trees of every kind on earth that bear fruit with the seed in it." Since crops are harvested in autumn, Eliezer explains, "you must say that this is Tishrei." Yehoshua, on the other hand, says the verse is referring to when the first shoots appear, which is in Nisan.

Regardless of which month they choose, the rabbis believe that the date of Creation shaped the whole course of Jewish history. "Rabbi Eliezer says: In Tishrei the world was created; in Tishrei the Patriarchs were born; in Tishrei the Patriarchs died . . . on Rosh Hashana Sarah, Rachel, and Hannah were remembered by God and conceived; on Rosh Hashana Joseph came out from prison" (10b), and so on down to the coming of the Messiah, which will take place in Tishrei as well. Rabbi Yehoshua agrees that all these things happened on the same date, but places it in Nisan instead.

The Talmud justifies these symmetrical datings with Biblical interpretations. The Gemara says that the Patriarchs died on the same date they were born—but how do we know this? In Deuteronomy 31:2, Moses says on the day of his death, "I am a hundred and twenty years old today," implying that he died on his birthday. If Moses was granted this sign of divine favor, surely Abraham, Isaac, and Jacob would receive it as well.

Months in the Jewish calendar begin with the new moon, and while experts knew how to predict the lunar cycle—"I am able to fix the calendar for the entire Diaspora," Shmuel claimed—the ancient custom was for the priests to certify the appearance of the new moon based on the testimony of two witnesses. "There was a large courtyard in Jerusalem which was called Beit Ya'azek," says the Mishna in Rosh Hashana 23b, "and there all the witnesses would gather and the court would examine them there. And they would prepare great feasts for them, so that they would be willing and accustomed to coming."

Testifying about the new moon was such an important mitzva that witnesses were permitted to violate Shabbat to get to Jerusalem on time. On one occasion, forty pairs of witnesses showed up, and since only one pair was needed Rabbi Akiva was going to send the rest home. But Rabban Gamliel stopped him, saying that if the rabbis started discouraging people from testifying, a day might come when nobody showed up at all.

People of low character weren't allowed to serve as witnesses, including dice players, pigeon racers, moneylenders, and slaves. In addition, witnesses had to be personally known to the members of the court, or vouched for by someone who was. This precaution was introduced on account of the Boethusians, a schismatic Jewish sect with its own ideas about how the calendar should be calculated. They would sometimes give false testimony to the court, even bribing a pair of witnesses four hundred dinars to claim they had seen the new moon on the wrong day. Fortunately, one of them turned out to be a double agent who was loyal to the rabbis. "I heard that the Boethusians were seeking to mislead the sages," he explained, "and I said to myself, I will go and hire myself out to give false testimony, and I will inform the sages of the truth, lest unworthy people come and mislead the sages." He was allowed to keep his bribe as a reward, while the other witness was flogged.

Why do the judges need witnesses to testify about the moon in the first place? Couldn't they look for themselves? The Talmud debates whether this is permitted, since in principle it is forbidden to act as a judge and a witness in the same case. Rabbi Akiva says that even if a murder is committed in front of a panel of judges, they would have to recuse themselves from judging the case: "They are all rendered witnesses, and a witness cannot become a judge." There can be no fair trial without the possibility of acquittal, and "once they have seen [the defendant] kill a person, they will be unable to find grounds to exonerate him" (26a). If a panel of three judges sees the new moon, then, two of them should step down and be replaced, allowing them to testify.

Once the new moon was certified in Jerusalem, the news was spread by torch relays. A messenger would light a torch on top of a mountain, "and wave it back and forth and up and down, until he would see his colleague doing likewise on the top of the second mountain," and so on. The Talmud says that this network of relays extended all the way to Babylonia, where the final messenger "would see the entire Diaspora before him alight like one large bonfire."

To help witnesses describe exactly what they had seen in the night sky, Rabban Gamliel had a diagram of the phases of the moon hanging in his attic: "And he would say to them: Did you see a form like this or like this?" The Gemara wonders how he squared this with Exodus 20:19, which prohibits making "gods of silver or gods of gold," traditionally understood to mean images of the sun and moon. Abaye defends Rabban Gamliel on the grounds that the Torah only prohibits making exact reproductions of holy things, such as the seven-branched candelabrum used in the Temple. A diagram doesn't try to reproduce the moon, only represent it, so a lunar chart doesn't fall afoul of the prohibition.

But the rabbis reject this argument, holding that any representation of a celestial body is prohibited. So how did Rabban Gamliel justify his chart? Perhaps it was permitted because he didn't make it himself, but purchased it from a gentile? The Gemara says that this wouldn't be a valid excuse, since even possessing a forbidden image is a sin. Finally, the rabbis decide that while images of the moon can't be used as decorations, they are permitted for the purpose of Torah study, which is the highest mitzva of all: "You may learn to understand and to teach" (24b).

For all its calendrical importance, the real significance of Rosh Hashana is that it begins the annual period of divine judgment, in which God decides who will be punished by death in the coming year. According to Rabbi Meir, "All are judged on Rosh Hashana and their sentence is sealed on Yom Kippur" (16a). The ten days in between are known as the Days of Awe because they are the last chance for prayer to avert God's judgment.

Other sages, however, take issue with the idea that judgment only happens once a year. Rabbi Yosei says "a person is judged every day," and Rabbi Natan says "a person is judged every hour." Rabbi Yitzhak offers another twist, saying that while God does issue sentences on Yom Kippur, he can be induced to cancel them later. "A person's sentence is torn up on account of four types of actions," he explains. Giving charity, praying, and changing one's behavior can all convince God to give us a second chance.

The fourth "type of action" is more surprising. Changing your name can avert God's judgment, Yitzchak says, and others add that changing your place of residence also works. This may sound like a trick, as if the angel of death wouldn't be able to find you if you go on the lam. But as the Talmud points out, there are Biblical precedents. Sarai was able to have a child after she changed her name to Sarah, and Abraham became the founder of a great nation after he left his native land.

Praying for God's forgiveness isn't enough, however. If you've wronged another person, you must seek their forgiveness as well. Rabbi Yosei offers a parable about a man who borrows one hundred dinars from a friend and takes an oath by the life of the king that he will repay the money. When the time comes and he defaults on the debt, he begs the king for forgiveness for breaking an oath made in the royal name. "For my insult I forgive you," the king replies, "but you must still go and appease your friend" (17b).

The Torah's description of Rosh Hashana, in Leviticus 23:24, is very brief: "a day of solemn rest for you, a memorial of blasts of a shofar, a holy convocation." It doesn't say what kind of animal horn can be used as a shofar, leaving the Talmud to clarify the issue. According to the Mishna, any kind of animal horn can serve as a shofar except a cow's horn, which is referred to by a different Hebrew word, keren. But Rabbi Yosei points out that elsewhere in the Bible, keren is also used to mean a ram's horn. So why is a cow's horn forbidden? The real reason, Rav Hisda explains, is that "A prosecutor cannot become an advocate." Cows were the downfall of the Israelites when they worshiped the golden calf, so it would be unwise to remind God of that episode by using a cow's horn as a shofar.

In the Temple, the shofar blown on Rosh Hashana was a straight ibex horn plated with gold, while on fast days a curved ram's horn was used. The Talmud offers a homiletic explanation for the difference: On Rosh Hashana a person should straighten his mind, while on fast days he should bend himself in prayer and humility. Any flaw that affects a horn's sound renders it unfit as a shofar. A horn that breaks and is glued back together can't be used, but a puncture can be sealed as long as the repair doesn't "impede the blowing." The horn can be shortened, scraped out, or plated with gold on the outside, but gold can't be applied on the inside or around the mouthpiece, because then the listener would effectively be hearing a metal instrument.

Most Jews don't have to worry about making a shofar or even blowing one; all they have to do is listen to it. But just hearing the sound isn't enough, the Talmud explains: "If one was passing behind a synagogue, or his house was adjacent to the synagogue, and he heard the sound of the shofar . . . if he focused his heart, he has fulfilled his obligation; but if not, he has not fulfilled his obligation" (27b). This distinction points to one of the central questions in Judaism. Is the performance of mitzvot inherently significant, or do they become significant because they are performed with pious intent? Is it the action or the intention that matters?

There's legal precedent for both possibilities. On Passover, even someone who is forced to eat matza against his will fulfills his obligation, supporting Rava's view that "mitzvot do not require intent." When it comes to reciting the Shema, on the other hand, conscious intention is required or else it doesn't count. Which rule applies in the case of hearing the shofar? The Gemara offers several possible answers. Perhaps the listener doesn't have to hear the shofar with intent to fulfill a commandment; he only has to realize that the sound he hears is a shofar, not some other noise. Or maybe what matters isn't the listener's intent, but the intent of the person who blows the shofar. If he blows it incorrectly or just to make music, rather than to fulfill the commandment, it doesn't count. In the end, the Gemara decides that both the person who blows the shofar and the one who hears it must consciously intend to perform the mitzva. For the Talmud, action without intention is as empty as intention without action.

Taanit On praying for rain, the importance of solidarity, and inauspicious dates.

On Yom Kippur, Jews fast to atone for their sins. Tractate Taanit, whose name means "fast," deals with a different kind of fasting—one that a community undertakes to convince God to change the weather. Praying for rain is common to religions around the world, and not just in the distant past. During a drought in 2014, the California Catholic Conference of Bishops called on the faithful to pray for rain. In Deuteronomy 28:24, God tells the Israelites that if they are obedient they will be rewarded with good weather, while disobedience will be punished by drought: "The Lord will make the rain of your land powder. From heaven dust shall come down on you until you are destroyed."

From Sukkot until Passover, Jews make an indirect request for rain by adding the words "He makes the wind blow and the rain fall" to the Amida prayer. But when exactly should the addition start? Rabbi Eliezer says it's the first day of Sukkot, but Rabbi Yehoshua points out that the last day would make more sense. We don't actually want it to rain during the holiday, which would make it impossible to dwell under the sukka's open roof.

The subject of rain leads to a wider discussion of meteorology, in which scientific thinking mingles with Biblical interpretation. When Rabbi Eliezer says "the entire world drinks from the waters of the ocean" (9a), he's basically summarizing the water cycle, in which ocean water evaporates into clouds and returns to the earth as precipitation. He bases this idea not only on logic and observation, but also on Genesis 2:6: "And there went up a mist from the earth and watered the whole surface of the ground." Rabbi Yehoshua lodges an empirical objection to this interpretation: How can rain come from the ocean, when seawater is salty and rain isn't? Eliezer replies that "the waters are sweetened in the clouds," which again is basically true; evaporation carries water to the clouds while leaving the salt in the ocean.

Less scientifically plausible is the assertion that God reserves the best rainwater for the land of Israel. "The land of Israel drinks first and the entire world afterward," the Talmud says, in the same way that "a person who kneads cheese takes the food and leaves the refuse." Some of the sages had lived in both the land of Israel and Babylonia, so they could have tested this theory against personal experience, but if anyone did the Talmud doesn't mention it.

If the addition to the Amida doesn't succeed in bringing rain, Taanit lays out a plan for more urgent action. If rain hasn't begun by the 3rd of Cheshvan—roughly the middle of October—an explicit request to "give dew and rain" is added to the Amida. This date is based on the agricultural needs of the land of Israel, but in other places the schedule can be altered to fit the local climate. In Babylonia, Jews began to request rain sixty days after the autumn equinox, in late November.

If two weeks go by and rain still hasn't fallen, it's time to start fasting. To begin with, "individuals . . . fast three fasts," but the Gemara warns that "not everyone who wishes to make himself an individual may do so." Only Torah scholars, the leading members of the community, can undertake a fast. The three fasts take place on Monday, Thursday, and the following Monday, during daylight hours only. The "individuals" can eat at night, and they can also continue to work, bathe, and have sex, all of which are forbidden on strict fast days such as Yom Kippur.

If two more weeks pass and the scholars' fasts haven't brought any rain, the whole community must join in, undertaking three days of lenient fasts. If the drought continues, a new set of three fasts begins on a stricter basis: No one may eat for a full 24-hour period, and work, bathing, and sex are all prohibited.

Finally, if rain still hasn't come, the entire community undertakes seven days of strict fasting, accompanied by public signs of distress including the sounding of alarms and the closing of stores. If even this fails to work, the community must go into mourning: "They decrease their engagement in business, in building and planting, in betrothals and marriages, and in greetings between each person and his fellow, like people who have been rebuked by God" (12b). Some sages would wear their shoes on the wrong feet to increase their discomfort.

Even as the Talmud sets out these rules, however, it is ambivalent about whether fasting is praiseworthy. According to Shmuel, "Whoever sits in observance of a fast is called a sinner," since inflicting suffering on oneself is inherently wrong. Rabbi Elazar makes the point with a striking image: "A person should always consider himself as though a sacred object is immersed in his bowels." In Judaism, unlike some other faiths, the body isn't an evil to be scourged but a holy vessel.

Certain people are particularly discouraged from fasting, since they need their strength for other purposes. According to Rav Sheshet, "The student of a Torah academy who sits in observance of a fast has let a dog eat his portion." The rabbis debate the status of pregnant and nursing women: Some say that they are exempt from the early fasts but must join in the later, more onerous ones, while others say the reverse.

But the rabbis agree that an individual can't opt out of a communal fast. "When the community is immersed in suffering, a person may not say: I will go to my home and I will eat and drink." Such a person is described by the Talmud as "middling," an average kind of sinner. One who goes further and actually enjoys himself during a fast—saying, in the words of Isaiah 56:12, "Come, I will fetch wine, and we will fill ourselves with strong drink"—is even worse, a "wicked person." Such a betrayal of solidarity will be exposed on the Day of Judgment, when "the stones of a person's house and the beams of a person's house testify against him."

Beyond the ethical issues involved, fasting also raises a theological problem. Do human beings have the power to coerce God into making it rain? The question is dramatized in a story in Taanit 19a about a holy man named named Honi. During a bad drought, Honi's neighbors asked him to pray for rain, and he cockily told them to bring their clay ovens inside so they wouldn't melt. When he prayed, however, nothing happened.

"What did he do? He drew a circle on the ground and stood inside it and said before God: Master of the Universe, Your children have turned their faces toward me, so I am like a member of Your household. Therefore, I take an oath by Your great name that I will not move from here until You have mercy upon Your children." A trickle of rain started to fall, but Honi told God that it wasn't good enough: "I did not ask for this, but for rain to fill the cisterns, ditches, and caves." Then rain started to fall in floods, but Honi wasn't satisfied with this either: "I did not ask for this," he told God, "but for rain of benevolence, blessing, and generosity." Having gotten the amount and quality of rain he wanted, Honi asked God to make it stop.

Honi's feat earned him the nickname "the Circle-Drawer," but the story leaves the rabbis uncomfortable. Surely we are supposed to beseech God humbly, not sulk until he does what we want. Shimon ben Shetach, the leader of the Sanhedrin, reproached Honi for his actions: "If you were not Honi, I would have decreed ostracism upon you, but what can I do to you? You nag God and He does your bidding."

This kind of spiritual haughtiness is a standing temptation for holy men. Rabbi Elazar, whose "head was swollen with pride because he had studied much Torah," once met an "an exceedingly ugly person" on the road and said, "How ugly is that man. Are all the people of your city as ugly as you?" The man shamed him by replying, "I do not know, but you should go and say to the craftsman who made me: How ugly is the vessel you made." Insulting a person's appearance means insulting God, who made human beings in his image. Elazar begged the man's forgiveness, and from then on he would teach, "A person should always be soft like a reed and not stiff like a cedar" (20b).

Other stories show that God prefers a humble but pious man to a haughty sage. Every year on Yom Kippur, Rava would "receive greetings from the yeshiva on high," the celestial academy where dead sages dwelled. Abaye, whose debates with Rava fill the Talmud, would receive greetings every Shabbat. But a man called Abba the Bloodletter, a mere barber-surgeon, received greetings from heaven every day on account of his good deeds. When he let a woman's blood, he covered her with a specially designed garment so he wouldn't see her bare skin; and he received payment in secret, so poor people wouldn't be embarrassed if they couldn't afford his fee.

A similar story is told about Rabbi Beroka Hoza'a, who stood in the marketplace with Elijah the Prophet and asked which of the passersby were worthy of the World to Come. Elijah pointed to a man who was not even wearing tzitzit. How could such a person deserve to go to heaven, the rabbi asked? The prophet explained that the man was a prison guard who looked out for the welfare of female prisoners, protecting them from assault. He didn't wear tzitzit because he passed as a gentile at work in order to get advance notice about decrees issued against the Jews, allowing him to warn the community. This made him even holier than those who devoted their lives to Torah.

Fasting is more than an emergency technique for ending a drought. In Taanit 27a, we learn about the fast of the "non-priestly watches." The priests who served in the Temple were divided into twenty-four watches, each of which had a corresponding watch made up of Israelites. When a priestly watch was serving in the Temple, its Israelite cohort would fast Monday to Thursday, with each day devoted to a particular cause. "On Monday they would fast for seafarers," because God created the sea on the first Monday of Creation; "on Tuesday for those who walk in the desert," because the dry land was created on Tuesday; on Wednesday "over croup, that it should not befall the children"; and on Thursday "for pregnant women and nursing women." On Friday they would break the fast to prepare for Shabbat, and of course they wouldn't fast on Shabbat itself.

But why didn't the non-priestly watches fast on Sunday, the Gemara asks? According to Rabbi Yochanan it was "due to the Christians": apparently Jews didn't want to give the impression that they were honoring the Christian Sabbath. If so, this could only have been a consideration in the last years of the Second Temple, since Jesus died around 30 CE and the Temple fell in 70. Reish Lakish, however, gives a different explanation: "An added soul is given to man on Shabbat eve, and at the conclusion of Shabbat it is removed from him." The day after Shabbat, Jews are still weak from their "woe for the soul that is lost."

These fasts ended with the Temple, but others are still observed today. The 9th of Av, the Talmud says, is the date when the First Temple was destroyed by Nebuchadnezzar in 586 BCE and also when the Second Temple was destroyed by Titus in 70 CE. As tractate Rosh Hashana showed, the Talmud likes this kind of calendrical symmetry, even if the dates need a little massaging to line up. The book of Kings actually says that the First Temple was burned down on the 7th of Av, while Jeremiah says it happened on the 10th.

In fact, the Gemara says, the fast could have been observed on a range of days, since on the 7th "gentiles entered the sanctuary," on the 8th they desecrated it, on the 9th they set fire to it, and on the 10th it burned down completely. Rabbi Yochanan says, "Had I been alive in that generation, I would have established the fast only on the 10th of Av, because most of the sanctuary was burned on that day." But the consensus is that "it is preferable to mark the beginning of the tragedy," on the 9th.

The destruction of the First Temple wasn't the first disaster to occur on the 9th of Av. "A meritorious matter is brought about on an auspicious day, and a deleterious matter on an inauspicious day," the Talmud says, and the 9th of Av had been cursed ever since the spies sent by Moses into Canaan returned on that day with discouraging reports. It was because of their lack of faith that God decreed that the whole generation of the Exodus had to die before the Israelites could enter the Promised Land. More than a millennium later, during the Bar Kochba rebellion of 132–135 CE, the city of Beitar fell on the 9th of Av and its inhabitants were massacred.

If this date is the worst in the Jewish calendar, however, "there were no days as joyous for the Jewish people as the 15th of Av, for on that day "the daughters of Jerusalem would go out in white clothes . . . and dance in the vineyards. And what would they say? 'Young man, please lift up your eyes and see what you choose for yourself for a wife. Do not set your eyes toward beauty, but set your eyes toward a good family.'" It would be a mistake to think of Jewish history solely through the lens of fasting; we must remember the feasting, too.

Megilla On divine inspiration, rewriting the Bible, and Haman's years as a barber.

The holiday of Purim is celebrated with a public reading of the megilla or scroll of Esther, which tells the story of the deliverance of the Jews of Persia from Haman's genocidal plot. As the name of tractate Megilla suggests, when it comes to Purim the Talmud's focus is less on the holiday than on the Biblical text behind it—what it says and how it should be read. Even the physical scroll itself is a subject of debate, since according to Shmuel it has an unusual status: "the book of Esther does not render the hands ritually impure" (7a). All the other books of the Bible transmit ritual impurity to those who touch them—a rule instituted by the rabbis to discourage people from handling sacred texts casually. So why not Esther? "Is this to say," the Gemara asks, "that Shmuel maintains that the book of Esther was not stated with the inspiration of the Divine Spirit?"

It's true that Esther is one of only two Biblical books not to include the name of God, which may explain why it doesn't render the hands impure. (The other is the Song of Songs, whose purity status is also disputed, according to Rabbi Meir.) And it's not just the name of God that's missing from the story; God himself seems to play no role. It may be that divine providence placed Esther on the throne of Persia, where she could intervene to save the Jews, and ensured Mordecai was in the right place to overhear the plot against Ahasuerus. But the text never says so explicitly; these are coincidences that never quite rise to the status of miracles.

The rabbis debate Esther's divine inspiration by engaging in close reading. For instance, Esther 6:6 says: "And Haman thought in his heart, 'Who is there that the king would rather honor than me?'" How could the author of the book of Esther have known what Haman was thinking if God didn't reveal it to him? For the Talmud, this is a sign of God's omniscience; today, a literary critic might say that the book uses an omniscient narrator to communicate a character's private thoughts. In fact, Rava says much the same thing, though in different terms: Divine inspiration wasn't necessary to understand Haman's thought process, since it could be deduced through "logical reasoning."

In the end, Shmuel offers a conclusive proof that Esther was divinely inspired. According to Esther 9:26, the Jews "confirmed and took upon themselves the obligation to celebrate Purim for all time." The redundancy of "confirmed and took upon themselves" is a sign that the verse needs to be interpreted, since for the rabbis there is no such thing as an extraneous word in the Bible. The phrase must signify that "they confirmed above in heaven what they took upon themselves below on earth," and how could the author of Esther know what was decided in heaven unless God told him?

This is a good example of the Talmud's paradoxical freedom in reading the Bible. Because the rabbis know in advance what they are going to find in the text—in this case, proof that the book of Esther is divinely inspired—they can diverge from its plain meaning as much as they need to. Much of tractate Megilla is devoted to a chapter-by-chapter analysis of the book of Esther that practically rewrites the story, adding new details and episodes that seem to spring from nowhere. Yet all these novelties are treated as necessary extrapolations from the text.

The analysis begins in Megilla 10b with the book's very first word, "Vayehi": "And it came to pass." "Anywhere that the word vayehi is stated, it is a term of nothing other than grief," the Gemara says, and goes on to list a dozen examples from across the Bible. Vayehi turns up in the Tower of Babel story, in the story of Hannah and Samuel, and in the story of Saul and David, each time in close proximity to some bad news: the Tower is destroyed, Hannah is unable to conceive, Saul turns against David.

Other words in Esther also have coded significance. The book opens with an account of a banquet where Ahasuerus displays "the riches of his glorious kingdom and the honor of his majestic greatness" (Esther 1:4). Rabbi Yosei bar Hanina points out that the words "glorious" and "majestic" are also used in Exodus 28:2 to describe the garments of the priests. This indicates that Ahasuerus was actually dressed in the garments of an Israelite priest, pillaged from Jerusalem at the time of the Babylonian conquest.

Semantic points soon give way to deeper questions. Esther tells the story of a barely averted genocide; why, the Gemara asks, were the Jews of that generation deserving of such punishment? One opinion is that they were guilty of participating in Ahasuerus's feast, where they ate non-kosher food. But even if they did, responds Rabbi Shimon bar Yochai, only the Jews of Shushan, the capital, deserved punishment, since people from other provinces couldn't have attended the feast. Another theory is that the Jews sinned by bowing down before an idol. But if they committed such a grave transgression, why did God finally spare them? Shimon replies that the Jews weren't sincere in their worship of the idol, but only did it to obey the king. In the same way, God didn't sincerely intend to punish them, but was angry "only for appearance" (12a).

If the Jews of Persia were punished for eating non-kosher food, what about Esther herself? Living in Ahasuerus's palace and concealing her Jewishness, she must have been served the same non-kosher dishes as everyone else. But to the rabbis, it is inconceivable that a Jewish heroine would have sinned in this way. When Esther 2:9 says "And [the king] advanced her and her maids to the best place in the house of the women," Rav says that this means "he fed her food of the Jews." As for how Esther could have observed Shabbat in the palace, Rava explains that she had seven maids and "would count the days of the week by them," so she always knew when Shabbat arrived.

The sexual irregularity at the heart of the story is harder to explain away. Esther was a concubine to a gentile king; the reason why Ahasuerus loved her more than the other women in his harem, Rav says, is that "if he wanted to taste in her the taste of a virgin, he tasted it, and the taste of a non-virgin, he tasted it." The rabbis even heighten Esther's transgression by declaring that she was not actually Mordecai's adopted ward, as the text states, but his wife.

This is accomplished by one of the Talmud's favorite interpretive techniques, adding a supposedly missing letter to the text. In Esther 2:7, where it says "Mordecai took her for his own daughter [bat]," Rabbi Meir adds a letter to turn the last word into bayit, "house," a metaphor for wife. This implies that Esther was sleeping with Ahasuerus and Mordecai at the same time: "She would arise from the lap of Ahasuerus, immerse herself in a ritual bath, and sit in the lap of Mordecai" (13b). Rabbi Abba partially extenuates this conduct, saying that Esther slept with Ahasuerus only "under compulsion."

With Haman, on the other hand, the Talmud adds new details to make him look even worse than he does in the Bible. The reason why Haman hated Mordecai is that he used to be Mordecai's slave. What's more, he was a cheap slave, "sold for a loaf of bread," with the lowly job of cutting his master's hair, because "Haman was the barber of the village of Kartzum for twenty-two years." In the Biblical story, Haman is forced to lead Mordecai's horse through the streets of Shushan. The Talmud adds that Haman's daughter saw the procession from her window and emptied a chamber pot onto her father's head, thinking that Haman was Mordecai and vice versa. When she realized what she had done, she fell off the roof and died (16a).

The rabbis take an almost antic freedom in reinventing the Biblical story. But when the book of Esther is read aloud on Purim it has to be treated seriously. It must be read from a scroll, not recited from memory, and ideally the scroll should contain only this book. If it includes other Biblical books, the Esther section must be visibly distinct from the rest, so the audience can see that the right text is being read.

The Mishna also says that one must hear the Megilla read aloud rather than reading it silently to oneself. The Gemara points out that Esther 9:28, where the Purim holiday is instituted, doesn't say anything about reading aloud, but simply instructs that "these days shall be remembered and observed throughout every generation, every family, every province, and every city." How do we know the story has to be read from a scroll? Rava explains by citing a verbal parallel: Esther commands us to "remember," and in Exodus God uses a related word to tell Moses, "Write this for a memorial in the book," which suggests that remembering requires a physical text.

This rule raises a problem, however. The book of Esther is written in Hebrew, but by the time of the Gemara most Jews spoke Aramaic, the lingua franca of the ancient Middle East. Is it permitted to read the book of Esther aloud in translation, so the congregation can understand it, or is the original Hebrew required? The Mishna is far from clear: "If he read it in translation or in any other language . . . he has not fulfilled his obligation. However, for those who speak a foreign language, one may read the Megilla in that foreign language. And one who speaks a foreign language who heard the Megilla read in Ashurit has fulfilled his obligation" (17a). Ashurit, "Assyrian," is how the Talmud refers to the Hebrew script adopted after the Babylonian Exile and still used today.

The Gemara tries to unravel these contradictions. Why does the Mishna first say that reading a translation is insufficient, and then that a translation is acceptable "for those who speak a foreign language"? According to Rav and Shmuel, "foreign language" here doesn't mean just any language but specifically Greek, which was so widely spoken by Jews in the ancient world that it enjoyed a special status, rather like English today. Indeed, Rabban Shimon ben Gamliel says that the Bible can be written in only two languages, Hebrew and Greek (18a). This sense that the Greek translation of the Bible, known as the Septuagint, has special status was apparently common in the ancient world. According to the Jewish historian Josephus, when King Ptolemy of Egypt ordered seventy-two Jewish sages to translate the Bible into Greek independently, they all produced exactly the same text—proof that the Septuagint is divinely inspired.

Even so, the Hebrew text is primary. Hearing Esther in Hebrew always fulfills a person's Purim obligation, even if they don't understand what they're hearing, like many "women and uneducated people." This may sound like rabbinic snobbery, but Ravina points out that the sages themselves didn't always know Hebrew perfectly. For instance, they didn't understand the word "seirugin" until a maidservant of Yehuda HaNasi "said to the sages who were entering the house intermittently rather than in a single group: How long are you going to enter seirugin seirugin?" This revealed the meaning of the word, which in turn clarified one of the rules of Purim—that the Megilla may be read seirugin, rather than all in one go. On occasion, even Torah scholars could be taught something by "women and uneducated people."

Moed Katan   On holidays, marking graves, and the right to be beautiful.

Passover and Sukkot are established in the Torah as seven-day festivals; outside the land of Israel they are extended to eight days, for reasons explained in tractate Beitza. The most important days are the first and last, when work is forbidden altogether. Tractate Moed Katan, which means "little festival," deals with the more limited restrictions that apply on the intermediate days known as Chol HaMoed.

The tractate begins, as usual, with a concrete problem: Is it permitted to irrigate a field during a holiday? Irrigation involves hard physical labor, which is usually prohibited on holidays, but if Jewish farmers couldn't water their crops for seven days they would sustain a serious financial loss. The Mishna tries to balance these concerns by allowing less strenuous forms of irrigation. It's permitted to use water from a naturally occurring spring, but "one may not irrigate a field with rainwater collected in a cistern . . . or with water drawn with a lever."

The Gemara tries to figure out the principle behind this distinction. Using a lever to pump water from a well is hard work, so it makes sense that it would be banned on a holiday. But "what excessive effort is involved in irrigating with rainwater?" Rav Ashi explains that this is one of those cases where the rabbis made a fence around the Torah by enacting a more stringent rule: "Rainwater itself will come to be water drawn with a lever" (4a). Once you start to empty a cistern, its water level may fall to the point where a lever will be needed; better not to start using it at all and avoid the temptation.

As the discussion moves to other kinds of agricultural labor—digging, weeding, clearing stones—the rabbis establish a general principle: "Loss yes, profit no." On intermediate festival days, you can only do work to maintain what you already have, not to gain more. You can't dig a new water channel on a festival day, but you can repair a damaged channel; piling manure for storage is permitted, but using it to fertilize a field is not. Most kinds of paid work are forbidden on Chol HaMoed, but the Talmud makes an exception for urgent need: a merchant can sell his wares and a laborer can receive wages if necessary to avoid hunger. These rules are clear enough to distinguish holidays from ordinary days, but not so onerous that they will provoke disobedience.

It's also permitted to do work for the public good rather than for individual benefit, such as repairing roads and marking graves. Making sure that graves are clearly marked is important because coming into contact with any part of a corpse larger than an olive-bulk—a standard Talmudic measurement of volume—communicates ritual impurity. Grave-marking isn't explicitly commanded in the Torah, but the rabbis find an allusion to it in Ezekiel 39:15: "As those who traverse the country make their rounds, any one of them who sees a human bone shall erect a marker beside it."

Grave markers shouldn't be placed directly on top of the burial site, "so as not to cause a loss of ritually pure food items." If you were walking in a field holding a bundle of dates in front of you, you might not see the grave until you were so close that the dates were over it, rendering them impure. But the marker shouldn't be too far from the site, either, "so as not to cause a loss of the land of Israel" (5b) by fencing off more ground than necessary. To distinguish a gravestone from an ordinary stone, it should be marked with lime. A trail of lime between two stones indicates that the whole area is impure, but two stones with no lime trail indicate two separate burial sites. At night, it must have been an eerie experience to come across ghostly white marks and realize you had wandered into a graveyard.

The discussion of graves leads the rabbis to consider other funeral practices. During the thirty days before a major festival it is forbidden to eulogize a dead relative, since this would heighten the grief of the mourners and prevent them from celebrating the festival with joy. But there is another reason for the rule as well, having to do with the custom of hiring professional eulogizers. According to Rav, it was common in the land of Israel for mourners to hire a speaker to provoke cathartic tears: "They would say: let all those of bitter heart weep with him." But it once happened that a wife spent all of her husband's savings to hire a eulogizer, leaving him unable to pay for his upcoming pilgrimage to Jerusalem. To avoid such situations, the rabbis prohibited hiring eulogizers before a festival—though presumably it would be just as easy to waste one's pilgrimage money in other ways.

A mourner should also abstain from wearing tefillin, greeting people, washing his clothes, bathing, working, and studying Torah. He should turn his bed upside down before sleeping on it, because when a person dies God says, "I have placed the likeness of my image within humans, and owing to their sins I have overturned it." For the most intimate losses—the death of a father, mother, or teacher—a man should tear his garment as a sign of mourning. One can also tear one's clothes upon seeing the destroyed cities of the land of Israel and the ruins of the Temple. Once these rips are made, they should never be completely repaired: "One may tack them together with loose stitches, and hem them, and gather them, and fix them with imprecise ladder-like stitches. But one may not mend them with precise stitches" (26a). Like trauma itself, the sign of mourning should always leave a scar.

The Talmud debates how this rule is applied to unusual cases. If a man tears his garment because his father has died, and then learns that his son has also died, can he extend the initial tear or is a separate one required? A man in this situation might not be expected to pay much attention to the rules of tearing, but the Talmud believes there is a correct course of action in any situation. There's a kind of consolation in this strictness, since it's based on the belief that God is always paying attention to what we do. In case of a double loss, a mourner can extend the tear, but he should remember which part of the tear was made for which purpose. A tear made for a son can eventually be mended, but one for a father can't be.

When "a Torah scholar dies, everyone is his relative" when it comes to rending their garments. This is true even if the deceased wasn't a famous sage but simply "an upright person." Neglecting to honor the pious can have fatal consequences: "For what reason do a person's sons and daughters die young? Because he did not cry and mourn over an upright person who died" (25a). This doesn't seem fair to the sons and daughters, but it reflects the Talmud's idea that a man's family is his possession, which can be taken from him as a punishment for sin.

And because the rabbis believe in a perfectly just God, they insist that no one is ever punished wrongly. "A man is suspected of having done something wrong only if he has indeed done so. And if he did not do it wholly, he did it partly. And if he did not do it even partly, he thought in his heart to do it. And if he did not think to himself to do it, he saw others doing it and was happy" (18b). Anything is preferable to admitting that grief and suffering might be simply random.

One shouldn't mourn excessively on Chol HaMoed, but celebrating a wedding is also forbidden. The Gemara queries this rule: "And if it is a joy for him, what of it?" Why shouldn't the bride and groom add the pleasure of a wedding to the pleasure of a holiday? The answer is that their rejoicing has to be for the right reason. As the Torah says, "you shall rejoice in your festival"—"in your festival and not in your wife," the Gemara emphasizes.

Rabbi Yitzhak Nappacha, however, has a more pragmatic explanation. Preparing for a wedding is expensive and time-consuming, and so is preparing for a festival. If weddings could take place on a holiday, people would be tempted to combine the two occasions, postponing the wedding until a holiday came around. This would delay the birth of children, violating the commandment to be fruitful and multiply.

The Talmud believes that women have a right to tend to their appearance, and on Chol HaMoed all kinds of grooming are permitted: "She may paint her eyelids, she may remove unwanted hair, and she may put rouge on her face" (9b). A woman may also groom her pubic hair, or in the Talmud's euphemism, "pass a comb over her lower face." Rav Hisda emphasizes that the right to beautification belongs not only to young women, who are concerned about attracting a husband, but to women of all ages: "Even your mother, and even your mother's mother, and even a woman so old that she is standing at the edge of her grave." After all, "a woman of sixty years, like one of six, runs at the sound of the timbrel," the rabbis say, with an edge of contempt for such frivolity.

Hagiga   On divine judgment
and the danger of prying
into God's secrets.

The official subject of tractate Hagiga, whose name means "festival offering," is the obligation to offer an animal sacrifice in the Temple on Passover, Shavuot, and Sukkot, the major pilgrimage festivals, as commanded in Exodus 23:17: "Three times a year all your males shall appear before the Lord God." But this short tractate is also the home of the Talmud's most intriguing speculations about God and the universe.

Hagiga pivots from pilgrimages to theology because of the Torah's phrase "appear before the Lord God." In its original context, this means that Jews must present themselves at the Temple, where God dwelled. But the Talmud interprets it metaphorically as a reference to the soul's appearance before the divine judge. Rav Huna and other sages would cry out when they read this verse, thinking of the fearsome prospect of coming before God for judgment. Rabbi Yochanan quotes Ecclesiastes 12:14: "For God shall bring every work into judgment concerning every hidden thing." If God judges us like "a slave whose master weighs his unwitting sins like intentional ones," Yochanan asks, how can we hope to be acquitted?

The Talmud is certain that even minor sins lead to punishment. In one case, a young student died because he spoke irreverently to his teacher. "Even frivolous speech between a man and his wife"—that is, talking intimately during sex—"is declared to a person at the time of death," when he has to defend his conduct in his lifetime. This particular rule was difficult for Rav himself to obey. On one occasion, Rav Kahana was lying underneath Rav's bed—how he got there, the Talmud doesn't say—and "he heard Rav chatting and laughing with his wife, and performing his needs," that is, having sex. When Kahana upbraided him for idle talk, Rav replied with understandable impatience: "Kahana, leave, as this is not proper conduct."

But sometimes people die without having committed even a small transgression. Proverbs 13:23 acknowledges that "there are those who are swept away without justice." Rav Yosef questions this verse: "Is there one who goes before his time?" If God decides when people die, doesn't that mean everyone dies just when they are supposed to?

In fact, death turns out to involve angels and spirits who are far from infallible. On one occasion, the Angel of Death told his "agent" to bring him a woman named Miriam who was a braider of women's hair. The agent made a mistake and brought him a different Miriam who was a nurse. The Angel of Death scolded his servant, but didn't bother to fix the error: "Since you have already brought her, let her be counted" toward the quota of the dead, he decided (4b).

Can death really be so random? Rav Beivai bar Abaye—who, we learned in tractate Berachot, used magic to contact demons—asked death's agent how he managed to kill Miriam the nurse if it wasn't her appointed time to die. The agent replies that Miriam accidentally burned her foot while cleaning out an oven, and he was able to take advantage: "Her luck suffered and I brought her."

This certainly doesn't sound like justice, and Rav Beivai challenges the Angel of Death: "Do you have the right to act in this manner?" Doesn't Ecclesiastes 1:4 say that "one generation passes away and another generation comes," suggesting that a human lifespan is predetermined and can't be changed by luck? The Angel replies that one way or another, the accounts are made to balance. If someone dies before their time, the unused years are given to a Torah scholar so he can live longer. Perhaps only a text composed by Torah scholars could consider this a good answer.

The Talmud warns that such investigations of the supernatural shouldn't be undertaken lightly. "Whoever looks at four matters, it would have been better for him if he had never entered the world: what is above and what is below, what was before and what will be after" (11b). This world is the limit of our knowledge; going beyond it means trespassing on God's secrets, and "anyone who has no concern for the honor of his Maker deserves to have never come into the world." For this reason, study of esoteric and mystical subjects is only permitted within strict limits. The "act of Creation" should only be taught to one student at a time, while "the Chariot"—the prophet Ezekiel's strange visions of the Godhead—shouldn't be taught at all. The subject can only be studied by a man who is at least fifty years old and who is "wise and understands on his own."

Yet these subjects are clearly hard to resist, since the rabbis have no sooner denounced mystical speculation than they start to engage in it them-selves. Rabbi Yosei remarks that there is more to reality than human beings perceive: "Woe to them, the creations, who see and know not what they see; who stand and know not upon what they stand." He explains by interpreting Biblical verses that the earth rests on pillars, which rest on waters, which rest on mountains, which rest on the wind, which rests on a storm, which hangs on the "arm of the Holy One."

This tendency to multiply the levels of the cosmos appears again when Reish Lakish explains that there are seven firmaments, each with its own name. Vilon, "curtain," "does not contain anything"; Rakia, "firmament," is where the sun, moon, and stars are fixed; Shehakim, "heights," is where "mills stand and grind manna for the righteous"; Zevul, "abode," is the lo-cation of the Heavenly Temple, where the angel Michael offers sacrifices to God; Ma'on, "habitation," is where choirs of angels sing at night; Makhon, "dwelling place," is where God keeps "harmful dews," storms and mists.

Finally, at the top of the ladder, is Aravot, "skies," where all of God's gifts are stored, "the treasuries of life, the treasuries of peace, the treasuries of blessing, the souls of the righteous, the spirits and souls that are to be cre-ated, and the dew that the Holy One, Blessed be He, will use to revive the dead." The account of the Chariot adds new elements to this cosmic picture. God is attended by "speaking animals of fire" and the angel Sandalfon, "who stands on the earth and his head reaches the divine creatures . . . he stands behind the Chariot and weaves crowns for his Maker" (13b).

All of this is much more exciting than the Talmud's usual debates—too exciting, in fact, since mystical knowledge is dangerous. In Hagiga 14b, the Gemara tells of four sages who "entered the orchard"—that is, delved into supernatural mysteries. Ben Azzai glimpsed God and immediately died; Ben Zoma glimpsed God and lost his mind; Elisha ben Avuya, an enigmatic figure referred to in the Talmud as Acher, "the other," "chopped down the shoots," meaning that he became an apostate. Only Rabbi Akiva came out safely, able to live with the knowledge he had gained. Yet as the long tradi-tion of Jewish mysticism shows, even this Talmudic warning couldn't stop generations of seekers from making their way into the orchard.

II

Seder Nashim

Marriage and Divorce

Yevamot On levirate marriage, converting to Judaism, and a camel that didn't dance.

Genesis 38 tells the story of Tamar, the wife of Er, one of the sons of Judah. Er dies childless, making it the duty of his brother Onan to marry Tamar, in order to "to raise up offspring for [his] brother." But Onan refuses to consummate the marriage, instead "spilling his seed upon the ground," and God punishes him with death. Onan's deed inspired the word "onanism" as a euphemism for masturbation, but in the Bible it seems clear that his real sin was refusing to continue his brother's family line.

A man's obligation to marry his dead brother's widow is the focus of tractate Yevamot, which takes its name from the Hebrew word for "sister-in-law." In English this practice is known as levirate marriage, from the Latin word for "brother-in-law." According to Deuteronomy 25:5, "When brothers dwell together and one of them dies and leaves no son, the wife of the deceased shall not be married to a stranger, outside the family. Her husband's brother shall unite with her: he shall take her as his wife and fulfill the duty of a brother-in-law to her."

But what happens, the Mishna asks, if the widow is forbidden to marry her brother-in-law because she's related to him in some other way? Say that a man has a daughter who grows up to marry his brother, her uncle—which is entirely permissible in Jewish law. If the brother dies without an heir, the father would be required to marry his own daughter, which is forbidden as incest. The Talmud explains that in this case, the prohibition overrides the levirate obligation. A man can never marry a woman who is forbidden to him by law, even if she is his brother's widow.

Polygamy adds another source of complication. In the Talmud as in the Torah, it is legal for a man to have multiple wives; in Yevamot 44a, the Gemara says that the maximum is four, so the husband can fulfill his sexual obligations to each wife. If a man dies leaving two wives childless, his brother would be obliged to marry both of them. But if one of the "rival wives," as the Talmud calls them, is forbidden to her brother-in-law, he is also freed from the obligation to marry the other one, even if there's no legal bar to their relationship. For example, if two brothers marry two sisters and one of the brothers dies, the surviving brother can't marry the widow, because she is his wife's sister, a forbidden relationship. If the dead brother also left a second widow, the surviving brother can't marry her either, even if they are unrelated, because she is his wife's sister's rival wife.

That was the view of Beit Hillel, at any rate, but Beit Shammai permitted marriage to rival wives. This disagreement raises the question of how the frequent differences between these two schools were handled in practice. If Beit Shammai performed marriages that were forbidden by Beit Hillel, the consequences could be disastrous. Beit Hillel might consider the offspring of such marriages to be mamzerim, illegitimate children, and refuse to marry with them. Before long the Jewish people would be split in two. (The same problem arises today because Orthodox rabbis don't recognize conversions and marriages performed by non-Orthodox rabbis.) But splitting the community is a sin, as Reish Lakish deduces from the words of Deuteronomy 14:1, "You shall not cut yourselves." In the Torah this refers to cutting one's flesh in mourning, but Reish Lakish points out that the Hebrew word for "cut" is related to the word for "faction," suggesting that it's forbidden to create factions among the Jewish people.

Did Beit Shammai and Beit Hillel constitute factions in this sense? The Gemara says no: "Beit Shammai did not refrain from marrying women from Beit Hillel, nor did Beit Hillel refrain from marrying women from Beit Shammai. This serves to teach you that they practiced affection and friendship between them" (14b). But Rabbi Shimon adds a qualification: "They did refrain in the certain cases, but they did not refrain in the uncertain cases." If a woman from Beit Shammai was offered in marriage, a man from Beit Hillel could safely assume she was not a mamzer. But if Beit Shammai knew that a woman was the child of a marriage Beit Hillel would have forbidden, they "would notify" Beit Hillel, and the match would be quietly called off. In this way, the problem of mamzerim never became public.

Still, there were many other areas of disagreement between the schools. Shammai believed that a child is obligated to perform the mitzva of dwelling in a sukka from the moment it is born, while Hillel did not. When a grandson was born to Shammai, he "removed the mortar covering the ceiling and placed sukka covering over the bed for the child." Wasn't this a public demonstration of disagreement with Hillel? Not necessarily, the Gemara replies: an onlooker might think that Shammai opened the roof for ventilation, "to increase the air" in the baby's room.

Clearly the main concern was to avoid making the disagreements between Beit Hillel and Beit Shammai public, which would have forced everyone to take a side. Even the greatest sages hesitated to get involved in these disputes. "They asked Rabbi Yehoshua: What is the law with regard to the rival wife of a daughter? He said to them: It is a matter of dispute between Beit Shammai and Beit Hillel." When pressed to say which side he agreed with, Yehoshua responded: "Why are you inserting my head between two great mountains?" (15b)

Perhaps out of sympathy with Onan, the Torah provides an escape clause for a man who doesn't want to marry his widowed sister-in-law. He can be released from his obligation by participating in a ceremony called halitza, "removal," which is described in Deuteronomy 25:9. "His brother's widow shall go up to him in the presence of the elders, pull the sandal off his foot, spit in his face, and make this declaration: 'Thus shall be done to the man who will not build up his brother's house.'"

The Torah plainly intends halitza to shame the unwilling brother-in-law. But in the Talmud, it's treated more as a welcome opportunity for both parties to get out of a burdensome and archaic obligation. Take the requirement of performing halitza in front of a group of elders. In the Torah, this seems like a way of providing an audience for the man's humiliation, which might make him change his mind. The Talmud, however, says that the role of the elders is to discourage an unsuitable marriage. "If he was a young boy and she was elderly, or if he was elderly and she was a young girl, they would tell him not to enter into levirate marriage . . . 'Go be with someone like yourself, and do not bring a quarrel into your household,'" they would counsel (44a).

The Talmud also tries to find a way around the gender inequity that gives the man alone the right to refuse a levirate marriage. If a widow didn't want to marry her brother-in-law but he refused to perform halitza, the rabbis would conspire with her to deceive him, putting justice above the law. On one occasion, Rabbi Hiyya was approached by a woman whose brother-in-law refused to release her. Counting on his ignorance of the law, Hiyya told the man that the ceremony of halitza would marry the couple, when in fact it prevented them from marrying. Once the ceremony was over, Hiyya sprang the truth on him: "Now she is disqualified for you" (106a).

When it comes to the ceremony itself, the Talmud inquires about technical details that the Torah leaves unaddressed. The woman is supposed to remove the man's footwear, but what footwear is valid for this purpose? Any shoe or a sandal is acceptable, as long as it is made of leather and has a hard heel; a soft shoe made of cloth doesn't qualify. Which foot should the shoe be removed from? The right, but if the man doesn't have a right shoe, he can put his left shoe on his right foot and have his sister-in-law remove that (101a).

Even the remotest contingencies have to be accounted for. What if a woman is physically unable to remove the man's shoe because she has no hands? This problem once stumped a sage named Levi, who turned to his fellow rabbis for advice. "Does it say in the Torah, she shall remove the shoe by hand?" they replied. As long as the shoe is removed from the man's foot, it doesn't matter how the woman does it; if she has no hands, she can do it with her teeth. Conversely, if the man's foot has been amputated, his sister-in-law can remove a shoe from his prosthetic foot.

The Talmud assumes that most men won't want to perform levirate marriage. Apparently it was common for men to put off the obligation with the excuse of being ill or needing to take a long journey, something the Talmud specifically discourages. Yet if a man is actually eager to marry his yevama, the rabbis seem equally displeased. According to Abba Shaul, "one who consummates a levirate marriage with his yevama for the sake of her beauty, or for the sake of marital relations, or for the sake of another motive [that is, to inherit her husband's estate], it is considered as though he encountered a forbidden relation" (39b). Levirate marriage is not supposed to gratify the surviving brother's desires, but to satisfy a commandment.

In fact, while halitza might sound like an evasion of duty, the Talmud suggests that it is preferable to going through with a levirate marriage. That is because the moral standard of the Jewish people has declined since Biblical times—an idea that recurs in the Talmud in many different contexts. In the past, "they would have intent for the sake of fulfilling the mitzva" of levirate marriage, the Talmud says, so it was a holy deed. But "now that they do not have intent for the sake of fulfilling the mitzva," things are different, and "the mitzva of halitza takes precedence over the mitzva of consummating levirate marriage." Eventually, halitza became mandatory in Ashkenazi tradition.

If a man and his yevama have sex, however, they are automatically married. It doesn't matter whether they do so intentionally or "unwittingly"—that is, if one partner is unaware of the identity of the other. Nor does it matter if coercion is involved. If "he was coerced and she was not coerced, or she was coerced and he was not coerced," the marriage is valid. This raises a question in the Gemara: "What are the circumstances the Mishna is referring to when it mentions a man who was coerced?" (53b) It's easy to understand how a woman might be forced to have sex against her will, but how could this happen to a man?

The first possibility the Gemara considers is that a man could be coerced "by gentiles," who threaten to kill him unless he has sex. (Naturally, the rabbis assume that Jews would never come up with such an idea.) Does this constitute coercion? According to Rava it doesn't, since a man needs to have an erection to go through with the act, and "there is no erection without intent." Perhaps, then, coercion means sex with "one who was sleeping." If a man has an erection in his sleep, a woman might take advantage of this and force herself on him. But according to Rav Yehuda, sex with an unconscious man doesn't count at all: "A sleeping man has not acquired his yevama."

The Gemara even wonders if it's possible for a man to have sex purely by accident—for instance, if he fell off a roof and happened to land on a woman and penetrate her. Such a well-aimed fall could never happen in real life, but the Talmud uses it to show that a collision of genitals doesn't constitute a voluntary sex act. Sex only counts if at least one of the partners intends for it to happen.

What if a man has an erection but doesn't intend to have sex with anyone, only to "press into a wall" (54a) and achieve orgasm that way? This would be a sin, of course, since it involves spilling seed. But if he ended up accidentally having sex with his yevama—maybe she was hiding behind the wall?—would he acquire her in levirate marriage? Again, the rabbis aren't trying to solve a real problem; rather, they're trying to figure out if it's possible to separate the intention to have an orgasm from the intention to have sex. The answer is yes: in this case, there is no voluntary sex act, so "he has not acquired her." However, if the man intends to penetrate an animal—another serious sin—but ends up penetrating his yevama, the law is different. In this case the intention to have intercourse, even with an animal, is enough to make the sex voluntary, so "he has acquired her, as he intended to act for the purpose of sexual intercourse in general."

The Talmud's remarkable frankness about sex continues when it discusses the definition of intercourse. "The Torah did not distinguish between intercourse and intercourse"—that is, between vaginal and anal sex, both of which count for purposes of levirate marriage. How much penetration is required to constitute a sex act? According to Shmuel, "the initial stage of intercourse is a kiss"—by which he means not a kiss with the lips, but genital-to-genital contact. Just as "a person who places his finger on his mouth, it is impossible that he not press the flesh of his lips," so when a penis touches a vagina there will inevitably be some degree of penetration, however slight; and this is enough to effect levirate marriage. Rabbi Yochanan, however, says that more is required: "the initial stage of intercourse is the insertion of the corona" of the penis (55b).

Halitza isn't needed to free a man from his levirate obligation if his sister-in-law is infertile, since the whole point is to produce children who will continue the dead brother's lineage. Even if the dead man had children whose halakhic status is "flawed"—because they were born outside of marriage, or from a legally forbidden relationship—no levirate marriage is necessary, since these offspring are enough to perpetuate his family line.

The only kind of child who isn't considered legal offspring is "a child born from a Canaanite maidservant or from a gentile woman." Because Jewishness is inherited matrilineally, a child born to a Jewish father and a gentile mother has no halakhic relationship to his father. As the Talmud explains, "Your son from a Jewish woman is called your son, but your son from a gentile woman is not called your son, but her son" (17a).

The child of a Jewish mother and a gentile father, by contrast, is "unflawed," fully Jewish. But in practice things weren't so simple, as a pointed anecdote in the Gemara shows. A man who was the child of a gentile father and a Jewish mother once asked Rav about his own halakhic status. Rav replied that he was legally unflawed. But when the man went on to ask the sage for his daughter's hand in marriage, he refused: "Even if he were as great as Joshua son of Nun, I would not give him my daughter in marriage." Rav's refusal suggests that mixed birth was a handicap in fact, if not in law. Actions speak louder than words, or as Rabbi Shimi bar Hiyya puts it, "People say that a camel in Medes [a remote town] can dance upon a kav [a small plot of ground]. This is a kav, and this is a camel, and this is Medes, and yet the camel is not dancing" (45a).

The only way to ensure that the child of a Jewish man and a gentile woman is Jewish is for the mother to convert, so that she becomes what the rabbis call "a different body," a new legal person. But Rabbi Nechemya is suspicious of anyone who converts to Judaism out of love rather than religious conviction. "Both a man who converted for the sake of a woman and a woman who converted for the sake of a man, they are not converts," he insists (24b).

Nechemya also rejects conversion for worldly reward. In the rabbis' time there was no advantage to converting to Judaism—quite the opposite—so this wasn't a common problem. But the Talmud says that "they did not accept converts in the days of David or in the days of Solomon," when the Israelite kingdom was powerful and conversion might have seemed like a profitable move. Nor will converts be accepted "in the days of the Messiah," when the Jewish kingdom is restored.

To make sure that a potential convert is acting out of pure motives, the Talmud explains that he or she is to be discouraged at first. "What did you see that you come to convert?" the rabbinic court must ask. "Don't you know that the Jewish people at the present time are anguished, suppressed, despised, and harassed, and hardships are visited upon them?" If the prospective convert still wants to go ahead, the judges offer a reminder of all the laws a Jew must obey: "Be aware that before you came to this status and converted, had you eaten forbidden fat, you would not be punished ... and had you profaned Shabbat, you would not be punished by stoning" (47a). Only once the convert has accepted the laws can he proceed with circumcision and immersion, in the case of a man, or immersion alone, in the case of a woman.

To Rabbi Helbo, however, even a sincere and informed convert to Judaism is undesirable: "Converts are as harmful to the Jewish people as a leprous scab on the skin." Later commentators offered various explanations for this ugly saying. According to Maimonides, it means that converts tend to lapse into their old ways, encouraging laxity among other Jews. Others say just the opposite: Converts tend to be stringent in their observance, which makes other Jews look bad by comparison. In any case, the Talmud makes clear that a convert is "a Jew in every sense"—there is no halakhic distinction between converts and other Jews.

A man who dies without having children has failed to carry out one of the most impotant mitzvot, and levirate marriage is meant to give him a kind of posthumous second chance. The commandment to "be fruitful and multiply" is older than Judaism itself; God addresses it to the first human beings, Adam and Eve, in Genesis 1:28. But how many children does God want us to have? According to Beit Shammai, a man shouldn't stop until he has two sons, following the example of Moses, who separated from his wife Zipporah after fathering Gershom and Eliezer. Beit Hillel, however, look to the Creation story, where God created human beings "male and female," suggesting that it's necessary to have at least one son and one daughter (61b).

Even having two children, however, is no guarantee that one's family line will continue, since they may die young or turn out to be infertile. According to Rabbi Yochanan, a man in that situation hasn't fulfilled his obligation to be fruitful and multiply, so he must try to have more children. But Rav Huna disagrees, because he takes a more mystical view of the command-ment. The "son of David [that is, the Messiah] will not come until all the souls of the body have been finished," he believes. That is, God created a finite number of souls, and the world won't come to an end until they are all born. By having children, a man does his share to hasten the coming of the Messiah, even if his family line dies out.

Is it only men who are commanded to have children, or are women equally obligated? The Mishna in Yevamot 65b records both views: "A man is commanded with regard to the mitzva to be fruitful and multiply, but not a woman. Rabbi Yochanan ben Beroka says that a woman is also commanded." At first this might seem like a strange distinction—after all, a man can't reproduce without a woman, and vice versa.

But as the Gemara explains, the issue has implications for divorce cases. If a man has been married for ten years and his wife hasn't given birth, he is required to divorce her so he can remarry and try again. Can a woman ask for a divorce on the same grounds? Once a woman came before Rabbi Yochanan in the synagogue at Caesarea and demanded a divorce from her husband after ten childless years. Yochanan ruled in her favor, suggesting that he believed a woman also has an obligation to be fruitful and multiply.

Other sages disagree about the commandment, but believe a childless woman should be granted a divorce for practical and emotional reasons. As a childless woman once pleaded to Rav Nachman, "Does this woman not require a staff for her hand and a hoe for her burial?"

If a husband and wife each insist that the other one is infertile, the judge should accept the woman's testimony, because as Rabbi Ami says, "She is certain whether his semen shoots like an arrow, whereas he is not certain whether his semen shoots like an arrow." This isn't the Talmud's only doubtful idea about biology; it also suggests that a man can become infertile by holding in his urine for too long. That is what happened to the sixty students of Rav Huna, whose long lectures prevented them from going to the bathroom. They all became impotent, and the only one to be cured was Rav Acha bar Ya'akov, who was willing to undergo an unpleasant treatment: "They suspended him from the cedar column that supported the study hall, and a substance that was as green as a palm leaf emerged from him" (64b). Zeal for the Torah is a good thing, but not at the price of bodily harm.

The requirement that a Jewish man have intact genitals is found in Deuteronomy 23:1: "He that is crushed or maimed in his private parts shall not enter into the congregation of the Lord." The Talmud explains that this includes any man whose testicles have been injured or punctured, but not "a eunuch by natural causes" (75a). A historian might explain this as one of the Torah's devices for distinguishing the ancient Israelites from other Near Eastern cultures, where castrated men often served as priests and officials. The Talmud, however, interprets it to mean that men with testicular injuries are forbidden from getting married because they are unable to have children.

But does a genital injury always lead to infertility, the rabbis wonder? Apparently not: "A certain man was climbing up a palm tree, and a thorn punctured him in the testicles, and semen resembling a thread of pus issued from him, and yet he later had children." Rav wasn't convinced by this story: "Go inquire about his children where they come from," he said, implying that the injured man couldn't have been their actual father. If a man's penis is injured and then heals, how does he know whether it's safe for him to ejaculate? The Talmud strongly forbids masturbation, so it recommends a different technique for causing ejaculation: taking "warm bread and placing it upon his anus." Alternatively, Abaye's suggests, you could "pass before him the colorful garments of a woman," which would be so exciting that he would ejaculate spontaneously.

All of this discussion is predicated on the idea that a sex act requires an intact penis. But what about lesbian sex, or as the Talmud describes it, "women who rub against each other"? This is frowned upon, but it isn't as serious a sin as forbidden sex between a man and a woman. According to Rabbi Elazar, an unmarried woman who has sex with another woman is still fit to marry a priest, while if she had sex with a man she is rendered unfit (76a). In this way, the rabbis' phallocentrism turned out to be good for Jewish lesbians—an ironic twist in the Talmud's complicated treatment of sexuality.

Even though the main purpose of marriage is childbearing, the Talmud also believes that being married is good in itself. According to Rabbi Hanilai, "Any man who does not have a wife is without joy, without blessing, without goodness" (63a). And the benefits of marriage aren't only emotional. Once Rabbi Yosei asked Elijah the Prophet to explain why God created Eve as a helpmate for Adam. Elijah responded, "When a man brings wheat from the field, does he chew raw wheat? When he brings home flax, does he wear unprocessed flax?" Cooking and sewing are the wife's contributions to the household economy.

If a marriage is miserable, however, there's no reason to prolong it. "It is a mitzva to divorce a bad wife," says Rava, since "a bad wife is as troublesome as a day of heavy rain." Rav had a notoriously unpleasant wife: "When he would say to her: Prepare me lentils, she would prepare him peas; if he asked her for peas, she would prepare him lentils." Things went on like this until their son, Rabbi Hiyya, hit upon a clever strategy: he would intentionally give his mother the wrong instructions for dinner, so she would end up cooking the dish Rav really wanted. Hiyya himself had an unhappy marriage, but he counseled resignation: "When he would find something [his wife would like as a gift], he would wrap it in his shawl and bring it to her. Rav said to him: Doesn't she aggravate you? Hiyya said to him: It is enough for us that our wives raise our children and save us from sin."

Ketubot On marriage contracts, the value of virginity, and how to deal with a disgusting spouse.

A wedding is meant to be one of the greatest joys in a Jewish life, and the Talmud emphasizes that nothing should be done to spoil the celebration. If there's a funeral procession on the same day as a wedding, it should be rerouted so the bride and groom won't encounter it. Even Torah study takes a backseat: "One suspends the study of Torah to attend the removal of a corpse for burial and to attend the entry of a bride into the wedding canopy" (17a).

Celebration makes a wedding festive, but what makes it legal is the ketuba, the marriage contract signed by bride and groom. Today, most Jewish couples treat the ketuba more or less as a piece of art, something to frame and display on the wall. But it's meant to be an enforceable contract, laying out the legal and financial responsibilities of husband and wife. Tractate Ketubot subjects this contract to detailed analysis, while also using it as a springboard for discussing broader questions about marriage and sexuality.

The basic provisions of the ketuba are simple. The husband agrees to provide food and clothing for his wife, have conjugal relations regularly, and set aside money for her in case the marriage ends in divorce or death. But of course, there are many other financial and legal issues that might arise between a married couple. For instance, the ketuba obligates the husband to provide for his wife, but is he also legally required to provide for their children?

This turns out to be a more complicated question than it might appear. The Mishna in Ketubot 49a says that "a father is not obligated to provide his daughter's sustenance," from which the Gemara infers that "with regard to providing his son's sustenance, he is obligated." But several authorities argue that even sons have no legal claim on their father—at least, not during his lifetime. It is only when the father dies and his estate is being divided up that his children can make a legal claim on his property.

However things may be in theory, however, the Gemara explains that in practice, fathers must provide for their children. "In Usha," the site of an important rabbinic court in the second century CE, the Sages "instituted that a man should sustain his sons and daughters when they are minors." If a father had the means to support his children but refused, the court could compel him. The rabbis also used shame as a motivator, comparing deadbeat fathers unfavorably to jackals and ravens, who feed their children even though they are scavengers.

The Talmud offers different rationales for supporting daughters and sons. Girls must be spared the dishonor of begging for their bread, while sons need to be supported so they can engage in Torah study. And Torah study begins early: in Rav's words, "If he is six years old, stuff him like an ox" with learning. Starting earlier than that is a wasted effort, since very young children can't sit still. "Anyone who brings his son to school when he is younger than six years old will run after him and not catch him," Rav Ketina says. If a boy resists going to school, the Gemara advises that he should be treated patiently until he is twelve years old: "From this point forward, [his father] harasses him in all aspects of his life."

A husband owes his wife material support, and in exchange he gains control over her income. The purpose of this rule, the Talmud explains, is to avoid the resentment that the man might feel if she hoarded her money while he was supporting her. If the wife chooses, however, she can live off her own earnings: "A woman may say to her husband: I will not be sustained by you and in turn I will not work for you" (58b).

A wife's main responsibility is running the household. "And these are the tasks that a wife must perform for her husband: She grinds wheat into flour, and bakes, and washes clothes, cooks, and nurses her child, makes her husband's bed, and makes thread from wool by spinning it" (59b). She doesn't have to do all this personally; "if she brought four maidservants [into the marriage], she may sit in a chair" and delegate all the work to them. According to Rabbi Hiyya this is the ideal setup, since he believes "a wife is only for beauty and a wife is only for children." Rabbi Eliezer disagrees, however, warning that idleness leads to licentiousness. Even a woman with a hundred servants should do some kind of work, such as making thread. Other rabbis say that it's enough for a woman to keep busy with pastimes such as "small dogs or games."

The sexual relationship between husband and wife is also legally regulated. The Talmud thinks of sex as something a husband owes to his wife, so a husband who takes a vow not to have sex must give his wife a divorce. As for the frequency, the Talmud establishes a sliding scale based on the man's occupation. If his job keeps him away from home or is physically demanding, he can have sex less often than if he lives a sedentary life. Thus men of leisure must have sex with their wives every day, while laborers do it twice a week, camel drivers once every thirty days, and sailors once every six months (61b). A Torah scholar should have sex with his wife every Shabbat—though the Talmud praises the wife of Akiva, who encouraged him to study in a distant city for twenty-four years, sacrificing her sexual fulfillment for his scholarly achievement.

A man is obligated to think of his wife's happiness in other respects, as well. He can't be miserly, giving her a bare minimum of sustenance, because this leads to social disgrace: "People hear about her and the matter is demeaning for her." Nor can he deprive her of small pleasures: "One who vows and obligates his wife not to taste a particular type of produce must divorce her" (70a). Divorce is necessary in this case because a wife can't nullify a vow taken by her husband, while a husband does have the power to nullify his wife's vows. For instance, if a woman vows not to adorn herself "with regard to matters that are between him and her"—that is, her appearance when naked, particularly the grooming of her pubic hair—then the husband has the right to nullify that vow. Rav Adda bar Ahava, however, believes that a wife's refusal to groom her pubic hair doesn't constitute any real injury to her husband, as he explains with a vivid metaphor: "We have not found a fox that died in the dirt of a hole" (71b).

More serious transgressions by a wife are grounds for divorce. The Talmud divides them into two categories. A woman who "violates the precepts of Moses" causes her husband to commit a sin—for instance, by lying about her menstrual status in order to have sex while she is ritually impure. A woman who fails to follow "the precepts of Jewish women" is guilty of more general immodesty, such as going outside with her hair uncovered or talking to strange men. Rabbi Tarfon adds another example—being "loud." In this context, the Gemara explains, a "loud woman" isn't simply one who raises her voice, but a woman who talks immodestly about "matters relating to intercourse." Alternatively, it could mean a woman who is loud during the act itself: "when she engages in intercourse in this courtyard and her voice is heard in another courtyard."

Irritating or immodest behavior can be changed, if the parties are willing. But what if the objectionable thing about a spouse is their appearance? The Talmud envisions marriages arranged by the spouses' families, where the couple might not see each other until shortly before the ceremony. If you discover that your spouse is physically repulsive, is that a valid reason to dissolve a marriage?

Unsurprisingly, the Talmud offers different standards for what qualifies as a blemish in men and women. The rabbis assume that a woman is willing to put up with defects that a man would find disqualifying, since even an unimpressive husband is a big social advantage for a woman: "One whose husband is as an ant places her seat among the noblewomen," as Abaye puts it (75a).

A wife can be divorced for major disfigurements like broken or maimed limbs, but also for minor imperfections such as "sweat, a mole, and odor from the mouth." The rabbis go into great detail about what kind of mole constitutes a blemish. A small one is acceptable, unless it's in the middle of a woman's forehead, but a large mole or one with a hair growing out of it is grounds for divorce. A man who discovers that his bride has one of these defects can dissolve their betrothal, or if they are already married, divorce her without paying the marriage contract.

But this is only the case if the defects existed before the betrothal and were hidden from him. If they were plainly visible and he went ahead with the marriage anyway, he can't change his mind afterward. Even if the groom never laid eyes on the bride, it is assumed that that his female relatives would have seen her in the public bath and related any imperfections, such as breasts that are too far apart ("three fingers" width between the breasts is considered ideal) or too big.

In a husband, minor blemishes like moles aren't grounds for divorce. Only serious defects count—"for example, if his eye was blinded, or his hand cut off, or his leg broken." In such a case, the court can compel a husband to grant his wife a divorce. So too if he engages in a trade that makes him permanently malodorous, like a tanner or a coppersmith. Even if a woman knew about these defects in advance and agreed to put up with them, Rabbi

Meir would allow her to change her mind: "She can say: I thought I could accept this but now I realize I cannot accept it" (77a). The rabbis, however, say that "she must accept it against her will," with only one exception—if her husband develops boils, making sex painful.

A bride's appearance can also raise a different kind of problem. At weddings it's customary to make speeches in praise of the bride's beauty. But "in a case where a bride was lame or blind, does one say with regard to her: A fair and attractive bride?" Beit Hillel and Beit Shammai disagree about whether such a white lie is permissible. Beit Hillel, generous as always, believe that every bride should be described as attractive, regardless of her actual appearance. Beit Shammai, typically strict, believe that one should praise "the bride as she is" by finding something flattering to say about her character or her family background, rather than her appearance.

In such disputes Hillel's views almost always prevail, as they do here. The rabbis say it is better to err on the side of kindness, since "a person's disposition should always be empathetic with mankind." And it's not just the bride's feelings that are at stake; after all, the Gemara adds, one wouldn't want to make the groom feel like "one who acquired an inferior acquisition from the market."

The most important responsibility for newlyweds is to consummate the marriage on the first night. This is such a high priority that even if a parent of the bride or groom dies on the day of the wedding, the couple must have sex before entering mourning, which requires them to separate for seven days. Speed is crucial because the groom needs proof that his wife is a virgin, as all Jewish women (except for widows and divorcees) are expected to be before marriage.

If the wedding night makes a groom suspect that the bride isn't a virgin, he would want to bring the matter before a court immediately. For this reason, the Talmud says weddings should take place on Wednesdays, since courts customarily sat on Thursdays (3b). The charge is very serious: according to Deuteronomy 22:21, if a bride is found not to be a virgin, "the girl shall be brought out to the entrance of her father's house, and the men of her town shall stone her to death; for she did a shameful thing in Israel, committing fornication while under her father's authority."

Because the stakes were so high, the wedding night was carefully monitored. Groomsmen were stationed outside the bedroom, and in the morning they would inspect the sheets for blood, to prove that the bride's hymen had been broken during intercourse. The Talmud notes that this measure was for the bride's sake more than the groom's; if the groom made a false accusation, the groomsmen could serve as witnesses to the bloody sheets (6b).

It takes more than sheets to determine if a marriage can be invalidated. A man who has sex with his wife for the first time might claim "I encountered an unobstructed orifice," suggesting that her hymen had been broken by intercourse with another man. But the rabbis note that a man can't always tell if a woman's "orifice" is obstructed or not. Indeed, if he's a virgin himself, as he ought to be, he would have no standard for comparison. By making such a claim, the groom opens himself up to a charge of sexual misbehavior. Once, when a new husband complained to Rav Nachman that he "encountered an unobstructed orifice" on his wedding night, the sage replied: "Flog him with palm branches; prostitutes are common around him" (10a).

It's also possible for a man to have intercourse with a woman who has an intact hymen and simply fail to penetrate it. He could have "diverted his approach," in the Talmud's words, by inserting his penis at an angle.

Even the absence of blood on the sheets isn't necessarily conclusive. A pair of newlyweds once came before Rabban Gamliel with a dispute. The man claimed there was no blood on the wedding-night sheets, but the woman insisted that she had been a virgin. Gamliel took the sheet and "soaked it in water and laundered it and found upon it several drops of blood," which proved that the wife was telling the truth. Furthermore, some women are predisposed not to bleed; as one bride pleaded, "I am from the family of Dorketi, who have neither menstrual blood nor blood from the hymen."

But Rabban Gamliel's understanding of gynecology wasn't exactly scientific. On another occasion, he tested a woman's virginity by having her sit on top of an open wine barrel. If she didn't have a hymen, he reasoned, the fumes would enter her vagina, travel through her body and come out of her mouth, so her breath would smell like wine. In this case, the woman's breath had no odor, proving that she was a virgin. Odd as this might seem, it's another example of how the Talmud raises the evidentiary bar so high that accusations of unchastity are almost impossible to prove.

If a bride lost her virginity by being raped, it is not grounds for divorce. This point leads Ketubot to a discussion of the law of rape, which shows that the Talmud thinks very differently about this crime than we do today. For us rape is a crime of violence, but for the rabbis it was more significantly a crime against a woman's social standing and marriage prospects. To repair this damage, the rapist is punished by paying compensation to the victim's father and marrying the woman he raped. As the Mishna says in Ketubot 39a, "The rapist drinks from his vessel." Horrifying as this may sound, the Gemara explains that the marriage only takes place with the consent of the woman (and her father).

In addition to paying a fine for the crime of rape, the rapist pays compensation for his victim's pain, humiliation, and degradation. In discussing these penalties, which are also paid to the victim's father, the Gemara inquires about what rape actually involves. "For what pain" is the rapist obliged to pay? According to one sage, it is the pain caused when "he slammed her into the ground." But as Rabbi Zeira points out, if this were the case then a rapist who "slammed her onto silk" would not be liable. Surely it's not the type of bedding that matters, but the sexual act.

But is the sexual act painful for the woman only because she is a virgin? If so, wouldn't she eventually have suffered just as much when she first had sex with her husband? That is the reasoning of Rabbi Shimon: "A rapist does not pay for the pain due to the fact that she will ultimately suffer under her husband." But the rabbis reject this line of reasoning, pointing out that "one who has intercourse against her will is not comparable to one who has intercourse willingly." Several sages cite their wives' opinions that the pain of consensual sex is trivial: "Rav Pappa said: My wife, Abba Sura's daughter, told me that it is like the feeling of hard bread on the gums" (39b).

What about the payment for humiliation? The Talmud makes clear that this isn't meant as compensation for the victim's emotional suffering, but for her loss of social status. Since not all women have the same degree of status to lose, it stands to reason that the payment varies depending on the standing of the victim. "Rabbi Zeira said: If one who engaged in forced intercourse with a daughter of kings pays fifty sela, does one who engaged in forced intercourse with the daughter of commoners pay fifty sela?" To calculate the damage that loss of virginity causes to a woman's reputation, the Talmud looks to the slave market: "One estimates the difference between how much a person is willing to give to purchase a virgin maidservant and how much a person is willing to give to purchase a non-virgin maidservant."

In Jewish law, incest is a much more serious crime than rape. A rapist pays damages, but "one who engages in intercourse with his daughter, with his daughter's daughter, with his son's daughter," or certain other female relatives receives the death penalty (36b). As the Talmud observes, this raises a question about the punishment for a man who commits a rape that is also an act of incest. Does he have to pay a fine, or does the death penalty cancel out the lighter penalty?

According to the Gemara, "you can hold [a criminal] liable for one iniquity, but you do not hold him liable for two iniquities." When one act violates two statutes, it can only be punished under one of them. These questions are further complicated by the fact that executions could only be carried out by the Sanhedrin, the supreme Jewish court. But in the Talmudic era the Sanhedrin lacked the power to enforce its verdicts, so a sentence of capital punishment was effectively no sentence at all. Should a rapist or thief be excused from paying an actual fine because of a merely theoretical death sentence? More fundamentally, how can halakha function as a code of law if there's no way to punish people for breaking it?

The answer, according to Rav Yosef, is that God will enforce his own sentences. "From the day that the Temple was destroyed, although the Sanhedrin was abolished the four death penalties were not abolished," he maintains. Jewish law provides for four types of execution—stoning, burning, decapitation, and strangulation—and a criminal who deserves one of these punishments will end up receiving it from "the hand of Heaven."

"One who was liable for stoning either falls from the roof or a beast tramples him. And one who was liable for burning either falls into a conflagration or a snake bites him. And one who was liable for decapitation is either handed over to the monarchy or bandits attack him. And one who was liable for strangulation either drowns in a river or dies of diphtheria" (30b). Of course, the rabbis must have known that not every criminal meets with such a fitting end. But the idea of divine punishment allows them to keep the scales of justice balanced in theory, however lopsided they may appear in practice.

In addition to laying out a husband's responsibilities during the marriage, the ketuba makes provision for the wife if she becomes a widow. A widow doesn't inherit her husband's estate, but she has two options for support. Either she can claim "sustenance" from her husband's estate, in which case his heirs are responsible for supporting her, or she can demand full payment of the amount guaranteed in her marriage contract. If a widow continues to live in her husband's household, she has the right to sustenance indefinitely. But if she decides to go back to her father's house, she can only claim sustenance for twenty-five years, after which she forfeits her marriage contract.

Abaye wonders how strictly this deadline should be enforced: "If she came before the setting of the sun at the end of the twenty-five-year period, she collects her marriage contract, but if she came after the setting of the sun she may not collect it? In that slight period of time did she waive her rights?" (104a) It seems absurd that after twenty-five years, one hour should make a difference. But Rav Yosef replies that "all the measures of the sages are such"—that is, they are exactly defined. Terms of measurement might be arbitrary, but without them any legal system would be unworkable. If twenty-five years plus an hour is all right, what about twenty-five years plus a day? A month? Who would decide what's reasonable?

If a widow decides to stay in her husband's house and be supported by his family, the Talmud warns them against making her situation uncomfortable. "The heirs are not able to say to her: Go to your father's house and we will sustain you. Rather, they sustain her and they give her living quarters befitting her dignity." She is entitled to all the comforts she had before: "the slaves and the maidservants," "the pillows and the sheets," "the silver utensils and the golden utensils." This list gives a sense of what kinds of insults a widow might be subjected to by her in-laws—forcing her to sleep with the worst bedding, making her drink out of clay cups when everyone else uses silver ones. The Talmud recognizes that, in domestic life, such pettiness and spite can be as intolerable as outright cruelty.

Nedarim and Nazir
On how to take a vow—
and why you shouldn't.

Kol Nidrei is one of the best-known parts of the Yom Kippur liturgy, in part thanks to its distinctive melody. It's less a prayer than a legal formula: the name means "all vows," and it is recited to nullify all the vows one will make over the coming year. But as tractate Nedarim makes clear, a vow or neder has nothing to do with obligations to human beings. It is a voluntary personal commitment to God, and to be binding it must use a particular verbal formula.

First, a vow has to be formulated negatively, as a promise to avoid or refrain from some person, thing, or activity, like eating a certain food. Second, the object of the vow should be "something that has actual substance" (15a)—a concrete object, rather than an action or abstraction. For instance, rather than vowing "not to sleep," one must say "sleeping is konam for my eyes." Which leads to the third rule: instead of simply vowing "I will not" do something, the prohibition must be associated with a sacred object, most often a Temple sacrifice or korban, which is forbidden to human beings because it belongs to God. The Gemara explains that the word konam was widely used as a synonym for korban, though the sages aren't sure whether it's a foreign equivalent or a term specifically devised for use in vows.

Vows that don't follow this formula are invalid, as are vows that are impossible to fulfill. Thus a man can vow not to sleep for a day, but if he vows not to sleep for three days, he is flogged for taking a vow in vain and released from what appears to be an unkeepable promise.

If a vow is binding, the Torah says there is no way to get out of it. "If a man makes a vow to the Lord or takes an oath imposing an obligation on himself, he shall not break his pledge; he must carry out all that has crossed his lips," says Numbers 30:2. But Nedarim is largely about finding ways to free people from their vows, since the Talmud recognizes that they are often made hastily and without a full understanding of their consequences.

Indeed, even as the Talmud analyzes the rules of vowing, it strongly warns against taking a vow in the first place. "It is better not to vow at all than to vow and not fulfill," says Ecclesiastes 5:4. A vow might seem like a display of piety, but in the Talmud's view it is "a stumbling-block," an obstacle you put in your own way. Someone who never vows doesn't have to worry about committing a sin by violating his vow: "Never be accustomed to taking vows, because ultimately you will disregard them" (20a). Hillel would never vow to sacrifice a particular animal to God; instead, he would bring an unconsecrated animal to the Temple courtyard, consecrate it, and immediately slaughter it. That way no accident could prevent him from fulfilling his promise.

Just as taking vows is borrowing trouble, the Talmud warns, "do not talk extensively with a woman, because ultimately you will come to adultery." Rabbi Acha makes the threat more concrete: "Anyone who looks at the heel of a woman will have indecent children" as a punishment. Reish Lakish explains that "heel" is used as a euphemism here: "The heel that is mentioned is the place of uncleanness, as it is situated opposite the heel."

Rabbi Yochanan ben Dehavai goes into detail abvout the links between sexual indecency and birth defects. If a child is born lame, it's because his father "overturned his table"—that is, had sex in an unconventional position. Muteness is punishment for "kissing that place," or cunnilingus, and deafness is punishment for talking out loud during sex. But all this was too puritanical for the rabbis, who declare: "The halakha is not in accordance with Yochanan ben Dehavai. Rather, whatever a man wishes to do with his wife he may do." Sex acts are a matter of personal preference, like "meat that comes from the butcher": "If he wants to eat it with salt, he may eat it; roasted, he may eat it; boiled, he may eat it" (20b).

In fact, the Gemara continues, what spouses should be worried about isn't sexual experimentation but hostility and coercion. "Children of fear," conceived by a wife who is afraid of her husband, and "children of a hated woman," conceived by a husband who doesn't love his wife, are likely to become sinners. So too are "children of drunkenness," conceived by a man who is too drunk to know who he's having sex with. This may not be a sound theory biologically, but if you think of it as a reflection on family dynamics, it makes a kind of sense. Conversely, the best children result when the woman is an eager participant in sex: "Any man whose wife demands [sex] of him . . . will have children the likes of whom did not exist even in the generation of Moses our teacher." Still, the Talmud says that it is immodest for a wife to demand sex openly; rather, she should "entice" her husband.

If a person takes a vow and then realizes he shouldn't have, does he have any recourse? The Talmud frowns on using equivocations to get out of a vow. A standard vow formula is to declare the object cherem, meaning "dedicated," the way sacred items were dedicated to God in the Temple. But a person having second thoughts might try to claim that he hadn't said cherem but chermo, meaning "a net," which is legally meaningless. Or he might take refuge in technicalities, swearing not to have anything to do with "my wife," and then claiming he really meant his ex-wife. If people try to use this kind of trick, Rabbi Meir says, "the court punishes them and treats them stringently."

Even so, the Talmudic consensus is that instead of punishing people for trying to get out of their vows with bad excuses, a judge should try to give them a better excuse. Courts "dissolved four types of vows: vows of exhortation, vows of exaggeration, vows that are unintentional, and vows depending on circumstances beyond one's control." For instance, a man might decline an invitation to dinner by saying, "a drop of cold water is konam for me" (21a). This doesn't mean he's actually forbidden to drink water; it's only an exaggerated way of saying that he's so full he can't eat or drink any more. "A person speaks this way," the Gemara says, but it is only a manner of speaking.

Rav Huna took a more straightforward approach. He would ask a petitioner, "Is your heart upon you?"—that is, do you still feel the same way you did when you took the vow? If the answer was no, he would dissolve the vow. Rabbi Yochanan once released a mother from her vow to cut off her daughter because she changed her mind after the neighbors began to gossip about it.

Some sages took this leniency to an extreme. Rabbi Shimon once came before a court asking to be released from his vow, and the judges spent all day looking for a loophole that could free him. Finally, a rabbi called Botnit found the solution. Would Shimon have made the vow if he had known that dissolving it would cause so much trouble to the rabbis? No, he said—so the rabbis dissolved it. Ingeniously, the vow was declared invalid because it was so hard to find a reason why it was invalid.

Vows can also be invalidated on the grounds of hyperbole. For example, a man might say that he will give up a certain food or activity "if I did not see on this road as many as those who ascended from Egypt" (24b). Since six hundred thousand Jews participated in the Exodus, it's clear he didn't mean the comparison literally. He was just trying to emphasize that he saw a lot of people, so the vow isn't binding.

The Gemara goes on to add another complication. What if the man claimed that when he said he saw "as many as those who ascended from Egypt," he wasn't referring to people but ants? It's conceivable, at least to the rabbis, that he did see six hundred thousand ants in an anthill. As often happens, the Talmud is using a seemingly frivolous example as a way to approach a serious issue: Do I determine the meaning of my own words, or is meaning established by the consensus of the community? Rav Ashi, anticipating twentieth-century philosophers such as Ludwig Wittgenstein, says that language can't have private meanings: "When he takes an oath, he takes an oath based on our understanding." In the case of the vow about "those who ascended from Egypt," "we do not entertain the possibility in our mind that he is referring to ants."

As an example of the danger of private meanings, the Gemara mentions a case known as "the cane of Rava." Rava was judging between a debtor who claimed that he had repaid his debt and the creditor, who insisted it was still owing. The debtor filled a hollow cane with coins and tricked the creditor into holding it by saying he needed his own hands free. The debtor then swore that he had given the creditor back all his money. Technically this was true, since at that moment he was holding the money in the cane; but of course the creditor didn't know this, and the debtor intended to take the cane back. The charade was exposed when the creditor got angry and broke the cane, causing the money to fall out (25a). It is to prevent this kind of chicanery that the Talmud insists on following the ordinary meaning of words.

Other common hyperbolic vows included forswearing "those who see the sun," "those who have dark heads," and even "those that are born." These are all understood as ways of saying "everyone," not a reference to specific groups; if you swear not to derive benefit from those who see the sun, that doesn't mean you're making an exception for the blind. Apparently it was not uncommon for a Jew to get so exasperated with other Jews that he vowed not to have anything to do with them, using expressions like "those who rest on Shabbat," "the offspring of Abraham," or "those who are circumcised" (31b). The Talmud takes these formulas to mean Jews as a whole, making no exception for a Jew who was not circumcised for medical reasons or who fails to observe Shabbat. Conversely, a vow to avoid "those who are uncircumcised" refers to all gentiles, even ones who happen to be circumcised, because "uncircumcised is used only to name the nations of the world"—that is, the nations other than Israel.

The reference to circumcision prompts a digression on the subject of this mitzva. The foreskin, says Rabbi Elazar ben Azarya, is "repulsive," and "the wicked are disgraced" by having it. Rabbi Yehoshua ben Korcha brings up the famously weird episode in Exodus 4 where God tries to kill Moses and is dissuaded by Zipporah, who circumcises their son and touches Moses's feet with the bloody foreskin. The Talmud sees this as a lesson about the importance of circumcision: "So great is circumcision that all the merits of Moses our teacher . . . did not protect him when he was negligent about it." Yehuda HaNasi goes furthest of all: "So great is circumcision that if not for it, the Holy One, blessed be he, would not have created his world."

In addition to hyperbole, vows can also be declared invalid if they're made under duress. "One may take a vow to murderers, or to robbers, or to tax collectors" if necessary for self-preservation. The Gemara wonders about this grouping: are tax collectors really as bad as murderers and thieves? According to a famous dictum of Shmuel, "The law of the kingdom is the law": wherever they live, Jews are obligated to obey the government. Accordingly, the Talmud clarifies that legitimate tax collectors can't be lied to. It is only "a tax collector who establishes himself as such independently," or "a tax collector who has no fixed amount," whom it is permitted to evade (28a). At a time when taxes were collected by independent tax farmers as a kind of freelance extortion, the Talmud permits resisting their illegitimate authority.

Torah scholars are exempt from paying any kind of tax, but despite this perk, the Talmud insists that sages shouldn't derive material benefit from their learning. Rabbi Tarfon took this principle to an extreme. On one occasion, he was eating figs from a tree when its owner caught him and stuffed him into a sack, intending to throw him in the river. "Woe to Tarfon, for this man is killing him!" the rabbi cried out, whereupon the man, realizing that he had bagged a famous sage, set down the sack and ran away. Afterward, Tarfon blamed himself for drawing on his scholarly renown: "Woe is me, for I made use of the crown of Torah" (62a).

As this story suggests, great sages were the celebrities of Jewish society, and many Torah scholars must have been motivated at least partly by simple ambition. Knowing this, the Talmud dwells on the importance of learning Torah for the right reasons: "A person should not say: I will read so they will call me a sage; I will study so they will call me rabbi; I will review so that I will be an elder and sit in the academy." Instead, "learn out of love, and the honor will eventually come."

Certainly a man doesn't become a Torah scholar for the sake of his health. Sages were expected to be pale and frail. A heretic once insulted Rabbi Yehuda by saying that he looked like a pig breeder, meaning that his ruddy glow was unbecoming for a scholar. Yehuda replied that he owed his good health to having regular bowel movements: "There are twenty-four bathrooms on the way from my home to the study hall, and I enter each and every one of them" (49b).

In addition to being frail, some sages were also famously ugly. "The daughter of the emperor" once told Rabbi Yehoshua ben Chanania that he was "magnificent Torah in an ugly vessel." He responded by asking her whether in her household she kept wine in plain earthenware jugs; when she said yes, he advised her to try switching to gold and silver jugs. She did, but the wine spoiled. "The same is true of the Torah," Yehoshua concluded; ugliness is a protective shell for knowledge. When the princess retorted that, after all, some scholars were both learned and good-looking, Yehoshua replied, "If they were ugly they would be even more learned" (50b).

The Talmud also discusses the standard of beauty for Jewish women. On one occasion, a husband was so disgusted by his wife's appearance that he vowed, "Benefiting from me is konam for you until you show some beautiful part of your self to Rabbi Yishmael." Yishmael was hard put to find even one good quality: "He said to his students: Perhaps her head is beautiful? They said to him: It is round. Perhaps her hair is beautiful? It resembles stalks of flax. Perhaps her eyes are beautiful? They are narrow. Perhaps her ears are beautiful? They are double in size. Perhaps her nose is beautiful? It is stubby. Perhaps her lips are beautiful? They are thick. Perhaps her stomach is beautiful? It is swollen. Perhaps her legs are beautiful? They are as wide as a goose's." By implication, beauty consists of soft hair, wide eyes, small ears, full nose, thin lips, flat stomach, and narrow legs.

Finally, Rabbi Yishmael asked if the woman at least had a beautiful name. Unfortunately, her name was Likhlukhit, which, in addition to being a mouthful, is related to the Hebrew word for "dirty." But here Rabbi Yishmael found his opening: "It is fitting that she is called Likhlukhit, as she is dirty with blemishes," he decided (66b). Since her name was so fitting it could be considered pleasing, allowing Yishmael to rule that she had passed her husband's insulting test.

Not until near the end of Nedarim does it become clear why this tractate belongs in Seder Nashim, the section of the Talmud devoted to the laws of marriage and divorce. According to Numbers 30, a husband has the right to nullify a vow taken by his wife, provided he does so on the same day he hears about it. The Talmud analyzes this rule: does "the same day" mean by sunset on the day the husband hears about his wife's vow, or within a full twenty-four-hour period? Can a husband nullify his wife's vow in advance, with a blanket statement, or does he have to wait until she makes it? And what if he can't actually hear it at all, because he is deaf? To this last question the Talmud offers a strictly literal answer: A deaf man can never annul his wife's vows, because he can never satisfy the Torah's requirement of hearing them.

Many of the vows mentioned in Nedarim are thoughtless or petty, which helps to explain the Talmud's disdain for vowing in general. More venerable and serious is the nazirite vow, which is the subject of tractate Nazir. Naziriteship is established in Numbers 6 as a special form of dedication to God. The nazir, male or female, promises to abstain from drinking wine, cutting their hair, or coming into contact with a corpse for a specified amount of time. When the term expires, the nazir offers a special sacrifice and cuts off their hair, burning it in a sacrificial fire.

Becoming a nazirite sounds like a pious act that should earn God's favor. The most famous nazirite in the Bible is Samson, whose extraordinary strength was linked to his vow not to cut his hair (which is how Delilah proved to be his downfall). But the Talmud looks no more positively on nazirite vows than on other kinds. If a nazirite breaks his vow he is supposed to bring a guilt offering to a priest, but Shimon the Righteous, a high priest in the Second Temple period, refused to accept such offerings, since he didn't want to encourage the practice of naziriteship.

Despite their seriousness, nazirite vows were often taken frivolously, much as we use the solemn words "God damn it" to express irritation. The Talmud says that a farmer dealing with a refractory cow might vow that he would become a nazirite if the cow stood up. People also used the term without understanding what it really meant, treating it as a simple vow of abstention, as in "I am hereby a nazirite and therefore will refrain from dried figs" (10a). If someone uses the term this way, the Talmud asks, is he a nazirite? Beit Shammai says he is, but Beit Hillel thinks such a vow is meaningless.

A married woman who vows to become a nazirite effectively needs her husband's permission, since he has the power to nullify her vows. This raises an interesting moral problem. Say a woman takes a nazirite vow and her husband nullifies it without telling her, so that she believes she's a nazirite even though she isn't. If she drinks wine, has she committed a sin? Technically she hasn't, because her vow wasn't binding, so the Talmud says she's not liable to receive the forty lashes ordinarily given to a sinning nazirite. But since she intended to sin, it seems unfair that she should be rescued by a technicality. Rabbi Yehuda says "she should incur lashes for rebelliousness," but the rabbis are milder: "She requires atonement and forgiveness" (23a).

The intention to sin can make even a permissible action sinful. Rabbi Akiva gives the example of eating non-kosher food: "One who intended to pick up pork in his hand and in fact he picked up the meat of a lamb in his hand requires atonement and forgiveness." Even though he didn't violate the dietary laws, his intention to violate them is still sinful.

Rabbi Nachman bar Yitzhak goes further, saying that "a transgression committed for the sake of Heaven" is preferable to "a mitzva performed not for its own sake." The Talmud offers several Biblical examples of this kind of virtuous sin. When Lot's daughters had sex with their father, believing that it was the only way to preserve the human race, they were acting meritoriously. So was Tamar when she posed as a prostitute in order to get pregnant by her father-in-law Judah, and Yael when she seduced the enemy general Sisera in order to kill him. For the Talmud, what we do matters greatly, but sometimes why we do it is even more important.

Sota On magic potions, unfaithful wives, and a worm that chews through stone.

The Torah is full of supernatural events, but there's only one legal process that actually depends on magic. According to Numbers 5, if a husband suspects his wife of adultery, she must appear before a priest and drink a potion known as "the water of bitterness." If the accused woman, known in Hebrew as a sota, is not guilty, the water won't hurt her; but if she has sinned, it "shall enter into her and become bitter, and her belly shall swell, and her thigh shall fall away." This spectacular death is proof of the woman's guilt and turns her memory into "a curse among her people."

This sounds like a sadistic and irrational ritual, but it's possible to find a humane motive behind it. In a sense, the water of bitterness helps to protect women by defusing male jealousy. If a wife comes through the ordeal, God himself has publicly declared her innocence, so her husband can't continue to suspect her. "Then she shall be free, and shall conceive seed," says Numbers 5:28. In theory, of course, the potion can also lead to her death, but only if it really does have magic powers.

Torah laws that make the modern reader squirm often had the same effect on the rabbis, though they responded differently. While we might see the water of bitterness as an archaic, mythical element in the Torah, the rabbis saw it as the word of God, just like every other commandment. But the Talmud is adept at nullifying Torah laws through interpretation without presuming to explicitly abolish them, and that's what happens in tractate Sota.

Like many rituals that could only be performed in the Temple, the ordeal of the bitter water had been a dead letter for centuries by the time the Talmud was composed. But that doesn't stop the rabbis from analyzing it with their usual rigor. They begin by applying some standard principles of halakhic jurisprudence. In general, a person can't be convicted of a crime under Jewish law unless they were warned in advance both that an act is criminal and what punishment it carries.

Accordingly, a suspicious husband must warn his wife that he suspects her of adultery with a particular man. "How does he issue a warning to her? If he says to her in the presence of two witnesses, do not speak with the man called so-and-so." Several sages comment that "in the present," even this preliminary step is discouraged: "A man issues a warning to his wife only if a spirit entered him. What spirit? The rabbis say: a spirit of impurity" (3a). The Talmud turns the moral implications of the ritual upside down: it is the husband, not the wife, who is shamed by an accusation.

A warning can be issued against any man, Jewish or gentile, even one who is impotent. The formula for the warning says "do not speak with the man," but merely conversing isn't sufficient grounds to suspect a woman of adultery. Rather, she must have "entered a secluded place and remained with that man long enough to become defiled." The rabbis clarify that this doesn't require enough time to complete an act of intercourse, just long enough for the "initial stage" of penetration—about as much time as it takes to swallow an egg, walk around a palm tree, or drink a cup of wine, according to the analogies offered by different sages (4a).

If a husband learns that his wife has defied the warning and secluded herself with her suspected lover, he must divorce her immediately, even before the ordeal that is meant to prove her guilt. Most transgressions are only proved by the evidence of two eyewitnesses, but in this case a wife must be divorced as soon as her husband hears a rumor about her—"even if he heard about it from a flying bird" (31a), as Rabbi Eliezer puts it.

As for the ordeal itself, the Torah lays out the basic procedure. The accusing husband brings the priest an offering of barley flour, and then the wife drinks the potion, which is made by writing a curse on a scroll and submerging it in holy water sprinkled with dust from the floor of the Temple. The experience was designed to be degrading, in ways both subtle and obvious. The sota offering uses unsifted barley flour, rather than the usual fine wheat flour, because barley was usually fed to animals. "Just as her actions were the actions of an animal, so too her offering is animal food," says Rabban Gamliel. If a woman refuses to drink, her mouth is forced open with an iron hook (19a).

Even a sota who was found innocent must have felt violated and humiliated by this process. A guilty one was supposed to suffer a horror-movie death: "She does not manage to finish drinking before her face turns green and her eyes bulge, and her skin becomes full of protruding veins," the Talmud says. She begins to menstruate, because "fear relaxes" her muscles and causes her blood to flow, and then she drops dead.

However, there's a way for even a guilty sota to avoid this gruesome fate. If she has gained merit in the eyes of God through Torah study, her punishment can be delayed for up to three years. For this reason, Ben Azzai says that parents should teach their daughters Torah as a kind of insurance policy. But Ravina disagrees, saying that women gain merit not by studying Torah themselves, but by enabling their husbands and sons to study it. Rabbi Eliezer takes an even more uncompromising position: "Anyone who teaches his daughter Torah is teaching her promiscuity."

The Gemara takes issue with this harsh statement: "Could it enter your mind to say that teaching one's daughter Torah is actually teaching her promiscuity?" (21b) This idea doesn't reflect very well on the Torah, never mind the daughter. But Abbahu explains that it's not the content of the Torah that is dangerous; it's the fact that "wisdom dwells with cunning," in the words of Proverbs 8:12. A woman who becomes wise by studying Torah might also become clever enough to get away with adultery. Of course, this concern never arises when the rabbis are exhorting men to study Torah. But the Talmud often implies that women are more driven by sexual desire than men; as Rabbi Yehoshua says, "A woman desires a kav of food and a sexual relationship rather than nine kav of food and abstinence." (A kav is a measure of volume, roughly the same as a quart.)

After analyzing the ritual at length, the rabbis explain in the last chapter of Sota that it was actually defunct even before the destruction of the Temple rendered it moot: "From the time when adulterers proliferated, the performance of the ritual of the bitter waters was nullified" (47a). Apparently, sexual immorality had become so widespread that it was impossible to single out individual offenders. The change was instituted by Yochanan ben Zakkai, who quoted Hosea 4:14: "I will not punish your daughters when they commit harlotry, nor your daughters-in-law when they commit adultery."

The Gemara offers many more examples of the moral decline of the Jewish people, from an increase in murders to sloppiness about tithing crops. Arrogant people began to "draw out their spittle," apparently a sign of haughtiness, and women in search of husbands began to "look only at the face," judging men by appearance rather than character. Even Torah scholars had "boastful hearts," engaging in unnecessary disputes until no one could be sure what the law said, and "the Torah became like two Torahs."

As punishment for these sins, God canceled many of the pleasures and privileges of Jewish life. Fruit lost its flavor and the honeycomb its sweetness. "Song was nullified from the places of feasts," making celebrations dreary. And "from the time when the Second Temple was destroyed the shamir ceased to exist." This mythical creature was a tiny worm capable of chewing through the hardest material. Because the stones used to build the Temple couldn't come into contact with iron, which is used to make weapons, the shamir hewed them into the right shape. (The five-foot-tall Israeli prime minister Yitzhak Shamir, born Yezernitsky, named himself after this small but irresistible creature.)

The Talmud paints a frighteningly bleak picture of the Jewish people in exile. Since the destruction of the Temple, Rava says, "Each and every day is more cursed than the previous one." Finally the rabbis ask, "Why does the world continue to exist?" (49a) It's a moving reminder that the Talmud, and the Judaism it helped to define, emerged out of an experience of historical disaster at least as shattering as the Holocaust. In the second century as in the twentieth, all that remained was faith: "Upon whom is there for us to rely? Only upon our Father in Heaven."

Gittin On divorce, the destruction of the Temple, and the real meaning of tikkun olam.

Just as a Jewish marriage begins with a document, the ketuba, so it ends with a document, a bill of divorce known as a get. In the Torah, the procedure for divorce is so simple it's covered in a single verse, Deuteronomy 24:1: "A man takes a wife and possesses her. She fails to please him because he finds something obnoxious about her, and he writes her a bill of divorce, hands it to her, and sends her away from his house." But it takes all of tractate Gittin (the plural of get) to translate this into a workable legal process.

The Torah refers to a bill of divorce as if everyone knows how to draw up such a document, but the Talmud demands concrete instructions. Does it have to be written on parchment or paper? Not necessarily; a get can be chiseled on stone, written on a cow's horn, or even tattooed onto the skin of a slave (19a). Of course, this doesn't mean that people often, or ever, wrote legal documents in the form of tattoos. Rather, the point is that anything that can be handed over to a woman can be used to write a get, while stationary objects are unfit for the purpose. Thus a get can be written on an olive leaf that has fallen, but not one still attached to the tree, since trees can't be moved.

The Torah seems to envision that a bill of divorce is written by the husband himself. A woman cannot issue a get, an asymmetry that can still create serious problems in Orthodox communities. But in Gittin, it's taken for granted that this is a job for a professional scribe, because many people were illiterate. This creates a problem even if a scribe is doing the writing, since a get must be read and signed by two witnesses. If the witnesses don't know how to read, it's permitted to read the document aloud to them; if they don't know how to write, the scribe should make a stencil of their names and have them fill it in with ink (9b).

While the Torah imagines a husband handing his wife a bill of divorce in person, the Talmud makes clear that this was usually done by an agent, a kind of process server. This introduces a potentially serious complication, since a husband might dispatch an agent to give his wife a get and then decide he didn't want a divorce after all. Originally, the law held that he could nullify the get by appearing before a court and declaring that he had changed his mind. But what if he nullified the get and was unable to inform the agent, who might already be on his way to find the wife? She might receive the get and remarry in the belief that she was legally divorced, only to find out later that she had been married all along. This possibility meant that a woman could never completely trust a get she received via an agent.

To eliminate this uncertainty, Rabban Gamliel reformed the process so that a get couldn't be revoked simply by the husband's declaration. Instead, the husband had to send a direct message to the wife, and it had to reach her before the get itself: "Once the bill of divorce had entered her possession, he can no longer render it void." A second reform required the get to include not only the names of the spouses but all their aliases and nicknames, or else the blanket phrase "so-and-so and any other name that he/she has." This change made it harder to get married under different names in different places.

The Talmud explains that these reforms were instituted by the rabbis "mi'pnei tikkun olam," for the sake of the betterment of the world (32a). Today, the phrase tikkun olam is often used by American Jews to signify the improvement of society in the name of social justice. But this is a recent spin on a phrase that, in the Talmud, simply refers to a practical improvement in legal procedure. In Kabbalah, meanwhile, tikkun olam developed yet another meaning—repair of the cosmos through mystical contemplation. Such transformations of the meanings of words are one of the ways Judaism balances continuity and change.

The rabbis go on to discuss another important reform introduced by Hillel "for the sake of the betterment of the world." The Torah states that just as every seventh day is a day of rest, so in every seventh year the land of Israel must lie fallow and all debts among Jews are wiped out. The Sabbatical Year embodies Jewish ideals of generosity and mutual care, but it also creates a strong disincentive to lend money, especially as the seventh year approaches. This problem is already anticipated in Deuteronomy 15:9:

"Beware lest you harbor the base thought, 'The seventh year, the year of remission, is approaching,' so that you are mean to your needy kinsman and give him nothing."

To avoid this problem, Hillel created a legal instrument known as a prosbul, which allows a creditor to temporarily assign his claim to a court. Unlike an individual, the court could collect debts in a Sabbatical Year, allowing it to seize the debtor's property and return it to the creditor. The practical utility of the prosbul is obvious, but it's also a pretty bold way of using a legal fiction to circumvent Torah law. Shmuel called the prosbul a disgrace and wished that he had the power to abolish it (36b), but by his time it had proved too useful to do without.

Another example of tikkun olam has to do with the ransoming of captives, an important religious duty and one that Jewish communities had to perform regularly. "For the betterment of the world," the Talmud says that "captives are not redeemed for more than their value" (45a). Paying extortionate ransoms could bankrupt a community—the Gemara mentions one case in which a father paid thirteen thousand gold dinars to free his daughter—and encourage more kidnapping.

The discussion of captives leads to a story about Reish Lakish, an outsize figure among the sages both physically and mentally. Before he was convinced by Rabbi Yochanan to devote himself to Torah, Reish Lakish led an adventurous life. Anecdotes scattered throughout the Talmud make him sound more like Samson or Ulysses than a standard Torah scholar.

On one occasion, he was hard up and agreed to take money to join a troop of gladiators. Evidently there was a tradition that before a gladiator went into combat, he had to be granted his last wish. Reish Lakish's wish should have set off alarm bells for his captors: "I want to tie you up and have you sit, and I will strike each of you one and a half times." But they agreed, whereupon he took a bag in which he had hidden a heavy stone and smashed them all to death. When he returned home, the story continues, Reish Lakish devoted himself to "sitting, eating, and drinking," even though he didn't own so much as a pillow to sleep on. When his daughter asked him if he needed one, he replied, "My daughter, my belly is my pillow" (47a).

A different kind of anecdote is told in Gittin 55b as an explanation of how the catstrophe of 70 CE came about. The historian Josephus, who participated in the Jewish revolt against the Romans, wrote a long book about the political, social, and religious factors that caused the Jews to start the war and then lose it. But the Talmud reduces the cause to a single sentence: "Jerusalem was destroyed on account of Kamtza and bar Kamtza."

The story goes that a man was giving a banquet, and instead of inviting his friend Kamtza, he accidentally sent an invitation to his enemy, the similarly named bar Kamtza. Finding the unwanted guest at the party, "the host took bar Kamtza by his hand, stood him up, and took him out." Bar Kamtza was incensed by this public humiliation, and particularly by the fact that none of the sages present at the banquet made any protest. To get revenge, he embroiled the Temple priests with the Roman authorities by deliberately mutilating a calf that was to be sacrificed on the emperor's behalf. When the priests, seeing the blemish on the calf's upper lip, refused to sacrifice it, the Romans interpreted this as an insult to the emperor—and so the war began. This is implausible as history, but the tale of Kamtza and bar Kamtza is a powerful parable about the need for solidarity. Internal division can lead to the downfall of the whole people.

Ordinarily, if a husband hires a scribe to write a bill of divorce but doesn't explicitly order it to be delivered to his wife, the law assumes that he didn't intend to divorce her, only to "mock her" by threatening a divorce. However, the Talmud makes an exception for a man on his deathbed, who presumably wouldn't waste time with a get if he didn't mean it. In this case, any bystander is authorized to deliver the get without direct instructions from the dying man. Even if a man has fallen into a pit so that he can't be seen, only heard, bystanders are supposed to follow his verbal instructions to write out a get, on the assumption that he is seriously injured and about to die.

But in this scenario, the Gemara asks, how do people know that the man in the pit is who he claims to be? What if the voice actually belongs to a demon trying to make mischief? Fortunately, there's a test to distinguish a human being from a demon: the former casts a shadow and the latter doesn't (66a). The rabbis also ask about a situation where a man tries to divorce his wife because he's temporarily insane on account of demonic possession. In this case his orders are disregarded, and he can get rid of the demon by wearing an amulet containing its name, which the Talmud says is Kordeyakos.

In the Torah, divorce is effected immediately: the husband gives his wife a get and at the same time "sends her out of his house." Again, the Talmud suggests that the reality is more complicated. For various reasons, both parties might prefer a conditional get, in which divorce takes effect only under specified circumstances. A man going on a long journey might write, "This is your bill of divorce if I do not come back from now until the conclusion of twelve months." That way, if he died far from home and the news didn't reach his wife, she wouldn't be left in a legal limbo, unable to remarry.

Other conditions are more like divorce settlements, in which the get is used to make financial and custody arrangements. A husband might grant a divorce "on the condition that you will give me two hundred dinars," or "on the condition that you will nurse my son." But a problem arises if such a condition proves impossible to fulfill. For instance, if the get says that the wife will nurse the child for two years but the child dies before the term is up, the rabbis say that the get is nullified. Shimon ben Gamliel, however, says that the wife shouldn't be responsible for circumstances beyond her control: "Any hindrance to the fulfillment of the condition that does not result from her, then it is a valid bill of divorce" (75b).

A spiteful husband who wanted to make divorce difficult could take advantage of this rule by adding impossible conditions to the get. The Talmud lists several examples: "This is your bill of divorce on the condition that you ascend to the sky, or on the condition that you descend to the depths of the sea, or on the condition that you swallow a four-cubit reed." Such unfulfillable requirements render a get null and void, the rabbis say. But this rule gives a malicious husband the power to make divorce impossible, and Rabbi Yehuda ben Teima offers an alternative view: The get itself remains valid, and only the impossible condition is voided.

Flying into the air or diving to the bottom of the sea is physically impossible. But what about a condition that is only morally impossible? The Talmud gives the example of a get that goes into effect only if the wife eats pork. Can such a condition be enforced, or should it be voided under Yehuda ben Teima's rule? According to Abaye, a forbidden act is equivalent to an impossible one, so the condition is void and the divorce is effective.

Rava disagrees, but the Gemara challenges him by raising the stakes. What if a husband divorces his wife on the condition that she commits incest with her father? This is a much more serious sin, punishable by death; should the wife be deprived of her divorce because of her refusal to perform such an act? Rava rebuts the challenge, however, arguing that incest actually is impossible, on the grounds that the father would never consent to it. As a result, the condition is nullified, since asking a woman to commit incest is like asking her to fly (84a).

The Torah makes clear that only a husband can initiate a divorce, and in the many hypothetical cases discussed in Gittin, it's always the husband who issues the get and the wife who receives it. When the Talmud discusses the grounds for divorce, then, it only considers the husband's motives (though there are certainly ways for a wife to provide the impetus for a divorce, even if she can't issue a get).

The Torah's description of the grounds for divorce is ambiguous. Deuteronomy 24:1 first says "she fails to please him," suggesting that a husband can initiate a divorce if there's anything he doesn't like about his wife. But this is followed by "because he finds something obnoxious about her," which implies that the wife must be culpable in some way. The Hebrew phrase translated as "something obnoxious" is "ervat davar," literally "a matter of nakedness," and elsewhere in the Torah the word ervah is associated with sexual transgression, as when Ham uncovers the nakedness of his father Noah.

Accordingly, Beit Shammai says that "a man may not divorce his wife unless he finds out about her having engaged in forbidden sexual intercourse." Beit Hillel, on the other hand, interprets ervat davar to mean anything displeasing: "He may divorce her even because she burned his dish" (90a). Akiva is still more permissive: "He may divorce her even if he found another woman who is better looking." If it would make him happier to have a different wife, he should divorce and remarry.

But the rabbis insist that a man shouldn't use this power just because he possesses it. A frivolous divorce is legally valid—"What he did, he did," the Gemara says—but Rava warns against it with a citation from Proverbs 3:29: "Devise not evil against your neighbor, seeing he dwells securely by you." Divorce in general is displeasing to God, according to Malachi 2:16: "For I hate sending away, says the Lord, the God of Israel." Worst of all is when a man divorces his first wife; according to Rabbi Elazar, "Anyone who divorces his first wife, even the altar sheds tears over him." When it comes to divorce, the rabbis didn't feel able to rewrite Torah law "for the betterment of the world," as they effectively did with the prosbul. But they made clear that husbands have a responsibility to behave ethically as well as legally.

Kiddushin On betrothal, the duties of parents and children, and why women don't have to wear tefillin.

Kiddushin is the last tractate in Seder Nashim, but it deals with the first step in the marriage process, betrothal. Betrothal is more significant in Jewish law than a secular engagement, which today is just an informal declaration of intent to marry. By contrast, kiddushin—which comes from the same Hebrew root as the word for "holiness" and could be translated as "consecration"—is a legal contract that binds the parties with financial obligations.

The modern understanding of marriage as an agreement between equal partners is very different from the one found in ancient legal systems, including the Talmud. The Mishna in Kiddushin 2a begins "a woman is acquired in three ways," which makes betrothal sound like a kind of purchase: a man acquires a wife, just as he might acquire a slave or a piece of land. But the Gemara, paying close attention to word choice, explains that the Mishna actually means that a woman has equal agency in the transaction. "If the Mishna had taught: The man acquires the woman, I would say that he can acquire her even against her will. Therefore the Mishna taught: The woman is acquired, from which it may be inferred that with her consent, yes, he can acquire her as a wife, but without her consent, no."

As for the three methods of acquisition, they are "through money, through a document, and through sexual intercourse." A document is the most straightforward method, since it makes clear exactly what financial commitments are expected from the bride and groom. Most marriages arranged between families would have involved this kind of written betrothal. By including money and sex as means of betrothal, however, the Talmud offers legal protection to a woman who becomes involved with a man in a less strategic fashion. A man can't seduce a woman and abandon her, since the act of intercourse makes them betrothed.

Not all gifts of money constitute betrothals; the man must also use the correct verbal formula to make his intentions clear. A gift accompanied by the words "You are hereby betrothed to me" or "You are to me as a wife" is a valid betrothal. But if the man says "I am hereby your betrothed" it is invalid, since only a woman can legally be "acquired" by betrothal. For the same reason, if a woman makes a declaration of betrothal it is legally meaningless. As for more poetic statements of betrothal, such as "You are my helper" or "You are my rib," the Gemara declares, "it shall stand unresolved" (6a).

The minimum sum that can be used for betrothal is a peruta, a low-denomination copper coin, but the examples in the Talmud's discussion suggest that the usual sum was much higher. The rabbis imagine a case in which a man is counting out a hundred dinars as a betrothal gift. Can the woman break off the betrothal while he's still counting? The sages offer different opinions. Some say the first dinar is enough to effect betrothal, while others say the whole hundred is required.

The same kind of question can be asked about betrothal by sexual intercourse. At what point during the sex act does the woman become betrothed? To illustrate the point, the Talmud imagines an unlikely scenario in which a woman is having sex with one man when a second man places a betrothal document in her hand. Which one is she betrothed to? Rabbi Ameimar says that the second suitor prevails, since "anyone who engages in sexual intercourse has the completion of the act of intercourse in mind" (10a). Since sex doesn't count until it's completed, the first man hasn't betrothed the woman until the act is finished.

For the Talmud, an important part of making matches is ensuring that the children will have a good lineage. Members of the primary Jewish castes—priests, Levites and ordinary Israelites—can marry one another freely, and the offspring inherit the status of their father. But members of any of these groups are supposed to avoid marrying spouses with flawed lineage, meaning that their ancestry includes converts, emancipated slaves, mamzerim (children of forbidden relationships), or children of unknown paternity. People with flawed lineage should marry one another, so as not to introduce flaws into a pure lineage. According to Rabba bar bar Chana, addressing the matter of ill-matched lineage, "Anyone who marries a woman who is not suited for him, the verse ascribes blame to him as though he plowed the entire world and sowed it with salt" (70a).

That's the theory, anyway. In actuality, in the Talmudic era lineages were already hopelessly confused. The rabbis explain that when the Jews returned to the land of Israel from their Babylonian exile, in the late sixth century

BCE, family lineages had been forgotten. As a result, anyone might have a problematic ancestor somewhere in their family tree. Recalling Lamentations 5:11, Ulla says (71b), "Perhaps we are from those about whom it is written: 'They have ravished the women in Zion, the maidens in the city of Judah.'" That is, even a Torah scholar might be descended from a woman raped by gentile invaders. But no one cares much, because in practice, marriages are arranged on the basis of wealth rather than lineage. As Rabbi Yehoshua ben Levi observes, cynically or realistically, "Money purifies mamzerim."

The subject of betrothal leads to a broader discussion of marriage and family. A Jewish father has several religious responsibilities. He must circumcise his son, redeem his firstborn son from the priesthood by paying a tax, and teach his son Torah (29a). There are also practical obligations. A father must make sure his son learns a trade, so he can make an honest living. As Rabbi Yehuda says, "Any father who does not teach his son a trade teaches him banditry." Ideally, he should pick a trade that is "clean and easy." It's better to be a perfumer than a tanner, who spends his life among foul-smelling hides and chemicals. Surprisingly, despite the long-standing affinity of Jews for medical careers, the Talmud thinks of doctoring as one of the worst professions. "The best of doctors goes to Gehenna," says Rabbi Yehuda (82a).

That's because doctors have to deal intimately with women, exposing them to sexual temptation. The Talmud tells a number of stories about Torah scholars who made great efforts to avoid such temptation. Once Rav and Rav Yehuda were walking on a road behind a woman, and Rav advised, "Raise your feet and walk away from Gehenna." Just walking behind a woman could provoke uncontrollable lust. Yehuda objected that Rav himself had said this wasn't dangerous for men of "fit morals." But Rav replied, "Who said that I was referring to you and me?" Even a sage shouldn't trust his ability to resist temptation.

That's the moral of the story of Rav Amram, known as "the pious," who allowed a group of women just redeemed from captivity to stay in his house. For their protection, the women slept on the upper floor with the ladder removed. But in the middle of the night, Rav Amram caught a glimpse of one of them and was so aroused that he "grabbed a ladder that ten men together could not lift, lifted it on his own and began climbing."

Fortunately, he came to his senses halfway up the ladder and began crying, "There is a fire in the house of Amram!" This woke the household and the neighbors, who came running and found Amram on the ladder, clearly on his way to the women's room. His fellow sages scolded him for bringing disgrace on Torah scholars, but he replied, "Better that you be shamed in Amram's house in this world, and not be ashamed of him in the World to Come." Then Amram cast out his evil inclination, which emerged in the shape of a pillar of fire. "See, you are fire and I am mere flesh, and yet I am superior to you," Amram boasted (81a).

Because men are prey to such strong temptations, the Talmud advises them to marry as early as possible. A father is obligated to find a wife for his son before he is twenty years old: "Until twenty the Holy One, blessed be he, sits and waits for a man, saying: When will he marry a woman. Once he reaches twenty and has not married, he says: Let his bones swell." But the earlier a man gets married the better. Rav Hisda explained, "I am superior to my colleagues [in virtue] because I married at sixteen," and wished he had gotten married still earlier: "If I had married at fourteen, I would say to the Satan: an arrow in your eye" (30a).

In turn, children have duties to their parents. The Talmud explains that the fifth commandment, "Honor your father and your mother," requires treating your parents like God. This reflects the fact that "there are three partners in the forming of a person: the Holy One, Blessed be He, and his father and his mother." The rabbis give several examples of such filial piety. One story involves a man named Dama ben Netina, who was visited by Jewish priests on a mission to buy jewels for the breastplate of the high priest. Dama would have made six hundred thousand dinars on the deal, but the key to the chest holding the jewels was hidden under his sleeping father's pillow. Rather than disturb him, Dama gave up the sale.

Happily, he was rewarded later when a red heifer was born in his flock. The priests needed this rare animal for certain purification rites, and they bought it for the same price as the jewels would have earned (31a). If Dama was rewarded for honoring his father when, as a gentile, he wasn't bound by the fifth commandment, a Jew can expect even greater rewards, says Rabbi Hanina: "Greater is one who is commanded to do a mitzva and performs it than one who is not commanded to do a mitzva and performs it."

Mothers don't have the same parental obligations as fathers; as the Talmud notes, the commandment to circumcise sons was given to Abraham, not Sarah. Nor are fathers obligated to do the same things for their daughters as for their sons, since only boys can be circumcised and only firstborn sons are eligible for the priesthood. As for teaching Torah, the Torah itself says in Deuteronomy 11:19, "And you shall teach [God's words] to your sons," not to your daughters.

More generally, "with regard to all positive, time-bound mitzvot, men are obligated and women are exempt" (35a). Any commandment that involves doing something at a particular time, such as dwelling in a sukka or putting on tefillin, applies only to men. Women are obligated by positive commandments that don't involve a designated time, such as honoring one's parents, and by prohibitions, such as the ban on working on Shabbat.

Later commentators argued that this rule is an acknowledgment that women have heavier domestic responsibilities than men, so they have less time for mitzvot. But this rationale doesn't appear in the Talmud himself. Instead, the rabbis try to deduce the general principle from specific examples. "Just as women are exempt from tefillin," the Gemara proposes, "so too, women are exempt from all positive, time-bound mitzvot."

But other rabbis note that the Torah never says women don't have to wear tefillin. Deuteronomy 6:4–9, the verses recited in the Shema prayer, mention three obligations in regard to the words of the Torah: to "speak of them" continually, to "bind them for a sign upon your hand . . . and between your eyes," and to "write them upon the doorposts of your house and on your gates." The Gemara points out that women are exempt from the first of these responsibilities, since teaching Torah is reserved for men, but they are obligated in the third, since women must put up mezuzot in their houses. It's not clear which category wearing tefillin belongs in: maybe women should wear them, just as they put up mezuzot.

The Gemara notes other contradictions as well. Women are obligated to eat matza on Passover, which is a positive time-bound commandment, so why aren't they obligated to dwell in a sukka on Sukkot? The Torah forbids Jews to "destroy the corners of your beard," so why doesn't this prohibition apply to women, who are allowed to remove their facial hair? The Talmud manages to refute these apparent contradictions one by one, using arguments about what constitutes a precedent and how to juxtapose

Torah verses. But the basic question—Are the commandments addressed to men more than to women?—is never resolved.

If you think of mitzvot as a burden, women might seem better off for having fewer of them to worry about. But the Talmud's view is the opposite. Men are privileged to have more obligations, because performing mitzvot brings rewards. (That's why, in the traditional morning prayer service, a man thanks God for not making him a woman.) The rewards aren't only spiritual: "Anyone who performs one mitzva has goodness bestowed upon him, his life is lengthened, and he inherits the land. And anyone who does not perform one mitzva does not have goodness bestowed upon him, his life is not lengthened, and he does not inherit the land," the Talmud says (39b).

Yet the Gemara points out that this isn't always borne out by experience. Take the case of a boy whose father ordered him to climb up on a roof to fetch some chicks. Before taking them, the boy made sure to send the mother bird away from the nest, as commanded in Deuteronomy 22:7: "Let the mother go, and take only the young, in order that you may fare well and have a long life." Yet "on his return he fell and died. Where is the goodness of the days of this one, and where is the length of days of this one?" the Talmud demands.

The rabbis struggle to find an answer. At first they say "perhaps this never occurred," but Rabbi Ya'akov insists that he saw it happen. Then they suggest that the boy might have deserved to die because of a hidden evil thought. But this would violate the principle that "the Holy One does not link a bad thought to an action": people are only punished for what they do, not what they think.

Finally, the rabbis explain the case with a different principle: "The danger was established; and anywhere that the danger is established one may not rely on a miracle." God works through the real world and the laws of nature; he doesn't change them to rescue people from predictable dangers. In this case, the Talmud speculates, perhaps the boy used a rickety ladder to climb down from the roof, exposing himself to danger.

But it's still possible to have faith in God's promises if you believe that reward and punishment take place in the next life rather than in this one. According to Rabbi Ya'akov, "There is not a single mitzva in the Torah whose reward is stated alongside it which is not dependent on the resurrection of the dead." The boy who fell off the roof didn't enjoy a long life in this world, but he will in "the world where all is well," the World to Come. Without this conviction, faith in God's justice would be too hard to sustain.

III

Seder Nezikin
Civil and
Criminal Law

Bava Kamma On negligence, restitution, and the problem with being robbed by a Jewish bandit.

For all their length and complexity, Seder Moed and Seder Nashim focus on quite limited areas of Jewish life. Festivals take place once a year and a marriage usually once in a lifetime. It is in Seder Nezikin, meaning "damages," that the Talmud deals with the issues that occupy most of the world's courtrooms every day. The first three tractates, Bava Kamma, Bava Metzia, and Baba Batra—in Aramaic, the "first gate," the "middle gate," and the "final gate"—are divisions of what was originally one very long tractate devoted to torts, in which one person brings a claim against another for property damage, financial loss, or personal injury.

Nowhere is the gulf between the Torah and the Talmud clearer than in these tractates. The Ten Commandments define the basic principles of ethics—do not kill, do not steal—and the Torah is full of instructions about ritual matters that are now obsolete, including the design of the Tabernacle and the protocols for animal sacrifice. But detailed and practical laws, the kind needed to govern an actual society, are scarce.

The closest thing to a civil code in the Torah is found in Exodus 21–22, which lays down rules on everything from lending money to freeing slaves. But in the Torah's usual style, these rules are tersely stated, using examples that suited the ancient Israelites but were less useful later on. For instance, rather than offering general rules about compensation for theft, Exodus 21:37 says: "If a man shall steal an ox, or a sheep, and kill it, or sell it; he shall restore five oxen for an ox, and four sheep for a sheep." It's not clear how to apply this rule even to stealing cows, much less to the kinds of theft and fraud that occur in urban, commercial societies.

The Talmud was the product of such a society, and Bava Kamma works to adapt the Torah to its legal needs in the areas of personal injury and property damage. The Torah discusses how to deal with several types of cases in which one person inadvertently causes harm to another, including the owner of an ox that gores another animal; a landowner who digs an open pit, causing someone else's ox or donkey to fall into it; and a man who sets a fire that burns out of control and destroys someone else's grain.

The Mishna in Bava Kamma 2a transforms these specific cases into broad legal categories. "Ox" covers any case "in which there is a living spirit" that causes damage of its own volition; "Fire" covers hazards that can spread even though they're not alive; and "Pit" refers to stationary hazards where "the typical manner is not to proceed from one place to another and cause damage." The common denominator of all these categories "is that it is their typical manner to cause damage," so that "their safeguarding [is] upon you." Anyone who creates or maintains these hazards without due care is liable for the damage they cause.

This principle is established in Exodus 21:28–29, where different punishments are prescribed depending on whether an ox has gored before. If an ox kills someone with no warning, the animal is stoned to death but its owner isn't liable. If the ox has a pattern of goring people, however, and the owner hasn't taken precautions to keep it penned up, then the owner also receives a death sentence.

The Talmud usually moderates the Torah's harsh sentences, and in this case it replaces the death penalty with payment of monetary damages. An ox is considered "innocuous" unless it gores three times on three different days, whereupon it becomes "forewarned," a known menace (23b). If an innocuous ox gores another animal, the ox's owner must pay the victim's owner half the value of the dead animal. But if the ox is forewarned, its owner is liable for full damages.

The same principle extends to other kinds of damage caused by an animal. The owner pays in full for damage that is "commonplace" and therefore predictable, but only half for damage that is "not commonplace." An ox typically wears a harness and carries a burden, so it's reasonable to hold the owner fully responsible if it causes damage with these appurtenances. But if the ox kicks a rock that flies through the air and hurts someone, the owner pays only half the damage, because it's not commonplace for oxen to kick rocks (3b).

Figuring out exactly what's commonplace and what's unusual gives the rabbis a chance to engage in some thought experiments. What if a dog steals a loaf of bread while it's baking on hot coals, and one of the coals is still attached, and while the dog is eating it the coal ignites a stack of grain? In this case, the rabbis decide that the dog's owner is fully liable for the bread, since it's typical for dogs to steal food, but only half liable for the grain, since it's rare for dogs to start fires (18a).

Rami bar Yehezkel offers another scenario. What if a rooster puts its head into a glass bottle and crows, and the sound shatters the glass? Deciding the liability here involves a series of follow-up questions. Is it typical for a rooster to put its head in a bottle? Does the answer change if there were seeds in the bottle and the rooster was trying to eat them? Is the crowing considered part of the rooster, like its feet, or a secondary force, like a pebble it kicks with its feet?

It's easy enough to calculate damages to property and livestock, but how do you put a price on injuries to human beings? Exodus 21:24 lays down a simple and famous rule: "eye for eye, tooth for tooth, hand for hand, foot for foot." This principle, known in Latin as lex talionis ("the law of retaliation"), first appears in ancient Babylonian legal codes, where it was an innovation meant to rationalize punishment. Instead of setting off a cycle of retaliation that could escalate into a blood feud, the law limits punishment so that it's equal to the original injury. But Christianity later interpreted this idea as an example of harsh Jewish legalism, in contrast to its own ethic of forgiveness. In the Sermon on the Mount, Jesus rewrites the verse from Exodus: "You have heard it said, An eye for an eye, and a tooth for a tooth. But I say to you, Do not resist evil. When someone strikes you on your right cheek, turn the other one to him as well" (Matthew 5:38–39).

In fact, the Talmud also repudiates the idea of punishing one injury with another. Instead, one who inflicts physical harm is liable to pay five kinds of monetary compensation: "for damage, for pain, for medical costs, for loss of livelihood, and for humiliation" (83b). The departure from the Torah's rule is so blatant that the Gemara comments on it: "The Merciful One states: An eye for an eye," and "you might say an actual eye" is what it means, but "that interpretation should not enter your mind." The rabbis find a scriptural basis for the apparent change in Leviticus 24:18–19, where punishment for striking a person is juxtaposed with punishment for striking an animal. In the latter case the guilty party pays monetary compensation, so the same must be true when the victim is a person. This doesn't exactly justify ignoring the Torah's explicit rule, but it gives the rabbis some scriptural anchorage for an innovation they clearly believed to be more just and humane.

For as they point out, a literal interpretation of "an eye for an eye" couldn't be applied equitably. Rabbi Dostai ben Yehuda observes that eyes can be different sizes, and putting out a large eye in exchange for a small one would be inequitable. The rabbis reject this argument, on the reasonable grounds that what matters isn't the size of the eye but its power of vision. But Shimon ben Yochai points out that this would make it impossible to punish a blind man who puts out a seeing man's eye, since the blind man has already lost his power of vision. Such impunity would violate the principle stated in Leviticus 24:22, "You shall have one manner of law" for all people. To avoid this inequity, damages must be assessed in money, which everyone can pay.

Theft is an easier kind of damage to remedy. According to Leviticus 5:23, someone who steals property by force or fraud must repay the owner, plus an additional one-fifth of the item's value as a penalty. (He must also sacrifice an unblemished ram as a guilt offering.) But the Talmud notes that this formula leaves it ambiguous whether a thief becomes the legal owner of the property he steals, with the compensation treated as a kind of purchase price, or whether it remains the legal possession of the original owner. This issue has repercussions if the stolen item increases or decreases in value while in the thief's possession. If a thief steals a cow and it becomes pregnant and gives birth to a calf, who owns the calf, the original owner or the thief? Conversely, what if the thief steals a coin and it breaks while in his possession, rendering it worthless? Does the thief return the broken pieces of the coin, or must he pay back the value of a whole coin?

The Mishna explains that "this is the principle: All robbers pay according to the value of the stolen item at the time of the robbery" (93b). This means that both profit and loss accrue to the thief: he gets to keep the calf from the stolen cow, but he can't give back a broken coin. Beit Shammai, on the other hand, hold that a stolen item remains the owner's property no matter how much alteration it undergoes. Support for that position can be found in the apparently unrelated commandment in Deuteronomy 23:19, "You shall not bring the fee of a prostitute or the price of a dog into the House of the Lord your God." The Gemara points out that a prostitute's fee can't be donated to the Temple regardless of whether it has undergone a change in form. If she is paid in wheat and then grinds it into flour, the flour can't be used in an offering. For Beit Shammai, the same principle applies to stolen goods: a changed item "remains in its place," legally speaking.

But the Gemara points out that Beit Shammai's strict interpretation of the law creates barriers to restitution. If a thief has to return not just the value of the stolen item but also any profit he earned from it, he will be less likely to confess his crime. For this reason, the sages instituted an "ordinance for the penitent," saying that a thief acquires stolen items and only has to repay their original value.

In fact, victims of theft are positively discouraged from accepting the stolen item itself, so as not to create a precedent. Rabbi Yochanan tells the story of a certain thief who wanted to come clean after a long criminal career, until his wife pointed out that it would be impossible to return every item he had stolen. "Even the belt you are wearing is not yours," she observed (94b). As a result, "he refrained and did not repent," leaving everyone worse off. The owners didn't get restitution and the thief didn't get to clear his conscience.

The Talmud is also concerned about another practical barrier to repentance. According to the Mishna in Bava Kamma 103a, if a thief takes a false oath that he didn't steal an item and then decides to repent, he is obligated to make restitution to the victim even if he has to go "after him to Medea." This was a region of northwestern Iran far from the Mesopotamian cities where the Babylonian Talmud was composed, implying that the penitent must make extraordinary efforts to find his victim. The sages, fearing that this obligation would discourage penitence, "instituted a great ordinance stating that if the expense required to return a stolen item to the victim is greater than the principal," the thief can pay restitution to a court instead (103b). Unlike a secular court, whose primary concern is compensating the victim, a Jewish court is also charged with helping wrongdoers repent.

When in-person atonement is possible, however, it is required. A thief can't make restitution to his victim's appointed agent or even his son, only to the victim in person. If the victim is no longer alive, then the thief can achieve repentance by paying back his heirs. But the Talmud notes that this is problematic in the case of a son who steals from his father; in that case he would be required to pay back the money to himself, which hardly seems fair. The rabbis offer several suggestions for getting around this problem, including donating the money to charity or giving it to other relatives. And what if the dead man has no other relatives? The Gemara flatly rejects this possibility: "But is there any Jewish person who has no kinsman?" (109a)

The rabbis can't imagine a situation in which a Jew is so cut off from his community that he can't find a single relative.

Restitution isn't the only reason why it's important to determine who has legal title to stolen property. If the owner of stolen goods continued to own them after they left his possession, then the thief would have no right to sell them to a third party. If he did sell them, the original owner could seize them from the buyer, even if the buyer didn't know they were stolen. This would introduce an element of insecurity into all commercial transactions, since any purchase could potentially be revoked if the item had been stolen at any time in the past. To avoid this situation, the Talmud introduces the principle that a victim of theft gives up ownership of the stolen item once he "despairs" of its return. If he no longer has a reasonable expectation of regaining the stolen property, he is still entitled to compensation from the thief, but he can't claim the property from a third party.

The Talmud gives examples of thefts where the victim automatically despairs of recovering his property. For instance, if the thief is a bandit the owner can't expect to get his goods back, because professional outlaws were unlikely to be caught. The Gemara suggests that the odds of a bandit being forced to return stolen property depend on whether he is a Jew or gentile, but the rabbis disagree about which type of bandit it's better to be victimized by. According to Rav Ashi, it's better to have your property stolen by a Jewish bandit, because he would obey the orders of a Jewish court. Rav Yosef argues the reverse: It's better to be robbed by a gentile bandit because then you can take him before a gentile court, and "gentiles judge with force," while "a Jew pronounces a verbal decision" (114a).

This dispute sheds light on an important question that the Talmud usually passes over in silence. Since the fall of the Temple, halakha has never been the law of a sovereign state—not even in modern Israel, which has a secular legal system. This means that Jewish courts have rarely been able to back up their verdicts with threats of force. Instead of imprisonment or execution, they can only employ excommunication and ostracism. Rav Yosef and Rav Ashi disagree about whether that is enough to make a hardened criminal obey.

When it comes to a legal dispute between a Jew and a gentile, Rabbi Yishmael argues that Jews should always stick together, regardless of which party is in the right. "In the case of a Jew and a gentile who approach the court for judgment in a legal dispute, if you can vindicate the Jew under Jewish law, vindicate him, and say to the gentile: This is our law. If he can be vindicated under gentile law, vindicate him, and say to the gentile: This is your law. And if it is not possible to vindicate him under either system of law, one approaches the case circuitously, seeking a justification to vindicate the Jew" (113a).

Not all the sages agreed with this troubling idea. According to Rabbi Akiva, acting "circuitously" to help a Jew prevail in court is contrary to "the sanctification of God's name"—that is, it would bring Jews and Judaism into disrepute. But the Talmud is quite certain that no Jew can hope for justice from gentile authorities. Appealing to a gentile government in a dispute with a fellow Jew is considered a deadly betrayal, and the rabbis went to great lengths to enforce a "no-snitching" rule. On one occasion, we read in Bava Kamma 117a, a Jew told Rav that he was going to denounce another Jew to the authorities, helping them to seize his property. Rav prohibited this in strong terms, but the man insisted on going ahead; whereupon Rav Kahana, another sage who was present, "dislodged the man's neck from him," killing him with a blow.

Rav justified this action by citing Isaiah 51:20: "Your sons have fainted, they lie at the head of all the streets, as an antelope in a net." He explained, "Just as with this antelope, once it falls into the net, the hunter does not have mercy upon it, so too with regard to the money of a Jew, once it falls into the hand of gentiles, they do not have mercy upon him." Denouncing a Jew to a non-Jewish court was as good as killing him, so Rav Kahana was justified in killing the denouncer first. Living in profound fear of their gentile neighbors and rulers, the rabbis saw Jewish solidarity as a precondition of justice.

Bava Metzia On ownership, exploitation, and when to ignore the voice of God.

In Bava Metzia, the second of the three "gates" devoted to civil law, the focus shifts from the responsibilities of property-owners to the meaning of ownership itself. The tractate begins by imagining a case in which "two people come to court holding a garment, and this one says: I found it, and that one says: I found it." How can the judges determine which party is the owner?

The detail that both parties are holding the garment makes it especially tricky to decide. Ordinarily in Jewish law the burden of proof rests on the plaintiff, since he's the one who wants the court to take action, while the defendant wants to maintain the status quo. In this case, however, there is no status quo, since neither party has physical possession of the garment. And since the property was found, rather than bought or sold, the judges also lack the kind of evidence that might be used to decide a standard property dispute, such as a contract.

In other words, the case is designed to boil down property disputes to their essence, which is the assertion of contradictory claims of ownership. It's the same kind of dispute that Solomon faced in 1 Kings 3, where he had to decide between two women who both claimed to be the mother of a child. In that case, Solomon ordered the baby to be cut in half, and the true mother revealed herself by protesting the decision.

The Talmud offers a similar solution here. Each party takes an oath that he has a right to at least half of the garment, and then they divide it in two. The stakes are much lower than in Solomon's case, of course, but even with a garment simply splitting it in two is an unsatisfactory solution, since half a cloak is useless to both parties. The Gemara therefore says that the parties should split the value of the item, rather than the item itself (8a).

But the Gemara's main focus isn't the division of property; rather, it's the oath each party is required to take. In American courtrooms, people who give testimony swear to tell the truth "so help me God," but this is usually treated as a formality. In a Jewish court an oath is much more serious, since violating it could bring eternal punishment in the afterlife. For this reason, Ben Nannas argues that "an oath is not administered to two parties in court when one of them is certainly lying," since the court shouldn't encourage either party to commit perjury. At the same time, the rabbis recognize that there has to be some deterrent to making a false claim in court. As Rabbi Yochanan says, "This oath is an ordinance instituted by the sages so that everyone will not go and seize the garment of another and say: It is mine" (3a).

Lawsuits over found property are rare; more common are disputes between a buyer and a seller. In the Talmud, the basic rule is that a transaction isn't complete until the buyer "pulls" the item, taking physical possession of it. Until the buyer receives the goods they remain the property of the seller, even if the buyer has already paid. This rule is meant to safeguard the interests of the buyer, as the Talmud explains: "And for what reason did the Sages say that pulling acquires an item and money does not? This is a rabbinic decree lest the seller say to the buyer after receiving the money: Your wheat was burned in the upper story" (46b). The seller has an incentive to safeguard the goods until they are delivered, since he will bear the loss if they're destroyed.

This rule also gives the buyer more opportunity to cancel a transaction: "If the buyer gave the seller money but did not yet pull produce from him, he can renege on the transaction." The seller, by contrast, can't renege once he has received money from the buyer. But the Talmud strongly discourages buyers from taking advantage of this loophole, saying that God punishes people who go back on their financial commitments: "He who exacted payment from the people of the generation of the flood, and from the generation of the dispersion [after the Tower of Babel], will exact payment from whomever does not stand by his statement" (44a).

Another kind of commercial dishonesty involves "exploitation," taking advantage of someone's ignorance in a negotiation. According to Leviticus 25:14, "When you sell property to your neighbor, or buy any from your neighbor, you shall not exploit one another." The Talmud translates this general principle into a precise formula: The purchase price of an item can't be more than one-sixth higher or lower than the market price. If the seller tricks the buyer into paying more than that, or the buyer tricks the seller into accepting less, the exploited party can either nullify the transaction entirely or demand a refund of the excess amount.

For buyers, there is a time limit for bringing a claim of exploitation, which the Talmud defines as the amount of time it would take "to show the merchandise to a merchant or to his relative" (49b). This allows the buyer to compare prices and find out whether he was ripped off. A seller who is defrauded is in a more difficult situation because he no longer has the item he sold, so he can't easily bring it to an expert for an estimate. As a result, there is no time limit for the seller to bring a claim.

The Talmud specifies that a claim of exploitation can only be brought by someone who is ignorant of the fair market value of the goods. This means that "there is no exploitation for a merchant," since he is expected to know how much his merchandise is worth. If he chooses to sell for a lower price than usual, Rav explains, it's only because "other merchandise happens to become available to him and he needs the money to purchase that item." More generally, partners in a transaction can waive the right to sue for exploitation if they are informed in advance that they aren't paying the market price.

In addition to "exploitation in buying and selling," the Talmud also prohibits "exploitation in statements" (58b). It's forbidden to say anything that will cause humiliation or anguish to another person, such as reminding a penitent of his past sins or telling someone who is suffering that his misfortunes are a punishment from God. The rabbis offer several comparisons to underscore the seriousness of this offense; according to Rav, "It is more comfortable for a person to cast himself into a fiery furnace than to humiliate another in public."

To illustrate the importance of not causing humiliation, the Gemara in Bava Metzia 59b tells one of the most significant stories in the entire Talmud. There was once a dispute among the rabbis about the ritual purity status of a type of clay oven known as an "oven of achnai," whose interior is made up of horizontal segments separated with mortar. Only intact vessels can contract ritual impurity, and Rabbi Eliezer argued that since such an oven is made up of discrete parts, it can't become impure. None of the other sages agreed, and in his frustration Eliezer asked God to prove that he was right by performing miraculous signs. First he caused a carob tree to jump a hundred cubits; then he made a stream flow backward; then he made the walls of the study house collapse. But the rabbis rejected each of these signs, saying that they didn't constitute an actual halakhic proof.

Finally a divine voice was heard to say, "Why are you differing with Rabbi Eliezer, as the halakha is in accordance with his opinion in every place?" Rabbi Yehoshua responded with a quotation from Deuteronomy 30:12: "It is not in the heavens." In its original context, the phrase signifies that the Torah isn't "too difficult for you or beyond your reach," as if it were necessary to go up to the heavens to discover it. Yehoshua uses the phrase to suggest that the power to interpret halakha resides with the sages on earth, not with God in heaven. As the Gemara explains, "Since the Torah was given at Mount Sinai, we do not pay attention to a divine voice." Once God gave the Torah to the Jewish people, it was up to them to determine its meaning.

The Gemara bolsters this idea with a phrase from Exodus 23:2, "incline after the majority." Here, again, the words have a different meaning in their original context, where the Torah is actually warning not to incline after the majority: "When you give testimony in a lawsuit, do not pervert justice by inclining with the majority." But the rabbis cite the phrase to suggest that the Torah entrusts the power of legal interpretation to the majority vote of the sages. Even direct signs from God can't prevail over their authority. When Rabbi Yehoshua made this argument, the Talmud says, God "smiled and said: My children have triumphed over me; my children have triumphed over me."

The story captures something profound about the Talmud's fusion of rationality and spirituality. In the Bible, God communicates with people directly, by means of miracle and prophecy. But the Talmud is a product of a disenchanted world like ours, where the best way to approach God is to think hard about his commandments. The sages have no doubt that all the miracles in the Torah really happened, but they don't expect them to happen again, and would even prefer they didn't. A divine voice can only upset the careful structure of halakha that took so many centuries to build.

The story is told here, as part of the Talmud's discussion of humiliation, because of its sequel. Unable to convince Eliezer to bend to the will of the majority, the rabbis decided to formally ostracize him, and they sent Akiva to deliver the verdict. He arrived dressed in black, an expression of mourning, and broke the news to Eliezer gently, using polite circumlocution: "My teacher, it appears to me that your colleagues are distancing themselves from you." This is offered as a model of good manners, but there was also an element of self-preservation involved, since Eliezer had supernatural powers: "There was great anger on that day, as any place that Rabbi Eliezer fixed his gaze was burned."

After banning unfair pricing and verbal humiliation, the Torah goes on to prohibit charging interest on a loan, which it sees as another kind of predatory behavior. "If any of your fellow Israelites become poor and are unable to support themselves among you . . . do not take interest or any profit from them, but fear your God, so that they may continue to live among you," says Leviticus 25:35–36. Instead of seeing someone's need as a profit opportunity, you should simply help them.

As the Talmud points out, however, charging interest isn't really analogous to the other property crimes discussed in Bava Metzia. Theft takes place against the will of the victim, and exploitation takes place without the victim's knowledge. But lending at interest requires the consent of the borrower, who agrees to pay back more than he has borrowed. So why is it considered a crime?

The answer reveals the difference between halakha and secular legal systems. Jewish law is ultimately about what God wants from us, not what we want for ourselves. That's why everyone who participates in charging interest is guilty—"the lender, and the borrower, and the guarantor, and the witnesses" (75b)—even if they are all taking part of their own free will. It's similar to the way American law bans the sale of organs, even if the seller is willing to give up a kidney in exchange for money.

It's hard to stamp out a crime that both parties are eager to commit, and the Talmud discusses several popular strategies for getting around the ban on interest. The lender might sell the borrower an item for a hundred dinars and then buy it back for ninety-six dinars, allowing him to record the four-dinar gain as profit rather than interest. A borrower might repay more than he borrowed without explicitly telling the lender, or he might repay the correct amount but then give the lender a gift. But Rav Nachman declares that all such techniques are prohibited: "The principle with regard to interest is: Any payment for [the lender's] waiting [to collect the debt] is forbidden" (63b).

Other ways of compensating a lender are harder to detect. The borrower might allow the lender to live rent-free on his property, or the lender might compel the borrower's slaves to work for him. That example prompts a discussion of whether slaves should be considered a net asset. If the lender takes over the borrower's slaves but also becomes responsible for feeding them, is he actually making a profit? The Talmud decides that he is profiting—obviously, one might think, or else no one would want to own slaves in the first place. But Rava grants that there are exceptions, such as Dari, a slave who did not do any useful labor but was a kind of entertainer, "dancing among the wine barrels" at Rav Nachman's shop.

While charging interest on a loan is forbidden, it's not clear that a borrower has any practical remedies. According to Rabbi Elazar, "fixed interest," which is stated explicitly in a contract, can be confiscated by a judge and returned to the borrower. "A hint of interest," on the other hand, which takes a clandestine form, can't be seized. Rabbi Yochanan goes further, saying that "even fixed interest cannot be removed by judges." Someone who lends at interest will be punished by God, but it's not possible for human beings to undo the transaction.

The Talmud often relates anecdotes about Torah scholars, from their supernatural feats to their domestic arrangements, but it seldom has anything to say about their physical appearance. They can easily come across as being all mind and no body. But Rabbi Yochanan is an exception. In Bava Metzia 84a, his beauty is evoked with an extravagant metaphor: "One who wishes to see the beauty of Rabbi Yochanan should bring a silver goblet from the smithy and fill it with red pomegranate seeds, and place a diadem of red roses upon the lip, and position it between the sunlight and the shade. That luster is a semblance of Rabbi Yochanan's beauty."

Yochanan's good looks particularly appealed to Reish Lakish, whose career as a gladiator is described in Gittin. In Bava Metzia we learn that it was Yochanan who convinced Reish Lakish to give up banditry and become a Torah scholar. They met when Yochanan was bathing in a river and Reish Lakish tried to rob him. Yochanan reproached the bandit, saying "Your strength is fit for Torah study," to which Reish Lakish flirtatiously replied, "Your beauty is fit for women." So Yochanan offered a bargain. If Reish Lakish would devote himself to Torah, Yochanan would give him his own sister, who was "more beautiful than I am," in marriage.

The men became brothers-in-law and study partners, but their quasi-romance was shattered one day when when they were arguing about whether a sword could contract ritual impurity. Losing his temper, Yochanan exclaimed, "A bandit knows about his banditry"—that is, Reish Lakish ought to be an expert about weapons because he was used to wielding them. As we have seen, bringing up a penitent's past crimes is explicitly forbidden in the Talmud, and with good reason: Reish Lakish was so aggrieved that he fell ill and died.

Yochanan was bereft, and to comfort him other sages volunteered to take Reish Lakish's place as his study partner. But they would always agree with his legal arguments, which only made Yochanan miss his friend more: "Are you comparable to the son of Lakish? In my discussions with the son of Lakish, when I would state a matter, he would raise twenty-four difficulties against me, and I would answer with twenty-four answers, and the halakha itself would be broadened." For the Talmud, this kind of sacred debate is much better than just being right, since it allows Torah study to be prolonged and enriched.

If Yochanan had a feminine kind of beauty, Yishmael and Elazar were paragons of manliness. For the Talmud, however, this doesn't mean lean and muscular, according to the Greek ideal. Rather, they were so fat that when they stood face to face, "it was possible for a pair of oxen to enter and fit between them [under their bellies] without touching them" (84a). A Roman noblewoman once insulted the pair by saying "your children are not your own," implying that Yishmael and Elazar couldn't have sex with their wives because their stomachs would get in the way. The rabbis replied by quoting Judges 8:21: "As the man is, so is his strength." As big as their bodies were, in other words, their penises were even bigger. The Talmud backs them up: "The organ of Rabbi Yishmael was the size of a jug of nine kav," while Rabbi Yochanan's was the size of five kav. A kav is equivalent to 1.2 liters, so those must have been some impressive jugs.

Bava Batra On real estate, inheritance, and surviving catastrophe.

As the first two "gates" show, owning property involves obligations as well as rights. A farmer must ensure that his livestock doesn't hurt people and a merchant must buy and sell at a fair price. Bava Batra, the "final gate," examines the responsibilities of owners of real estate, including houses, courtyards, and fields. Like the previous tractates, this one begins with a concrete problem: If two neighbors decide to partition their joint courtyard, how should the wall be built? The Talmud offers a logical answer: They should divide the courtyard in half and build the wall right down the middle, splitting the cost of the building material.

The difficulty starts when one person wants to build a wall and the other doesn't. Can one partner in a jointly owned courtyard compel the other to build a wall? Today we might say that what's at stake here is the right to privacy. The Talmud doesn't use the modern vocabulary of rights, but it gets at the same point by asking, "Is damage caused by sight called damage?" (2b) That is, can I claim that being observed by a neighbor is a form of injury that demands redress?

The rabbis find support for this idea in a law that prohibits building a house whose windows look into those of the house next door. This is meant to prevent the residents from being seen indoors, which suggests that damage caused by sight is real damage. Rav argues that even plants can be damaged by being seen, which is why "it is prohibited for a person to stand in another's field while the grain is standing." Here the problem isn't invasion of privacy but the evil eye: an envious look at a neighbor's crop might cause it to wither.

The rights and responsibilities of neighbors clash in a more tangible way in the case of a two-story house that's sinking into the ground. This is a major problem for the owner of the ground floor, but not for the owner of the upper floor, at least not immediately. In this case, however, the Talmud says that the downstairs neighbor can't compel the upstairs one to rebuild the house. Even if he offers to cover all the expenses, the upstairs neighbor can coldly reply, "Crawl on your stomach to go in, and crawl on your stomach to go out" (7a). But once the beams supporting the second story sink to within ten handbreadths of the ground, the situation changes. As we saw in tractate Sukka, a legal domain is ten handbreadths high, so at that point the upstairs neighbor has encroached on the domain of the downstairs neighbor, giving the latter the right to demolish the building. Of course, the first floor would have become uninhabitable long before this point.

Perhaps because these disputes involve neighbors who lack generosity, Bava Batra devotes several pages to praising tzedaka or charity, which Rav Asi says is "equivalent to all the other mitzvot combined." Rabbi Elazar says that "one who performs acts of charity in secret is greater than Moses our teacher" (9b). The Talmud sees charity as a kind of progressive taxation, requiring people to give according to their means. Charity collectors are empowered to "seize collateral for charity," even against the will of the owners; on one occasion, "Rava compelled Rav Natan bar Ami and took four hundred dinars from him for charity." Similarly, when a city is collecting funds to build a wall it should "collect based on net worth," with the rich paying more and the poor less. "Fix nails in this," Yochanan says, emphasizing that it is an ironclad rule.

Education is another public good that the community must pay for. As we saw in Kiddushin, the Torah holds fathers responsible for teaching their sons. But not every father is competent to teach, and orphans need instruction too. Accordingly, Yehoshua ben Gamla, one of the last High Priests before the destruction of the Temple, ordered that "teachers of children should be established in each and every province and in each and every town," and that children should start attending school at age six or seven. This was so successful that the Talmud credits Yehoshua ben Gamla with the preservation of Judaism itself: "If not for him the Torah would have been forgotten from the Jewish people" (21a).

The principle of mutual responsibility limits the rights of property owners in several ways. A person can't make improvements to his own land that might damage his neighbor's land, such as digging a new pit that could cause an existing pit to collapse or building a pond that could weaken the foundation of a wall. The same holds for indoor construction: "A person may not set up an oven inside a house unless there is a space four cubits high above it," to avoid causing damage to the dwelling upstairs. Conversely, someone living on an upper story can't build an oven unless the floor is three handbreadths thick, to avoid damaging the dwelling downstairs. The same principle applies in commercial properties: "A person may not open a bakery or a dye shop beneath the storeroom of another," since heat and fumes could damage the goods (20b).

On the other hand, there are certain annoyances that are unavoidable in communal life. A person can prevent his neighbor from opening a business in their shared courtyard on account of the disruption. "I am unable to sleep due to the sound of people entering and the sound of people exiting," he can say. But if the neighbor works inside his own home, he's within his rights, even if he makes a lot of noise. Likewise, you can't complain if your neighbor's children are making noise, or about the noise from a nearby school.

Sometimes a dispute arises about who actually owns a piece of property. According to the Talmud, hazaka, the presumption of ownership, is granted by actual possession. If you have lived in a house or worked a field for three consecutive years, you are presumed to be the owner. This rule doesn't appear in the Torah, but the rabbis manage to find an indirect Biblical justification for it in Jeremiah 32:44, where the prophet predicts that the Jews will return to their land after the Babylonian exile: "Men shall buy fields for money, and subscribe the deeds, and seal them." The Talmud interprets this to mean that Jeremiah himself bought a field before the Babylonian conquest, confident that one day he would return to it. And why did he sign a deed for the purchase? Because he knew that the conquest would take place in two years, which wasn't long enough for him to establish ownership by working the land. It follows that this requires a longer term of possession—three years, as the Talmud says.

This is an ingenious deduction, but Abaye wonders if it isn't too ingenious. "Perhaps there he merely teaches us good advice," Abaye suggests (29a), because it's sound business practice to record transactions in writing. Rava offers a more pragmatic explanation for the three-year rule. If someone owns a piece of land and sees an interloper working it, he might take no action for a year or even two years, but "he will not waive his rights for three years." By neglecting to take action in a reasonable amount of time, he's conceding that the property doesn't belong to him.

This rule isn't meant to legalize squatting, however. As the Mishna says,

"Any possession that is not accompanied by a claim is not presumption" (41a). In other words, in addition to actual possession, the claimant must be able to explain how the property came to belong to him in the first place, such as through purchase or inheritance. In particular, tenants and sharecroppers can't claim ownership of the land they are leasing, even if they've worked it for three years.

The principle that possession creates a presumption of ownership also doesn't apply to movable goods, which often leave their owner's possession for various reasons. A tailor or launderer can't claim ownership of garments in his possession, since the assumption is that they were meant to be returned. Even if a craftsman testifies that an item was given to him as a gift, his testimony has no weight: "He has not said anything," as the Gemara puts it (45b). Similarly, a husband can't establish legal possession of his wife's house simply by living in it, since spouses customarily live together.

Most of Bava Batra deals with issues that can also be found in secular real estate law. But one stipulation is unique to the Jewish world in which the Talmud was composed. Just as Judaism today lives in the shadow of the Holocaust, the rabbis of the Talmud lived in the shadow of the destruction of the Temple. To make sure that Jews never forget this, the Talmud says that "one may not plaster, and one may not tile, and one may not paint" any new building. It would be inappropriate to create a beautiful structure in a world where the Temple lies in ruins.

But the rabbis also warn against taking mourning too far. After the Temple was destroyed, there was "an increase in the number of ascetics among the Jews," people who said, "Shall we eat meat, from which offerings are sacrificed upon the altar, and now the altar has ceased to exist? Shall we drink wine, which is poured as a libation upon the altar, and now the altar has ceased to exist?" (60b)

Rabbi Yehoshua argued that this attitude was unsustainable. After all, he told a group of ascetics, there was also an offering of flour in the Temple; should Jews stop eating bread? The ascetics replied that they would give up bread and survive on fruit and vegetables. But there was also a water-libation in the Temple, Yehoshua continued; should Jews also stop drinking water? At this "they were silent," because it's impossible to survive without water.

Apparently some people did suggest that the Jews should respond to Roman persecution with national suicide: "By right we should decree upon ourselves not to marry a woman and produce offspring, and it will turn out that the descendants of Abraham our forefather will cease to exist." But the Talmud acknowledges that the urge to live is so strong that most people would never obey this harsh rule, even if it's justified in some sense. In a case like this, the rabbis' principle is to "leave the Jews alone" rather than give them an order that won't be obeyed.

When it comes to leaving buildings unfinished, the Talmud offers a compromise solution. It's not necessary to make every Jewish building unsightly, but one should "leave a small amount in it" unpainted and unplastered, as a reminder of the destruction of the Temple. Rav Hisda specifies that this should be one square cubit, visible from the entrance. Similar, Jews shouldn't stop enjoying meals, but they should "leave out a small item" to diminish the pleasure of feasting; Rav Pappa says this could be a side dish such as "small fried fish." Women should continue to make themselves beautiful, but leave one small patch of hair that they would ordinarily remove.

The subject of real estate is closely connected to Bava Batra's other main focus, which is how property is inherited. The Torah's statement on this subject comes in Numbers 27, where a man named Zelophehad dies leaving five daughters and no sons. At the time daughters couldn't inherit property, but the sisters went to Moses to plead their case. Interestingly, though they were mounting a challenge to a patriarchal system, they cast their appeal as a way of supporting that system. If Zelophehad's property was inherited by his male relatives rather than his daughters, his name would be forgotten, and "Why should our father's name disappear from his clan because he had no son?"

Moses took the problem to God, who ruled in the daughters' favor and established a new order of inheritance. A man's sons have the first claim on his property, with the firstborn taking a double portion, followed by his daughters, his brothers, and his uncles. If the deceased doesn't have any of these, the property goes to his nearest relative. But the Mishna in Bava Batra 108a changes this rule in one important respect, saying that a father can inherit his son's property, with his claim coming before that of the dead man's brothers. This means that a man can never inherit his brother's property as long as their father is alive.

This kind of direct contradiction between the oral Torah and the written Torah is a problem for the rabbis, and the Gemara engages in some complex hermeneutics to show that the rule about fathers inheriting from sons is implied in the Torah, even if it's not directly stated. In the list of heirs, the rabbis argue, the term "his nearest relative" is meant to refer to the father of the deceased. But in Numbers 27:11, "his nearest relative" comes last in the order of inheritance; so why should the father of the deceased inherit before his brothers? Here the Gemara looks for precedents in other areas of Jewish law. A father can designate a slave as a bride for his son, and a son can redeem a field that his father had consecrated, but brothers can't do these things for one another, which suggests that a father is a closer relative than a brother.

Finally, the Gemara points out that the Hebrew word translated as "relative" can refer to either sex. How do we know that this means the father of the deceased rather than his mother? The rabbis rule out that possibility because "family" is defined patrilineally: "It is the father's family that is called one's family, while one's mother's family is not called one's family." Still, the Talmud acknowledges that maternal relatives may be more important than paternal ones in real life. In fact, "Most sons resemble the mother's brothers," which is why "one who marries a woman needs to examine her brothers" (110a).

The statutory order of inheritance can't be changed: "One who says: So-and-so, my firstborn son, will not take a double portion, or one who says: So-and-so, my son, will not inherit among his brothers, he has said nothing, as he has stipulated counter to that which is written in the Torah" (126b). In general, any legal instrument that violates Torah law—such as a will that disinherits a son, or a ketuba that says a husband won't support his wife—is null and void.

But there's a way around this obstacle. A man can't bequeath his property however he likes, but during his lifetime he can give it away. The only condition is that the recipient must be "fit to inherit," meaning that he or she must belong to one of the categories of heirs listed in the Torah. Thus a dying man could choose to give his property to his brother instead of his son, but he couldn't give it to a stranger. Such gifts have to be made while the donor is still alive. If he dies and a deed of gift is found "bound to his thigh," proving that it's authentic, it still has no legal standing, since it's possible that the dying man changed his mind and deliberately held it back (135b).

Relying on gifts makes estate planning difficult, because a healthy person with years to live wouldn't want to give away his property in advance. The solution offered in the Talmud is to write a conditional deed of gift that takes effect on the death of the giver. Since gifts have to be given during the donor's lifetime, such a document must use the formula "from today and after my death," effectively backdating the gift.

Yet this language creates ambiguity about who owns the property before the giver dies, leaving it in a legal limbo. If a father writes a document leaving his land to his favorite son "from today and after my death," the rights of both parties are impaired: "The father cannot sell because it is written to the son, and the son cannot sell because it is in the possession of the father" (136a). The Talmud rules that the father can sell his right to the produce of the land, but upon his death the property will revert to his son. Conversely, the son can sell the land itself, but the purchaser has no right to use it until the father dies.

Deathbed gifts are treated more leniently than ordinary gifts in one key respect. A gift, like a purchase, usually isn't complete until the recipient takes physical possession of it. But since a dying man may not survive to see this happen, his verbal instructions are considered sufficient to effect the transfer. Rav Nachman explains that this rule isn't for the sake of the beneficiary but of the donor, who might "lose control of his mind" with frustration if he fears his wishes won't be carried out (147b).

Deathbed gifts can backfire, however, if the donor makes an unexpected recovery. If a dying man gets well, can he cancel his gift? The Talmud says he can, provided the gift was genuinely made in the expectation of imminent death. The test is whether the person gave away everything he owns or held something back. If he kept property for himself, the law views this as a provision in case he survived, so the rest of his gift remains in force.

Of course, it would be pretty low for an heir to insist on receiving a gift made by a dying man who recovered and asked for it back. But even the sages weren't always above using legal technicalities for personal gain. Rava, who lived in the fourth century CE, is one of the most important sages in the Gemara. In his debates with Abaye, his great contemporary, the law almost always follows Rava's opinion.

Yet the Talmud tells a disturbing story about how he once tried to seize a large sum of money, twelve thousand dinars, that was bequeathed to his fellow Torah scholar Rav Mari. Rav Mari's father, Issur, was a convert to

Judaism, and Rava figured out that Mari was conceived when Issur was still a gentile. This meant that he wasn't his father's heir under Jewish law, so when Issur died his property would be technically ownerless. Issur had trusted Rava, unwisely as it turned out, to keep the twelve thousand dinars as a deposit, assuming that he would hand it over to Rav Mari when the time came.

Rava declared that he intended to keep the money, resisting all of his colleagues' efforts to dissuade him. Finally, Rav Ika came up with a way for Issur to thwart Rava's plans. Rather than leave the money to his son as a gift, Issur should simply write a declaration that the money belonged to Rav Mari, leaving Rava no grounds for withholding it. Outwitted, Rava "became angry and said: They are teaching people claims and causing me loss" (149b). By including this unflattering story about one of its most authoritative figures, the Talmud acknowledges that no one is immune to the temptation to misuse the law—which makes the job of the sages all the more important.

Sanhedrin   On capital punishment, the World to Come, and using magic to make dinner.

According to the Talmud, the Sanhedrin was the supreme Jewish court in the land of Israel during the Second Temple period, responsible for appointing local courts and trying serious crimes. Modern scholars dispute whether the Sanhedrin ever really had the powers the rabbis ascribe to it. Certainly after the destruction of the Temple it would have lost its effective authority, though it seems to have continued to exist in some form. Tractate Sanhedrin discusses the structure of the court, but its real subject is criminal law and procedure in general, from rules of testimony to methods of execution.

The word Sanhedrin comes from the Greek synedrion, "sitting together," suggesting that the court was created when Judea was under Greek cultural influence, in the third century BCE or later. But Jewish tradition sees it as one link in a chain of authority that goes back to Moses. The Talmud explains that the Great Sanhedrin in Jerusalem had seventy-one members, in imitation of the seventy elders chosen by Moses to assist him in governing the Israelites—add Moses to the elders and you get seventy-one. As with the U.S. Supreme Court, having an odd number of members was also useful for preventing tie votes: "A court may not be composed of an even number of judges," the Talmud says (2b).

The full Sanhedrin was required for deciding on matters of state, such as declaring war or condemning an idolatrous city to destruction. But usually it delegated its authority to smaller panels. Three judges could try cases involving fines, while a case that might lead to corporal or capital punishment required a "lesser Sanhedrin" of twenty-three judges.

Judges have to be Torah scholars, naturally, since they are the only ones with a complete understanding of Jewish law. Serving on a court is a holy activity—"God stands in the congregation of God; in the midst of the judges he judges," says Psalm 82:1—and also a prestigious leadership role. The Gemara mentions that prominent judges were followed by a retinue of scribes and carried on the shoulders of crowds. Yet the Talmud tries to cool the ambition of would-be judges by dwelling on the job's unpleasant sides. For one thing, it's unpaid: a judge "does not do what is necessary to provide for the needs of his house, and he enters his house empty-handed," says Rav (7b).

But the real burden is the moral responsibility involved, since a judge is accountable to God for his decisions. "A judge should always view himself as if a sword is placed between his thighs and Gehenna is opened up beneath him," says Rabbi Yonatan. Yehoshua ben Levi adds that all the judges on a panel share responsibility for the verdict: "If ten judges are sitting in judgment, a prisoner's collar hangs around all of their necks." A dishonest judge doesn't just bring punishment on himself, but on the whole Jewish people: "Every judge who does not judge according to absolute truth causes the Divine Presence to withdraw from Israel."

Because a judge's responsibility is heaviest in a capital case, the Talmud sets the bar for conviction very high. In Sanhedrin 8b, the Gemara explains that "the court executes . . . only when the following elements are present: the congregation, and witnesses, and forewarning." That is, there must be a panel of twenty-three judges; there must be two eyewitnesses to the crime; and those witnesses must have warned the defendant in advance that the crime he is about to commit carries the death penalty. Rabbi Yehuda adds that the warning must include "by which form of the death penalty he is to be killed." Jewish law provides four methods of execution for various crimes: stoning, strangling, burning, and "killing" or decapitation.

Obviously, these requirements can seldom if ever be met in real life, particularly with crimes that take place in secret, such as adultery. But the Talmud adds still more barriers to execution. According to Rabbi Meir, the testimony of the two witnesses can be excluded if there is any inconsistency between them, even the most trivial. For instance, Yochanan ben Zakkai once grilled a pair of witnesses about the color of some figs (41a). Judges hearing a capital case should "intimidate" the witnesses by reminding them that procuring an execution, even of a guilty man, is a grave responsibility: "Adam was created alone, to teach you that anyone who destroys one soul from the Jewish people, the verse ascribes him blame as if he destroyed an entire world" (37a). This is one of the best-known sentences in the Talmud, frequently cited as an expression of Judaism's reverence for the individual (and often universalized by removing the reference to "the Jewish people").

The Talmud's extreme reluctance to execute criminals marks a clear departure from the Torah, which prescribes the death penalty for a wide range of crimes, from murder to violating Shabbat. Still, the Talmud finds a way to ground its position in a Torah verse. Deuteronomy 21:23 says that when a man is hanged for a crime he should be buried the same day, not left exposed to public view, because a hanged man is "a reproach to God." According to Rabbi Meir, this means that the execution of a sinner causes God to feel pain: "When a man suffers what expression does the divine presence use? I am distressed about my head, I am distressed about my arm" (46a).

Meir emphasizes the point with a parable about twin brothers, one of whom became a king while the other became a bandit. When the king had to order his brother's execution, he commanded that the corpse be taken down immediately, lest "anyone who saw the bandit hanging would say: The king was hanged." Just so, human beings are created in the image of God, and when a man is executed it brings disgrace on the divine image. Accordingly, the Talmud says that the whole process should be inconspicuous as possible: "They delay the verdict until it is near to sunset, and then they conclude his judgment, and they put him to death, and immediately afterward hang him. One ties him to the hanging post, and another immediately unties him."

This method wouldn't work when when the Torah prescribes execution by stoning, a brutal death that the Talmud does its best to palliate. The court is given every opportunity to revoke the sentence, up to the last minute; a flag relay is set up so that an order of clemency can be communicated directly to the executioner. If the condemned makes a last-ditch appeal, the execution must be postponed so the court can consider it, "even four or five times."

When stoning must be carried out, the Talmud offers ways to minimize the victim's suffering. First he's given a drink of wine mixed with frankincense "in order to confuse his mind," as a kind of anesthetic (43a). Then he is pushed off a high platform, in the hope that he will die instantly; as Rav Nachman says, this is a compassionate act, in the spirit of the commandment "Love your neighbor as yourself." If he survives the fall, the first stone must be thrown by the two witnesses who testified against him—another incentive to avoid testifying in capital cases. Only if this fails to kill the condemned man does the entire community join in the stone-throwing. But the Talmud says that this was never necessary, since the first stone was heavy enough to be lethal on its own.

Although Sanhedrin spells out the rules for capital punishment in detail, the tractate also acknowledges that by the rabbis' time, Jewish courts had lost the power to enforce executions. According to Rav Yosef, "From the day that the Temple was destroyed, although the Sanhedrin ceased to be extant, the four types of capital punishment have not ceased." To which the Gemara immediately replies: "Have they not ceased? But they have ceased" (37b). Like the ordeal of the bitter water in Sota, stoning is an entirely theoretical issue. While courts can no longer inflict the death penalty, however, God can: the Talmud suggests that a man liable to be stoned will fall from a roof or have his bones broken by an animal.

In addition to hanging and stoning, the Torah prescribes burning for certain sexual offenses, including adultery committed by the daughter of a priest. The Talmud explains that this doesn't mean burning the victim alive in a pyre, the way the Spanish Inquisition did in the auto da fe. In fact, the rabbis mention a case where a woman was burned in this manner—"they wrapped her in bundles of branches and burned her"—and emphasize that it was a mistake: "The court at that time was not proficient in halakha" (52a).

The correct procedure involves putting a long, thin piece of hot lead down the victim's throat, so they would be "burned" from the inside. This punishment, gruesome as it sounds, is considered preferable to actual burning because it's less painful and degrading. It also has a Biblical precedent. When Nadav and Abihu, the sons of Aaron, failed to follow the correct procedure for offering a sacrifice to God, "two threads of fire came out of the Holy of Holies" and entered their nostrils, killing them.

The fourth type of execution is decapitation, prescribed for murderers and residents of an idolatrous city. The rabbis have different views about how this punishment is carried out. Some say that Jewish courts follow Roman ones in using a sword, but Rabbi Yehuda argues that it's preferable to use a cleaver and chopping block, which he considers a less degrading method. The Gemara disagrees, saying that the cleaver is more degrading than the sword, but Yehuda replies that it should still be avoided, on the grounds that Jews are not supposed to "follow the statutes" of gentiles.

By the same token, gentiles are not supposed to follow Jewish law. Only seven commandments are binding on "the descendants of Noah"—that is, humanity as a whole, since all peoples trace their lineage back to Noah and his sons, the sole survivors of the Flood. One is requirement is positive—to establish courts of judgment—and the rest are negative: all human beings are forbidden to curse God, to worship idols, to commit incest, murder, and theft, and to eat a limb from a living animal.

The Torah's mitzvot, by contrast, are addressed only to Jews, and the Talmud strongly discourages non-Jews from practicing them. According to Rabbi Yochanan, "A gentile who engages in Torah study is liable to receive the death penalty." Rabbi Meir, however, takes the opposite view: "Even a gentile who engages in Torah study is considered like a High Priest" (59a).

Rabbi Yochanan's saying is one of several passages in Sanhedrin that are often cited in antisemitic attacks on the Talmud. Another is found in Sanhedrin 57a: "With regard to bloodshed, if a gentile murders another gentile, or a gentile murders a Jew, he is liable. If a Jew murders a gentile, he is exempt." This disturbing statement reflects the profound hostility between Jews and non-Jews in the ancient world, and it has troubled Jewish commentators ever since. Menachem ben Meiri, an important Talmudic commentator in thirteenth-century Spain, rejected the moral distinction between Jews and non-Jews, writing that everyone who obeys the seven Noachide commandments is considered pious and has a share in the World to Come.

Meiri also argued that the Talmud's hostility toward non-Jews was only meant for the idol worshipers of the Roman and Persian empires, and didn't apply to monotheistic Christians and Muslims. For Judaism, idol worship is the sin of sins. In the modern Western world it is easy to avoid, but in the ancient world, statues of gods and goddesses were everywhere. It would have been hard for a Jew to do business or deal with the government without encountering an image of some deity.

This fact informs Sanhedrin's discussion of capital punishment for Jewish idolaters, where a distinction is drawn between worshiping an idol and merely treating it respectfully. The death penalty is reserved for acts of worship like those performed for God in the Temple, such as bowing down, pouring a libation, or sacrificing an animal. But a Jew who "hugs or kisses" an idol, or tends to its appearance by washing or adorning it, is only liable to receive lashes (60b).

The Talmud also recognizes that even acts of worship aren't necessarily motivated by religious conviction. They can also be "due to love or due to fear," to curry favor or avoid punishment. Rava says that someone who bows to an idol for such reasons isn't a true idol worshiper and shouldn't receive capital punishment. But Abaye disagrees, holding that the act of idol worship itself is what matters, regardless of motive.

What if a Jew performs what he thinks is an act of disrespect to an idol, only to discover that this is how the god likes to be worshipped? Improbably, the Talmud claims that the Canaanite god Baal Peor was worshipped by defecating in front of his idol. On one occasion a Jew defecated in front of an idol of Baal Peor and "wiped himself with its nostril," which he intended as a gesture of contempt, but the priests were delighted, saying that no one had ever thought of such a clever act of homage before (64a). This kind of unintentional worship can be atoned for with a sin offering to God.

Sorcery, too, is a capital crime. The Talmud recognizes that some sorcerers are really just stage magicians. Rav Ashi mentions that he once saw a sorcerer "blow his nose and cast rolls of silk from his nostrils." Rav once saw "a certain Arab" slice a donkey in half and then bring it back to life, which Rabbi Hiyya points out must have been a trick, since the donkey didn't bleed. But other kinds of magic are apparently real. In Alexandria, Rabbi Ze'eiri once bought a donkey that turned into a wooden plank when he gave it water to drink. The seller agreed to refund Ze'eiri's money, though he considered him a rube: "Is there anyone who buys an item here and does not examine it first with water?" (67b).

Sometimes the rabbis themselves were miracle workers. Yannai once turned a woman into a donkey after she tried to make him drink a magic potion. Every Shabbat, Rav Chanina and Rav Oshaya would use "the halakhot of creation" to make a calf for dinner. Rabbi Eliezer once used magic to fill a field with cucumbers. The Talmud excuses these sages from the charge of sorcery on the grounds that while practicing magic is forbidden, it is permitted to study magical formulas and techniques: "You shall not learn to do, but you may learn to understand and teach" (the same principle invoked in tractate Rosh Hashana to excuse Rabban Gamliel for owning a diagram of the moon).

Usually the law can only punish a criminal after the crime is committed. But in a few cases the Talmud permits killing someone "on account of his ultimate end," for what he is going to do in the future. Thus it's permitted to kill a "pursuer," someone who is about to commit murder or rape. The Talmud doesn't consider this just a matter of self-defense; it's also good for the pursuer himself. "The death of the wicked is beneficial to them," since it spares them from committing sins that would endanger their souls (71b).

Another type of person who can be executed preemptively is a "stubborn and rebellious son." The procedure is laid out in Deuteronomy 21: "If someone has a stubborn and rebellious son who does not obey his father and mother and will not listen to them when they discipline him, his father and mother shall take hold of him and bring him to the elders at the gate of his town. They shall say to the elders, 'This son of ours is stubborn and rebellious. He will not obey us. He is a glutton and a drunkard.' Then all the men of his town are to stone him to death. You must purge the evil from among you. All Israel will hear of it and be afraid."

The idea that parents have the right to execute their children isn't unique to the Torah. The Roman paterfamilias had the same power, at least in theory. But the rabbis find this law so objectionable that they do everything in their power to qualify it out of existence. For instance, the Torah says nothing about the age of the stubborn and rebellious son, which might suggest that he can be killed at any age. But the Talmud observes that when a boy turns 13 he is a legal adult and beyond his parents' control, while if he's still a child he isn't bound to observe the mitzvot, so he can't be punished.

It follows that a boy can only be a stubborn and rebellious son when he is neither a child nor an adult—in other words, during puberty, which the Talmud defines in developmental terms as "from when he grows two pubic hairs until he has grown a beard around." (The Talmud refers euphemistically to pubic hair as the "lower beard.") According to the Gemara, this happens in three months or less, so a son can only be deemed "stubborn and rebellious" during that brief period (69a).

The rabbis go on to examine the adjectives themselves. Laws usually focus on concrete acts, such as murder or theft, but the description "stubborn and rebellious" is vague. How do we know when to apply it? The only clue in the Torah is that the parents call their son "a glutton and a drunkard," suggesting that this crime involves eating and drinking to excess. To make the law enforceable, the Mishna offers an exact definition of excess: one becomes a glutton and a drunkard by consuming "a tarteimar of meat and a half-log of Italian wine."

But eating and drinking doesn't count if it's "with a group assembled for the performance of a mitzva," such as a holiday. The meat has to be red meat, not fish or fowl. Rav Huna adds that the meat must be eaten raw and the wine must be undiluted, signs of an unrestrained appetite. What's more, the meat and drink must be stolen by the rebellious son from his father and eaten on someone else's property.

The Torah says that the death penalty must be requested by the father and mother together, which Rabbi Yehuda creatively interprets to mean that "if his mother is not suited for his father, he does not become a stubborn and rebellious son." According to the Gemara, this means that "if his mother was not identical to his father in voice, appearance, and height, he does not become a stubborn and rebellious son." Since no two people are ever identical, much less a husband and wife, it's clear that the law can never be enforced in practice, and finally the Talmud says so explicitly: "There has never been a stubborn and rebellious son and there never will be one in the future."

In that case, the Gemara wonders, "Why was it written?" Why did God put this law in the Torah if it can never be enforced? The answer captures something essential about the Talmud: "So that you may expound and receive reward." With secular laws what matters is obedience, but mitzvot, like every communication from God, exist to be interpreted.

On the very rare occasion when all the Talmud's conditions are met and the death penalty is actually carried out, the rabbis emphasize that the criminal's life is only ended in this world. "All of the Jewish people have a share in the World to Come," even the worst sinners (90a). The only transgressions that cause a Jew to forfeit the afterlife involve denying the truth of Judaism: "One who says there is no resurrection of the dead derived from the Torah, and one who says the Torah is not from Heaven, and an epikoros."

An epikoros is a skeptic or heretic; the term comes from Epicurus, the ancient Greek philosopher who taught that the world is strictly material, nothing but the movement of atoms in space. It's clear why this belief is incompatible with Judaism, and of course denying the divinity of the Torah removes the foundation of traditional Judaism. But it's not obvious why the Talmud considers belief in the resurrection of the dead to be equally essential, since that doctrine isn't actually taught anywhere in the Torah.

The Talmud finds scriptural support for it only by engaging in some ingenious interpretation. Numbers 18:28 instructs, "And you shall give the teruma [the tithed crops] of the Lord to Aaron the priest." This doesn't seem to have anything to do with the resurrection of the dead, but Rabbi Yochanan asks, "Does Aaron exist forever?" By using the future tense, the Torah wasn't just establishing a precedent for Aaron's descendants, the priests. Rather, it means that in the future Jews will give teruma to Aaron personally, which could only happen after they are resurrected in the World to Come.

What exactly is the World to Come, olam haba, in which all Jews have a share? At first it doesn't seem to be a spiritual afterlife but a transformation of this world, brought about by the arrival of the Messiah. The rabbis are certain the Messiah will come, though they disagree about when. Some believe that the schedule for redemption is set in advance: according to Rav Ketina, "Six thousand years is the duration of the world, and it is in ruins for one thousand years" (97a). Rav Yehuda is said to have learned from the prophet Elijah that the world will exist for eighty-five Jubilee cycles, which works out to 4,250 years. Another sage claims to know a man who discovered a secret scroll "among the Roman archives" that predicted the world will last exactly 4,291 years.

Other sages, however, say that it's impossible to know when the world will end. Rabbi Natan quotes Habakkuk 2:3: "For the vision is yet for the appointed time, and does not lie; though it tarry, wait for it because it will surely come." Natan says that "this verse penetrates and descends until the depths," by which he means that "the appointed time" of the Messiah is unknowable; he will come, but "not in accordance with our rabbis." Rabbi Yonatan agrees: "May those who calculate the end of days be cursed," he says, since when their calculations prove erroneous they might stop believing in redemption altogether.

If the Messiah isn't destined to come at a particular time, why doesn't he come now? "Since we are awaiting and the Holy One is awaiting, who is preventing the coming of the Messiah?" the Gemara asks. The answer is that no one is holding up redemption except the Jews themselves: "The matter depends only on repentance and good deeds." Rabbi Eliezer agrees: "If the Jewish people repent they are redeemed, and if not they are not redeemed" (97b). Rabbi Yochanan predicts that "the son of David will come only in a generation that is entirely innocent or entirely guilty." If the Jewish people are so good that they deserve redemption, he will come "with the clouds of heaven," in a miraculous fashion. If they are so evil that they need redemption but don't deserve it, he will come "lowly and riding upon a donkey."

This ambivalence leads some sages to hope they will never witness the messianic age, since it will be preceded by so much suffering. "Let the Messiah come, but after my death, so that I will not see him," says Ulla. Rav Yosef, on the other hand, believes that redemption will be worth it: "Let the Messiah come, and I will be privileged to sit in the shadow of his donkey's excrement." On this view, the only people who ought to fear the Messiah are the wicked, who will be punished in the World to Come. As Rabbi Simlai says, "It is comparable to a rooster and a bat who were looking forward to the light of day": the rooster welcomes the dawn while the bat flees from it.

But not all the sages believe that the messianic age is the same thing as the World to Come. According to Shmuel, "The difference between this world and the messianic era is only with regard to servitude to foreign kingdoms alone" (99a). The Messiah will restore Jewish sovereignty in the land of Israel, but he won't bring about the resurrection of the dead. According to Shmuel's definition, we might even be living in the messianic age today, since a Jewish state exists.

Nor will this period necessarily last forever. Rabbi Eliezer says the messianic age will last just forty years; others say seventy years or three generations. The World to Come, by contrast, is a supernatural phenomenon that can't be quantified or even described. According to Rabbi Yochanan, "all the prophets prophesied only about the messianic era, but with regard to the World to Come," the words of Isaiah 64:3 apply: "No eye has seen it, God, aside from you."

While the Talmud says that all Jews have a share in the World to Come, some rabbis see it as a reward for the pious alone. According to Reish Lakish, "one who leaves even one statute" unfulfilled is doomed to Gehenna, the underworld. But Rabbi Yochanan, Reish Lakish's soulmate, rebukes him for taking such a strict view: "It is not satisfactory to their Master that you said this about them." Rather, Yochanan reverses the equation: "If one learned only one statute," he has a share in the World to Come (111a). The eternal Talmudic debate between strictness and leniency continues even into the next world.

Makkot   On flogging, perjury, and forbidden tattoos.

Tractate Sanhedrin deals primarily with capital crimes; lesser infractions of Jewish law are usually punished with makkot or lashes. Tractate Makkot, which may have originally been part of the previous tractate, focuses on how and when this punishment should be carried out. It begins, however, by addressing a different topic in criminal procedure: how to punish witnesses who commit perjury.

As tractate Sanhedrin explained, a defendant can only be convicted of a capital crime on the testimony of two eyewitnesses. According to Deuteronomy 19:19, a witness who lies in a capital case is put to death: "You shall do unto him [the witness] as he conspired to do to his brother." The Talmud adds that the same principle applies in cases involving money. If a pair of witnesses falsely testified that a man owed someone 200 dinars, they must pay him 200 dinars, dividing the sum between them. In cases where the defendant would have been punished by lashes, each lying witness is lashed (5a).

Proving that a witness committed perjury isn't easy. The Talmud gives the example of a murder case in which a pair of witnesses testify "with regard to a man called so-and-so that he killed a person." If a second pair of witnesses come forward and say that they saw the victim alive after the time of the alleged murder, the first pair of witnesses is discredited, but that doesn't mean they lied; they could simply have been mistaken. But if the second pair of witnesses testifies that the first pair couldn't have witnessed the murder at all, because "you were with us on that day in such and such a place," then the first pair must have been lying, so they are liable for the death penalty.

Unless they are directly refuted, witnesses are presumed to be telling the truth. The Talmud asks about a case where "a certain woman brought witnesses to testify on her behalf, and they were proved to be liars." When she brought a second pair of witnesses, the same thing happened again. If she goes on to bring a third pair of witnesses, does the court have to treat their testimony as valid, or is there now a presumption that the woman is suborning perjury? Reish Lakish says that she has "assumed the presumptive status of dishonesty," so her third set of witnesses is automatically discounted. Rabbi Elazar disagrees, however: "If she has assumed the presumptive status of dishonesty, has the entire Jewish people assumed that presumptive status?" (5b) Just because the woman is a liar doesn't mean everyone she knows is a liar too.

As we saw in tractate Sanhedrin, the Talmud makes it almost impossible to carry out an execution, and the rabbis take pride in this leniency. The Gemara in Makkot 7a says that "a Sanhedrin that puts a man to death once in seven years is called bloody," a sign of how rare executions were. Rabbi Elazar ben Azarya goes even further, saying that this epithet is given to a court that executes once in seventy years. And Tarfon and Akiva say, "If we had been members of the Sanhedrin, no one would have ever been executed."

Accidental killings are punishable by banishment rather than death. But how exactly is this crime defined? In Numbers 35:22, the Torah doesn't offer a general rule, only concrete examples: "If he pushed him without malice aforethought or hurled any object at him unintentionally, or inadvertently dropped upon him any deadly object of stone, and death resulted." On this basis, the Talmud decides that whether a killing is accidental depends on the direction of the movement: "Any murderer who kills unintentionally through a downward motion is exiled, and one who kills not through a downward motion is not exiled" (7b).

It follows that if you're raising a barrel onto a roof and it falls, you are exempt from liability, but if you're lowering a barrel from the roof to the ground and it falls, you can be exiled. The basis for this distinction isn't totally clear, but it seems to have something to do with intentionality. The man lowering the barrel means for it to descend, so he's responsible for what happens in its descent. But a man raising a barrel doesn't intend for it to descend at all, so if it falls, it happens entirely against his will.

Another kind of involuntary manslaughter involves acting recklessly. If someone throws a stone in a public place and a bystander is struck and killed, how should be be punished? The Mishna in Makkot 8a treats this as a case of accidental killing, punishable by exile. Rabbi Eliezer ben Yaakov says that if the victim entered the public area after the stone left the thrower's hand, the thrower is exempt from responsibility, because the action appeared to be safe when he performed it. The Gemara, on the other hand, thinks the Mishna is too lenient, saying that the stone-thrower should be treated as an intentional murderer, since he should have known his actions could lead to someone's death. Similarly, we might say today that someone who fires a gun on the street is guilty of murder even if he didn't deliberately aim at the victim.

Throwing a stone in a public place is unjustifiable because there's never a good reason to do it. But what if you're demolishing a wall that borders a public place and a stone accidentally falls and kills someone? The Gemara says that this too should be treated as intentional murder, since it's the worker's responsibility to make sure the area around the wall is clear. But if the wall is being demolished "into a scrap heap," where there's no reason to expect people to be passing by, then the worker is "a victim of circumstances beyond his control."

In a few special cases, causing physical harm is actually part of a person's job, such as a court attendant who administers lashes. If this accidentally results in the victim's death, the court attendant is not legally responsible. The same goes for a father who kills his son while delivering corporal punishment, which is actually a mitzva: "Chastise your son and he will give you rest," says Proverbs 29:17.

After dealing with crimes punishable by death and exile, the Mishna in Makkot 13a turns to crimes that earn lashes. These generally have to do with violating taboos—sexual prohibitions such as incest and sex with a menstruating woman, or food prohibitions such as eating unkosher animals or eating leavened bread on Passover. Many of these crimes are also punishable by karet or "excision," a punishment mentioned in the Torah, which the Talmud defines in spiritual terms as separation from God in the World to Come.

But can a person be punished twice for the same crime, with lashes and with karet? The Gemara observes that a criminal who is liable for two punishments usually only receives the more severe one; a man sentenced to both death and lashes is executed but not flogged. Why doesn't the same logic hold when it comes to lashes and karet? According to Rabbi Akiva, it's because flogging is an opportunity for repentance. If a sinner repents after receiving lashes, "the heavenly court absolves him" and he doesn't receive karet in the afterlife. The Spanish Inquisition operated on the same principle: Pain is a gift to the criminal, because by suffering on Earth he is spared torment in the next world.

Another set of taboos has to do with altering the human body. Getting a tattoo, cutting your skin, and shaving are all punishable by lashes (20a). These rules seem to reflect a reverence for the natural human form, in keeping with the idea that human beings are created in the image of God. They can also be seen as ways of separating the Jews from pagan religious practices. In fact, Bar Kappara says that not all tattoos are banned, only those that contain "the name of an object of idol worship," a pagan god. Likewise, Rabbi Yochanan says that cutting the skin is only forbidden when it's done with a utensil, which is how the priests of Baal used to lacerate themselves.

Not until the end of Makkot do the rabbis address how the punishment is carried out. According to Deuteronomy 25:3, the standard sentence is forty lashes: "He may be given up to forty lashes, but not more, lest being flogged further, to excess, your brother be degraded before your eyes." The Talmud interprets "up to forty" to mean "a number adjacent to forty"—that is, thirty-nine. This bit of interpretive legerdemain leads Rava to remark ironically that people should rise in the presence of a sage just as they do in the presence of a Torah scroll, "as in a Torah scroll forty is written and the sages came and subtracted one."

A more practical reason for turning forty into thirty-nine is that the number of lashes needs to be divisible by three, since "the attendant flogs him with one-third of the lashes from the front of him, on his chest, and two-thirds from behind him, on his back." The prisoner stands bent over with his hands tied to a post, and the flogger uses a calf-hide strap one hand-breadth wide, delivering the blows "with all his strength" (22a). While the flogging is carried out, another attendant reads aloud Torah verses dealing with transgression and punishment.

Even in the midst of this brutal spectacle, the Talmud shows some concern for the victim's human dignity. If the prisoner urinates or defecates, the flogging is halted and he's spared the remaining lashes. After all, Rabbi Hanania ben Gamliel notes, by calling the criminal "your brother," the Torah implies that "Once he is flogged he is as your brother"—that is, he rejoins the community, having paid his debt. If the goal of punishment is rehabilitation, it shouldn't be so degrading that the criminal will be shamed forever.

Shevuot On taking oaths, the burden of proof, and when to throw a duck at a judge.

In Numbers 30:3, Moses impresses upon the Israelites the importance of keeping promises to God: "If a man makes a vow to the Lord or takes an oath imposing an obligation on himself, he shall not break his pledge; he must carry out all that has crossed his lips." Read casually, this might suggest that the terms "vows" (nedarim) and "oaths" (shevuot) are interchangeable. In the Talmud, however, they are treated as different forms of legal commitment.

As tractate Nedarim explains, vows have a negative form, declaring that something is forbidden to the vower. Oaths, by contrast, have a positive form, even when they involve a promise to refrain from doing something: "I will eat" and "I will not eat" are both valid oaths (3a). Oaths can also serve to confirm statements about past actions, such as "I ate" or "I did not eat." And oaths are administered to people who testify in court, which is why tractate Shevuot appears in Seder Nezikin.

Thanks to TV and movies, even people who have never been inside a courtroom know the wording of the oath used in American courts: "I swear to tell the truth, the whole truth, and nothing but the truth, so help me God." It's doubtful whether most people who repeat those words actually believe that God will punish them for lying. But for the Talmud, oath taking is a religious act of the utmost seriousness. A judge administering an oath must warn, "Be aware that the entire world trembled when the Holy One, Blessed be He, said at Mount Sinai: You shall not take the name of the Lord your God in vain" (39a). One who violates an oath isn't just punished himself, he also brings punishment on his family, his descendants in future generations, and the entire world, as in Hosea 4:2–3: "Swearing and lying ... break all bounds ... Therefore, the land mourns, and everyone who dwells therein languishes."

The first oath recorded in the Bible is the one Abraham makes his servant swear in Genesis 24:2, when he promises to find a non-Canaanite bride for

Isaac. That oath has a physical component: "Put your hand under my thigh and I will make you swear by the Lord," Abraham instructs. The Talmud interprets "thigh" as a reference to Abraham's circumcised penis, which was a kind of sacred object; accordingly, oaths must be taken while touching a sacred object, preferably a Torah scroll. As for swearing "by the Lord," Rabbi Hanina bar Idi believes that this means using God's personal name, YHWH, which Jews ordinarily don't speak aloud. But the rabbis say it is permitted to use any of the usual titles for God, such as Adonai.

Litigants are required to stand while their case is being heard, in accordance with Deuteronomy 19:17: "the two men involved in the dispute shall stand before the Lord, before the priests and judges." The judges can give them permission to sit down, but the Talmud says that they can't allow one party to sit while the other is required to stand, since this would give the impression of favoritism. For the same reason, the judges can't allow one litigant to "say everything he needs" but instruct the other to "curtail your statement."

The rule about standing can potentially conflict with another principle dear to the rabbis' hearts: respect for their own dignity. When a sage is seated, people who are his inferiors in learning are supposed to remain standing. So what happens, the Talmud asks, if a sage is involved in litigation with an am ha'aretz? How can the judge show the proper deference to the sage without seeming to compromise his impartiality?

This was the dilemma Rav Nachman encountered when he was a judge in a case involving the wife of Rav Huna. Ordinarily, Rav Nachman would have risen in her presence out of respect for her husband. (As with all but a few women mentioned in the Talmud, we never learn her actual name.) However, he knew that not everyone was familiar with this rule, so people might think he was compromising his impartiality. To get out of this bind, he came up with a slapstick solution, instructing his court attendant, "Go outside and cause a duck to fly and cast it onto me" (30a). This would give Rav Nachman an excuse to stand up, and no one could say whether he was doing it out of deference to Rav Huna's wife or to avoid the incoming duck. Sometimes to satisfy every point of Jewish law you have to think outside the box.

Ordinarily the burden of proof in a lawsuit rests on the plaintiff. The defendant is simply required to take an oath that he doesn't owe the plaintiff anything: "All those who take an oath that is legislated by the Torah take an oath and do not pay" (44b). But the Talmud makes exceptions in certain cases. If the plaintiff is a hired worker claiming his wages, or a victim of robbery or injury claiming compensation, then the roles are reversed: the plaintiff takes an oath that he is owed money and the defendant has to pay. This change seems intended to make it easier to remedy injustice by the strong against the weak. As the Talmud says, "the Sages uprooted the oath from the employer and imposed it upon the hired worker due to the fact that his wages are his livelihood" (45a).

Certain people, however, are "suspect with regard to oaths," so their statement under oath isn't automatically accepted. This includes anyone who has lied under oath in the past, as well as people with disreputable habits and professions, such as "a dice player, or one who lends with interest, or those who fly pigeons"—that is, who gamble on pigeon races. If a suspect person is party to a lawsuit, their opponent can take an oath and the court must accept it.

If both parties are suspect with regard to oaths, however, the sages aren't sure what to do. Rabbi Meir says that neither party takes an oath and the disputed sum is divided between them. Rabbi Yosei, however, says that with two suspect litigants, the oath "returns to its place." According to the Gemara, this formula can be interpreted two ways. The sages of the land of Israel took it to mean that the obligation to take an oath returns to the party originally liable to it—in most cases, that means the defendant. Since he's disqualified from oath taking, the court must rule in favor of the other party, which is usually the plaintiff.

But the sages of Babylonia interpret Rabbi Yosei's words to mean that "the oath returned to Sinai" (47a). When God gave the Torah on Mount Sinai, the whole Jewish people took an oath to obey it, including the laws forbidding theft and fraud. An earthly court may not be able to judge between the litigants, but God knows who is guilty of violating that oath, and will punish them in his own way.

Avoda Zara On idol worship, intermarriage, and the rabbi who used an emperor as a footstool.

Idol worship—which the Talmud calls avoda zara, literally "strange worship"—is the most serious sin in Judaism. A murderer pays for his crime with his life, but in the Ten Commandments, God says that the punishment of an idol worshiper will be visited on his descendants "unto the third and fourth generation." Even so, the Bible shows that it took a long time for the Israelites to give up the habit of worshiping idols. Even while Moses was receiving the Torah on Mount Sinai, the Israelites were making the golden calf. Centuries later they were still at it. According to Jeremiah 19:5, God allowed the Babylonians to conquer Jerusalem because the Jews "have built high places to Baal on which to burn their children in the fire as offerings."

By the Talmudic era, the battle against polytheism had been won. As we saw in tractate Yoma, when the Second Temple was built God took away the Jews' "evil inclination" to commit idolatry. But they still lived among idol worshipers, and in the Roman Empire everything from cities to days of the week was named after pagan gods. Accordingly, tractate Avoda Zara has less to say about actual idol worship than about avoiding contact with other peoples' gods. More broadly, it discusses how Jews can preserve their difference as a minority in a hostile culture.

In addition to shunning idol worship, Jews must avoid helping pagans worship their gods. For this reason, it's forbidden to do business with pagans for three days before any of their religious festivals, since if a pagan makes a profit he will give thanks to his god. The Gemara notes that this argument makes sense when it comes to lending money to a pagan, but not to borrowing money from him, which he presumably wouldn't celebrate. But Abaye explains that even borrowing is forbidden, since it might lead to lending.

The Talmud lists the particular Roman festivals that must be avoided: "Kalenda, Saturnalia, and Kratesis, and the day of the festival of their kings, and the birthday of the king, and the day of the death of the king." Kalenda is Kalends, the Roman name for the first day of the month; Saturnalia was a winter solstice festival; and Kratesis was a celebration of Rome's conquests. Of course, refusing to honor pagan holidays didn't endear the Jews to their neighbors. On one occasion, "a certain heretic" sent a coin to Rabbi Yehuda Nesia on the day of a festival. "What shall I do?" he asked Reish Lakish. If he accepted the coin, the heretic would be gratified and give thanks to his god; if he refused it, the heretic "will harbor enmity." Reish Lakish gave shrewd advice: he should accept the coin but then drop it into a pit, accidentally-on-purpose (6a).

Jews must take care not to give even the appearance of worshiping an idol. A Jew is forbidden to enter a city where a pagan festival is taking place, because onlookers might assume he's going there to celebrate. If a Jew gets a thorn in his foot while walking in front of an idol, he can't bend down to remove it, since onlookers will think he's bowing to the idol. If he must pick out the thorn, he should turn his back to the idol to make clear he's not worshiping it (12a).

Even on non-holidays it would have been difficult to avoid statues of gods, which could be found in most public places. The Talmud makes things easier by saying that a statue only has to shunned if "it has in its hand a staff, a bird, or an orb." The Gemara explains that these were symbols of divine power: "A bird represents dominion, as the idol grasps ... the entire world the way one grasps a bird" (41a).

It's permitted to visit a place that contains idols as long as it's not primarily devoted to worshiping them. Rabban Gamliel was once spotted in a public bath that contained a statue of Aphrodite; when challenged, he justified himself on the grounds that a bathhouse is not a temple. "People do not say, let us make a bathhouse as an adornment for Aphrodite; rather, they say, let us make Aphrodite as an adornment for the bathhouse." In addition, the placement of the statue showed that it wasn't intended to be sacred, merely ornamental: "this statue stands upon the sewage pipe, and all the people urinate before it" (44b).

The rabbis look forward to a time when the tables will be turned and Jews can stop putting up with idols. On the day of judgment, God will sit before the assembled nations with a Torah scroll in his lap. The Romans and Persians will come before him boasting of their achievements: "We have established many marketplaces, we have built many bathhouses, and we have increased much silver and gold." But God will scorn them: "Fools of the world . . .   Is there no one among you who can declare this?" he will ask, pointing to the Torah. As a rule, God doesn't laugh—"there is no making sport for the Holy One"—but he will make an exception to mock the gentiles. Passages like this explain why, starting in the sixteenth century, tractate Avoda Zara was often expurgated from printed editions of the Talmud, to avoid incurring the wrath of Christian authorities.

The rabbis usually express fear and hatred of Roman power, but they enjoy telling stories about Romans who honored individual Jews. An emperor referred to as Antoninus—possibly Marcus Aurelius of the Antonine dynasty, who reigned from 161 to 180 CE—was supposedly such an admirer of Yehuda HaNasi that he had an underground passageway built between their houses, so he could visit the rabbi in secret and ask his advice.

On one occasion the emperor said, "Important Romans are upsetting me; what can I do about them?" Yehuda HaNasi "brought him to his garden, and every day he uprooted a radish from the garden bed before him. Antoninus said to himself: Learn from it that this is what he is saying to me: You should kill them one by one, and do not incite all of them at once" (10a). Antoninus is even said to have kneeled down so that Yehuda HaNasi could climb on his back to get into bed, declaring: "Oh, that I were set as a mattress under you in the World to Come!" This surely never happened, but the story shows that Yehuda HaNasi was remembered as the rare Jewish leader whom the Romans respected.

The usual relationship between Romans and Jews was very different. Rabbi Yosei ben Kisma lamented that Rome "destroyed God's Temple, and burned His sanctuary, and killed His pious ones, and destroyed His best ones, yet it still exists." He concluded that Rome was "given reign by heaven," for reasons impossible to understand.

One of his friends, Rabbi Hanina ben Teradyon, was martyred by the Romans, as the Gemara describes in painful detail. Hanina was charged with teaching Torah in public, in defiance of a Roman ban, and sentenced to be burned alive. He was put on the pyre wrapped in a Torah scroll, which offered him a kind of consolation. "If I alone were being burned, it would be difficult for me, but now that I am burning along with a Torah scroll, He who will seek retribution for the insult accorded to the Torah scroll will also seek retribution for the insult accorded to me," he told his daughter (18a). Then the executioner "brought tufts of wool and soaked them in water, and placed them on his heart so that his soul should not leave his body quickly." But the executioner, evidently impressed by Hanina's faith, agreed to remove the tufts of wool in exchange for the sage promising him a place in the World to Come.

Sometimes the sages managed to outwit the Romans with the help of miracles. Rabbi Elazar ben Perata, arrested at the same time as Hanina, was charged with teaching Torah and being a thief. He protested that the two crimes were incompatible, giving a punning answer: "If one is an armed robber [safaya] he is not a scholar [safra], and if he is a scholar he is not an armed robber." Asked to explain why people called him Rabbi or "master" if he wasn't a Torah scholar, he explained that it was because he was a master weaver. The Romans challenged Elazar to prove it, bringing him two coils of wool yarn and asking him to tell the warp (which runs lengthwise) from the woof (which runs side to side). Fortunately, a sign from Heaven revealed the answer: a female hornet came and sat on the warp and a male sat on the woof. Finally Elazar was rescued by the prophet Elijah, who came to the trial disguised as a Roman nobleman and distracted a key witness.

Despite these stories of persecution, the Talmud insists that there is no such thing as undeserved punishment. If a Jew suffers, he must have commimtted a sin of some kind. That's the lesson of the story of Rabbi Eliezer, who was arrested by the Romans and charged with heresy. Eliezer was acquitted, but he was tormented by the thought that God wouldn't have made him undergo this ordeal if he hadn't been guilty of something. Rabbi Akiva agreed, suggesting that perhaps once in his life Eliezer had taken pleasure in heresy.

And Eliezer did remember one occasion, when a "student of Jesus the Nazarene" named Ya'akov offered an ingenious scriptural interpretation. The Torah says that a prostitute's earnings can't be consecrated to the Temple, but the Christian argued that they could be used to build a bathroom for the High Priest: "Since the coins came from a place of filth, let them go to a place of filth." "I derived pleasure from the statement, and due to this, I was arrested for heresy," Eliezer concluded (17a).

Clearly the safest course for Jews is to avoid gentiles altogether—a lesson that Avoda Zara drives home in a number of ways. A Jew shouldn't entrust his child to a gentile teacher "to teach him to read books or to teach him a craft." Jews may not go to places of amusement such as circuses, theaters, and stadiums, since "these matters bring a person to dereliction of the study of Torah" (18b).

Mixing with non-Jews doesn't only pose spiritual dangers. If a Jew is walking next to a gentile on the road, he should make sure to stay on the left, so he can use his right hand to draw a weapon for self-defense. And he should never bend down, which would give the gentile the chance to "break his skull." A Jewish woman must never be alone in the presence of a non-Jewish man, for fear of rape. Of course, a Jewish woman isn't supposed to be alone with a Jewish man, either; but the rabbis explain that, with a Jew, it's permitted if the man's wife is also present. A gentile's wife, on the other hand, "does not guard him" against sexual immorality (25b).

A Jewish mother can't employ a gentile midwife or nursemaid, since they might try to kill the child: the midwife "places her hand on the infant's temple and kills him," while the nursemaid "smears poison upon her breast." One gentile midwife was heard to boast that she had killed so many Jewish children that their blood was "like the foam of a river." Similarly, a Jew shouldn't allow a gentile to circumcise his son, since he might take the opportunity to cut off the penis.

Did these tales of pagan depravity have any basis in reality, or were they just hostile superstitions? For instance, did the rabbis really believe that pagans habitually had sex with animals? "One may not keep an animal in the inns of gentiles because they are suspected of bestiality," the Talmud says (22a). But the Gemara points out that Jewish law isn't consistent on this point; it's permitted to purchase an animal from a gentile for use as a sacrifice, which wouldn't be the case if bestiality is presumed.

The Gemara suggests that there are good reasons why gentiles would refrain from having sex with their own animals: a female would become barren and a male would be weakened. Likewise, a shepherd wouldn't molest the animals under his care because he might be caught and punished. But other rabbis reply that this would only deter a shepherd whose sheep belonged to a gentile. If a gentile shepherd had the opportunity to molest Jewish sheep, he would take it, because "we are not aware of them and they are not fearful of us." In general, the Talmud's assumptions about pagans communicate this sense that "we are not aware of them" and have no real sense of how "they" behave.

One of the ways Jews and pagans might come into contact is by socializing over food and drink. Jewish dietary laws already introduce a barrier here, but the Talmud says that even kosher food can't be eaten by Jews if it's prepared by pagans, since it may have been used as part of a religious ceremony. This is a special concern when it comes to wine, which was used as a libation in idol worship. For this reason, Jews can't drink wine that belonged to a gentile, or even buy and sell it.

The Gemara points out that there are some kinds of wine that pagans never use in their ceremonies, such as boiled wine. But this too is banned, on the grounds that gentiles aren't as careful as Jews about leaving wine or water exposed in an open container, where it might be contaminated by a poisonous snake. The Talmud discusses this concern quite seriously, unlikely though it sounds.

But when the rabbis extend the ban to beer, their real motivation becomes unmistakable. Beer isn't used in pagan rituals and it isn't liable to be poisoned by snakes, so why can't a Jew drink a gentile's beer? Rabbi bar Hama says frankly, "It is due to marriage" (31b). Drinking beer together promotes friendships, and friendships might lead to intermarriage. It's not idolatry that the rabbis are mainly worried about, but sociability.

For the same reason, Jews can't share bread with gentiles. Yehuda HaNasi was once offered a loaf of bread baked by a gentile and wished he could eat it: "How exquisite is this bread! What did the sages see that caused them to prohibit it?" he asked. Here too the answer is "marriage." Yehuda HaNasi wondered whether the ban applied even when there was no socializing involved, as when a Jew is by himself in a field. It does, as Aivu learned when he tried to get away with eating pagans' bread in a field and was shunned for it. "Do not speak with Aivu, as he eats bread of Arameans," instructed Rabbi Nachman bar Yitzchak (35b).

When it comes to oil, there is a disagreement among the sages. Rav forbids Jews from consuming oil that belongs to a gentile, but Yehuda HaNasi permits it. This perplexes the rabbis, who believe that the ban on oil was introduced by Daniel in the Bible. Since "a court cannot void the statements of another court unless it is greater than it in wisdom and in number," Yehuda HaNasi couldn't overturn Daniel's ruling. But it turns out that there's an even higher authority when it comes to law: the Jewish people themselves. The prohibition on oil "did not spread" among the Jewish people, and "the sages issue a decree upon the community only if most of the community is able to abide by it" (36a). This principle introduces a measure of democracy into halakha, allowing the Jews to vote with their feet.

Avoda Zara vividly communicates the Jewish experience of being outnumbered by hostile pagans. But why does God allow the world to be that way, the Mishna wonders? "The gentiles asked the sages in Rome: If it is not God's will that people engage in idol worship, why does he not eliminate it?" The sages had an ingenious answer: "Were people worshipping only objects for which the world has no need, he would eliminate it. But they worship the sun and the moon and the stars and the constellations. Should he destroy his world because of the fools?" (54b) Just because people are misguided enough to worship material objects doesn't mean that the material world is at fault.

But the objections didn't stop there. "If so, let him destroy objects for which the world has no need," the gentiles replied. Maybe God can't get rid of the sun and moon, but why can't he strike down a sacred grove or a statue of Apollo? Once again the rabbis have an answer: God could destroy these idols, but if he did so while leaving the sun and moon intact, people might believe that the sun and moon had the power to stand up to God. Rather than create such a false impression, God leaves all idols alone.

This answer is challenged by a Roman named Agrippas, who knew enough Torah to quote Deuteronomy 4:24: "For the Lord your God is a devouring fire, a jealous God." So why doesn't he devour the idols that compete with him for honor? Rabban Gamliel replies that it's because jealousy only applies to rivals: "A wise man might be jealous of another wise man, and a mighty man of another mighty man, and a rich man of another rich man." Since idols aren't gods, God has no need to be jealous of them.

The Talmud illustrates the point with a parable about a prince who named his dog after his own father, the king: "When the son would take an oath, he would say, I swear by the life of the dog, my father." In this case, the king wouldn't be angry at the dog, who doesn't understand what's going on; he would direct his anger at the prince who disrespected him. Just so, God doesn't take out his wrath on idols themselves, but on the people who worship them.

A last objection comes from a man named Zunin, who confided to Rabbi Akiva that he was skeptical about idols himself: "Both my heart and your heart know that there is no substance to idol worship." But how can we explain that sometimes sick people pray to idols and are cured? Akiva replied that this is just a coincidence. An illness takes an oath to last a certain amount of time, so if the sick person happens to pray at the right moment, it will seem as if his gods have healed him. In fact, the illness knows this and says to itself: "By right we should not leave him . . . Should we lose the fulfillment of our oath just because this fool is acting improperly?"

In the end, Rav Yehuda offers the most ingenious explanation for the persistence of idol worship: God allows pagans to sin "in order to expel them from the world" (55a). If the Jews are weak while the pagans are numerous and powerful, this isn't a sign that God favors the pagans. Rather, God is giving them the opportunity to sin so that one day he can wipe them out and give the whole world to the Jews. To a powerless and persecuted people, this must have been an appealing argument.

Horayot On mistaken judgments and why scholars outrank kings.

Halakha is perfect because it comes from God, but applying the law in particular cases is up to human beings, who are capable of error. Tractate Horayot, whose name means "decisions," discusses what to do when a court makes a mistaken judgment.

According to Leviticus 4:13, "If the whole Israelite community sins unintentionally and does what is forbidden in any of the Lord's commands," they must atone by bringing a young bull as a sin offering. The Talmud assumes that the only way this could happen is if the people were led astray by a court's incorrect ruling. In a case where an individual sinned because he "associated his action with the ruling of the court," then, the obligation to bring an offering falls on the court. After all, people are supposed to follow judges' rulings; as Deuteronomy 17:11 says, "You shall act in accordance with the instructions given you and the ruling handed down to you; you must not deviate from the verdict that they announce to you either to the right or to the left."

Are there matters where the law is so clear that even a layperson should be able to tell that a court's judgment is mistaken? What if a court rules that "there is no prohibition against engaging in intercourse with a menstruating woman" or "there is no prohibition against labor on Shabbat"? No Jew can plead ignorance on these matters; as the Talmud says, "it is a topic that you could go learn in a children's school" (4a). If people accept such rulings and commit a sin, therefore, they bear the responsibility themselves and have to bring individual sacrifices.

In the Talmudic era, legal decisions were made by courts composed of Torah scholars. But in earlier periods, kings and high priests were empowered to issue judgments, and they too had to bring an offering in case of error. As Leviticus 4:22 says: "When a ruler sins unintentionally and does what is prohibited by any of the commandments of the Lord his God, he incurs guilt." In discussing the nature of kingship, the Talmud says that when a king is afflicted with leprosy, he's no longer fit to rule. That was what happened to King Uzziah, who contracted leprosy and had to leave the palace and "live in a house apart" (2 Chronicles 26:21). The word "apart" can also be interpreted to mean "independent," which leads to an interesting observation: If Uzziah became independent after abdicating the throne, it follows that a king is dependent, like a servant (10a). This shows that a king is meant to be the servant of his people, rather than vice versa.

For Torah scholars, too, noblesse oblige. Rabban Gamliel, the head of the rabbinic academy, was once informed that two of his students were "so wise that they know how to calculate how many drops of water there are in the sea," yet they lived in poverty, with "neither bread to eat nor a garment to wear." He decided to honor the students by seating them in the front row of the academy, but they were so modest that they refused the promotion. Rabban Gamliel explained that leadership in the academy was not an honor but an obligation: "Do you imagine that I am granting you authority? I am granting you servitude." The more prominent a person becomes, the more right the community has to call upon his services.

In the course of this discussion, the rabbis digress to analyze Ecclesiastes 8:14: "There are righteous men to whom it happens according to the deeds of the wicked, and there are wicked men to whom it happens according to the deeds of the righteous." According to Rabbi Nachman bar Hisda, this means that good people get their suffering done in this life so they can enjoy perfect happiness in the afterlife, while bad people enjoy themselves in this world but are storing up torment in the next.

This is one of the Talmud's favorite explanations for the world's injustice, but Rava points out that it has a flaw: "Is that to say that if the righteous enjoyed two worlds it would be awful for them?" (10b) Why does God require a good person to suffer in this life so he can be rewarded in the next? Rava argues that good people can be happy in this life as well, but his definition of happiness is modest. He once asked a pair of sages, "Have you mastered this tractate and that tractate? Have you become somewhat wealthy?" Yes, they replied, they each studied the law and owned a plot of land that could sustain them. In that case, Rava said, "Happy are the righteous." A person needs nothing more than a livelihood and a chance to learn Torah.

Which of the different types of Jewish leaders has the greatest authority—kings, priests or sages? The Talmud explains that a king takes precedence over a high priest and a high priest over a prophet. A high priest from the First Temple, who was anointed with holy oil, has a higher status than a high priest from the Second Temple, who wore sacred garments but didn't have access to the oil. (Of course, there is no situation in which a First Temple high priest could confront a Second Temple high priest, but the Talmud believes in covering all the bases.) This hierarchical ordering of Jewish society extends to ordinary people as well. A priest precedes a Levite, who comes before an Israelite, who comes before a person of illegitimate birth, who comes before a convert.

But at the very top of the hierarchy the Talmud places the Torah scholar, who even outranks a king. After all, "in the case of a sage who dies, we have no other like him; but in the case of a king of Israel who dies, all Israel are fit for royalty" (13a). Anyone could be appointed king—there was nothing especially distinguished about Saul or David before they were chosen—but only a wise and learned man can be a rabbi. This idea reflects the Talmud's role in redefining what it means to be Jewish. Where there used to be Judah, a state ruled by a king and a high priest, now there is Judaism, a religion that can be practiced wherever there are Jews—and Torah scholars to lead them.

IV

Seder Kodashim
and Tractate Nidda
The Temple, Sacrifices,
and Ritual Purity

Zevachim and Menachot
On animal sacrifices, meal offerings, and how the Jewish people is like an olive tree.

Only the earliest sages quoted in the Mishna actually knew the Temple—the Beit Hamikdash or "sacred house"—as a functioning institution. For the rest, it could only be a subject of lore and speculation from an increasingly distant past. Ravina and Rav Ashi, who are credited with redacting the Gemara in the early fifth century CE, were as distant from the Temple as we are from the Mayflower.

Yet the Talmud devotes just as much effort to understanding the commandments related to the Temple as it does to matters like Shabbat observance or marriage and divorce. Seder Kodashim, which is devoted to the "holy things" of the Temple—in particular the laws of sacrifice—is omitted from most of the law codes compiled by later Jewish authorities for practical use, since Jews haven't sacrificed animals for two thousand years. But the Talmud is only partly concerned with applying the laws; mainly it strives to understand them, which is a sacred activity in itself. And when the Messiah comes it will be necessary to know how to conduct a sacrifice, since the Temple will be miraculously rebuilt and all its ceremonies restored.

Tractate Zevachim is named for the "slaughtered offerings" that were the core of the Temple service. According to a famous saying from Pirkei Avot, "The world stands on three things: Torah, avoda, and deeds of loving-kindness." The word "avoda" is usually translated as "divine service" and understood to mean worship in general. But in its original context, avoda specifically meant the Temple service with its cycle of sacrifices and rituals.

Rabbinic Judaism was created to fill the gap left when Temple sacrifices ended. It did this so well that later Jews found the idea of animal sacrifice bizarre. As the eleventh-century poet and theologian Yehuda Halevi wrote, "You slaughter a lamb and smear yourself with its blood, in skinning it, cleaning its entrails, washing, dismembering it, and sprinkling its blood. If this were not in consequence of a divine command, you would think little of these actions and believe that they estrange you from God rather than bring you near to Him."

Much of Seder Kodashim can still inspire this kind of estrangement. Its descriptions of the Temple sacrifices are like a highly detailed instruction manual for a technology that no longer exists. A sacrifice has several steps, which must be performed exactly the right way in order to be acceptable to God. First, an unblemished animal—a bull, sheep, goat or pigeon, depending on the type of sacrifice—is slaughtered in the Temple courtyard by slitting its throat with a blade (or, in the case of a bird, breaking its neck by hand). A priest collects the blood in a bowl and carries it up a ramp to the altar, where he sprinkles it on the corners. Depending on the type of sacrifice, some or all of the meat is burned on the altar, and whatever is left over is given to the priests to eat. Two lambs were sacrificed every day, one in the morning and one in the afternoon, and individuals brought their own sacrifices for many reasons—to atone for sins, celebrate a holiday, fulfill a vow, or give thanks for the birth of a child, among others.

Rather than laying out the process step by step, Zevachim begins by considering a specific problem: what is the status of an offering that is slaughtered "not for its own sake"? In a proper sacrifice, "the offering is slaughtered for the sake of the offering"—that is, the animal is intended as a particular type of sacrifice. If an individual brings a sheep to the Temple for a sin offering but the slaughterer kills it thinking it's a guilt offering—a related but different sacrifice established in the Torah—it "did not satisfy the obligation of the owner," and he must bring a new sacrifice. The easiest way to avoid this problem, Rava says, is for the slaughterer not to have any particular sacrifice in mind, since "if offerings were slaughtered without specification of intent, they satisfied the obligation of the owner" (2b).

Correct intention is just one of the six elements required for a proper sacrifice. The second is that it must be "for the sake of the one sacrificing": if the slaughterer forgets who brought the sacrifice and performs it with a different person in mind, it is ineffective. It must also be offered "for the sake of God," with pious intention, and "for the sake of the fires" that burn the animal's flesh on the altar. Finally it must be "for the sake of an aroma" and "for the sake of pleasing," since according to the Torah, the smell of cooked meat is what makes an offering pleasing to God. If any of these elements is missing, the sacrifice is flawed.

Offering sacrifices on the altar was the main duty of the priests, who inherited their office in a direct line from Aaron. But priests can be disqualified from Temple service for a number of reasons. An acute mourner—someone whose close relative has died but isn't yet buried—can't offer a sacrifice. Neither can an uncircumcised priest, which sounds at first like a contradiction in terms, but occasionally male infants are spared circumcision for medical reasons. The Talmud finds a basis for this prohibition in Ezekiel 44:7, where the prophet complains: "you have brought in strangers, uncircumcised in heart or uncircumcised in flesh, to be in My Sanctuary, to profane My house." The meaning of "uncircumcised in flesh" is clear, and the Talmud explains that "uncircumcised in heart" refers to "one whose heart is not directed toward Heaven" or "one whose actions are estranged from His father in Heaven" (22b).

Priests wear special garments while serving in the Temple, which must be new, unfrayed, and made of fine linen. Leviticus 6:3 says that these vestments must be worn "next to his body," which the Talmud interprets to mean that nothing can interpose between the cloth and the priest's skin. Rava wonders how far this rule should be taken: what if "a gust of wind entered the vestment," lifting it away from the priest's skin? (19a) What if there's a louse or a speck of dirt or a thread inside the vestments? Most of these questions go unanswered, but there's a kind of pathos in them. While the Temple stood, priests would have known how to deal with such problems, since they must have come up all the time. The rabbis, living centuries later, have to grope for answers.

The slaughter of sacrificial animals takes place in the Temple courtyard, with different offerings assigned to different locations. "Offerings of the most sacred order," including sin and guilt offerings, are slaughtered in the northern half of the courtyard (47a), as stated in Leviticus 1:11: "You are to slaughter it at the north side of the altar before the Lord, and Aaron's sons, the priests, shall splash its blood against the sides of the altar."

In Aaron's time, of course, the Temple hadn't yet been built by Solomon. Sacrifices took place at the Tabernacle, the portable tent where the Ark of the Covenant resided. But the Tabernacle was a forerunner to the Temple, and the rules governing the Tabernacle were applied to the Temple once it was built. (That's the traditional belief, at any rate; modern scholars, who believe the Torah was written much later, argue that its authors projected the dimensions and rituals of the Temple back onto the Tabernacle.)

Slaughtering animals is a messy process and many things can go wrong. For instance, what if a part of the sacrifice falls off the pyre—should it be put back in the flames or taken off the altar? According to Leviticus 6:2, a burnt offering should burn "all night until the morning," but the Mishna in Zevachim 86a says that until midnight is adequate. If a piece of the sacrifice is dislodged before midnight it must be returned to the altar, but not after.

The Gemara challenges this distinction: Why does the mitzva depend on time rather than the degree of burning? "If the limbs have substance, even after midnight the priest must return them to the fire," the Gemara says. Conversely, if a limb is fully burned before midnight, then if the ash falls it shouldn't need to be replaced. The rabbis conclude that the midnight rule applies only to a limb that's somewhere in between, "hardened" but not fully burned.

The altar confers sanctity, meaning that once a sacrifice has "ascended" onto the altar it is holy. The Talmud adds that the airspace above the altar is also sacred, since otherwise it would be impossible to lift the animal from the ramp onto the altar without causing it to enter profane space. The Gemara wonders if this could be avoided by dragging the carcass up the ramp and onto the altar, so it never loses contact with the surface; but apparently this method wouldn't work, because there was a gap between the ramp and the altar (87b).

If the airspace over the altar is sacred, the Gemara wonders, what would happen if you suspended a piece of meat over the altar by means of a pole? Would that render it sacred? At this point, however, the rabbis dismiss the subject with the words "Let it stand." Even in the Talmud, there comes a point when it's fruitless to keep speculating.

In addition to animal sacrifices, the priests also offered menachot or meal offerings, made of flour mixed with oil and frankincense. Both types of offering raise many of the same issues, and tractate Menachot often runs parallel to Zevachim; it also begins by asking about the status of offerings made "not for their own sake." Even the ritual protocol for meal offerings is similar to that for animal offerings. Instead of collecting blood in a bowl and presenting it on the altar, the priest scoops a handful of meal from a bowl.

This handful must be scooped with the priest's right hand; if he forgets and uses his left hand, he returns the meal to the bowl and starts over. The Gemara notes that this detail isn't mentioned in the description of Aaron's meal offering in Leviticus 9:17, which simply says, "And the meal offering was presented, and he filled his hand from it."

How do we know Aaron used his right hand? According to Rabba bar bar Chana, it's a general rule: "Any place in the Torah in which it is stated that an action is performed with a finger or by the priesthood, this teaches that it is performed only with the right hand" (10a). This can be deduced from Leviticus 14:26, where the ritual for cleansing a leper requires the priest to "take some of the oil and pour it in the palm of his own left hand." This is the only place in the Torah where the left hand is specified, which implies that when there's no specification, the right hand is meant.

According to Rava, the priest scoops up the offering "as people normally remove handfuls," by folding the fingers over the palm. But Abaye disagrees, saying that the priest "bends his middle three fingers until the tips of the fingers reach over the palm of his hand, and removes the handful." The thumb and the little finger, which have been left free, are then used to wipe away any excess flour from the top and bottom of the handful. This is such a tricky maneuver that scooping was considered "the most difficult rite in the Temple" (11a)—a title that is also given in Yoma to the high priest's act of transferring incense from a spoon to his hands.

The ingredients for a meal offering are listed in Leviticus 2:1–2: "And when one brings a meal offering unto the Lord, his offering shall be of fine flour; and he shall pour oil upon it, and put frankincense upon it." A few verses later, a fourth ingredient is mentioned: "You shall not omit from your meal offering the salt of your covenant with God." According to the Talmud, however, only the flour is indispensable: "If one did not pour the oil onto the meal offering, or did not mix the oil into the meal offering . . . or did not add salt," it is still fit to be sacrificed.

The Gemara wonders about this rule: "Doesn't the verse write that pouring the oil is indispensable?" Rather, the Mishna must mean that the oil doesn't have to be poured by a priest; a non-priest can also add it to the flour. But Rabbi Shimon disputes this leniency, saying that only a priest can perform any part of the sacrifice: "the mixing, the breaking, the salting, the waving, the bringing to the altar, the removal of the handful, and the burning of the handful upon the altar."

Not all meal offerings involve scooping raw flour. In some types the flour is baked into unleavened loaves, with different ingredients for different sacrifices. For the meal offering of the priests, the flour is kneaded with oil and frankincense; for the peace offering, only oil; and the showbread—the loaves that were perpetually on display in the Temple on a special table—uses only frankincense.

Loaves can be presented on the altar in two ways, by "waving" or "bringing near," depending on the type of offering. Bringing near means carrying the loaves to the western side of the altar, while waving is performed on the eastern side and involves holding up the loaves and waving them in all six directions—front and back, right and left, up and down. According to the Babylonian rabbis, the purpose of waving was to dedicate the sacrifice to "He to Whom the four directions belong" and "the heavens and the earth belong."

The rabbis of the land of Israel believed there was a more practical motive: waving was a way "to request a halt to harmful winds and storms that come from all directions" and "harmful dews" that come from above (62a). Rav Acha bar Ya'akov gave the ritual his own personal meaning, saying that waving the sacrifice was a way of "shooting an arrow in the eye of Satan." But the rabbis disapprove of this, because if you brag about defeating the devil he will "come to incite" the Jewish people even more.

The troubles of the Jewish people are the subject of a story told in Menachot 53b about how Abraham appeared in the First Temple when it was destroyed by the Babylonians. Abraham pleaded with God not to allow this to happen, in a speech clearly modeled on the episode in Genesis 18 where he tries to stop God from destroying Sodom and Gomorrah. Why are the Jews being punished, Abraham demands? God replies that it is because they are sinners. Perhaps they sinned unwittingly, Abraham pleads, but God insists their sin was deliberate. Perhaps only a minority of the people sinned? No, God says, all of them are guilty.

Finally, Abraham "placed his hands on his head," a gesture of mourning, and started "screaming and crying" over the fate of his descendants. To comfort him, God cites Jeremiah 11:16: "The Lord called your name a leafy olive tree, fair with goodly fruit." Then God promises, "Just as with regard to this olive tree, its final purpose is fulfilled" when it bears fruit, "so too with the Jewish people, their final purpose will be fulfilled at their end."

Rabbi Yehoshua ben Levi expands on this image: "Why were the Jewish people likened to an olive tree? It is to tell you that just as the leaves of an olive tree never fall off, neither in the summer nor in the rainy season, so, too, the Jewish people will never be nullified, neither in this world nor in the World to Come." Rabbi Yochanan, however, has a darker interpretation: "An olive tree brings forth its oil only by means of crushing," he observes, and "the Jewish people return to good ways only by means of suffering."

Different types of meal offerings have different recipes. A standard offering requires one-tenth of an ephah of flour, while the meal offering that accompanies the sacrifice of a bull uses three-tenths of an ephah, and the High Priest's daily griddle-cake offering is made from a tenth of an ephah divided in half, with one part offered in the morning and the other in the evening. (An ephah is a measure of volume equivalent to twenty-three liters, or according to other authorities thirty-six liters; so a tenth of an ephah is somewhere between 0.6 and 0.9 gallons.) Since most of these recipes called for multiples of one-tenth of an ephah, the Talmud reasons that the Temple must have contained a measuring bowl of that size.

As for the oil, it is measured in multiples of a log, which is equivalent to 0.3 liters or 10 ounces. Rather than a single bowl that measured one log, however, the Talmud says that "there were seven measuring vessels for liquids in the Temple" (87b). In addition to the one-log vessel for the oil of meal offerings, there was a six-log bowl for the oil accompanying a bull offering, a four-log vessel for a ram, and a three-log vessel for a lamb. Then there was a half-log vessel for the water of a sota and a quarter-log vessel for the water used in the purification of a leper.

But this is only six vessels—what was the seventh? The Mishna says that it was a large bowl that held one hin, which equals twelve log. But what was this vessel needed for, Rabbi Shimon asks, since no sacrifice requires a hin of oil? The only place in the Torah where this unit is mentioned is Exodus 30, where Moses uses a hin of holy oil to anoint the Tabernacle and the priests. It stands to reason that the hin-sized vessel in the Temple was the very one Moses used. Rabbi Shimon, however, argues that this vessel wouldn't have been kept in the Temple for so many centuries if it was never used again, but would surely have been stored away instead.

The easiest solution to the quandary would be to decide that there were only six vessels after all: "Is it not possible to not include a seventh?" the

Gemara asks. But the rabbis rule out this possibility: "It is learned as a tradition that there were seven measuring vessels for liquids in the Temple," so seven there must be. Tradition is always a more trustworthy guide than our own speculations about what's logical and probable.

Hullin and Bechorot On kosher slaughter, separating meat and dairy, and when a firstborn isn't a firstborn.

Animal sacrifices in the Temple were part of a sacred ritual, but when animals are slaughtered for food there are also precise rules that must be followed. In tractate Hullin—whose title means "profane," simply in the sense of "not sacred"—the Talmud establishes the laws that govern kosher slaughter or shechita to this day.

Temple sacrifices can only be performed by priests, but for everyday purposes, "Everyone slaughters and their slaughter is valid." That includes women, although in practice Jewish women have traditionally been barred from the profession of slaughterer. The only people who are legally forbidden to perform kosher slaughter are "a deaf-mute, an imbecile, and a minor," since they are presumed to be incapable of understanding the law.

When the Talmud says "everyone slaughters," it really means every Jew: "Slaughter performed by a gentile renders the animal an unslaughtered carcass," which is forbidden to eat. While a Jew can't eat such meat, however, he can "derive benefit" from it by selling it to gentile customers. There is only one condition: as Avoda Zara explained, a Jew is forbidden from deriving benefit from idol worship, and pagans often slaughtered animals as part of a sacrifice to their gods. According to Rabbi Eliezer, all meat slaughtered by a gentile falls into the category of idol worship unless proven otherwise.

Rabbi Ami, however, makes a distinction between gentiles and minim or Jewish heretics. It's only the latter whose slaughter is presumed to be for the sake of idol worship. He goes on to list other prohibitions related to heretics: Not only can a Jew not eat their bread or drink their wine, but their sacred writings are sorcery and should be burned, and their children are considered illegitimate because it can be assumed that their wives are adulterous. Heretics require special vigilance because, unlike pagans, they aren't obvious outsiders; as Rabba bar Avuh says, "There are no heretics among the nations of the world" (13b). For Judaism, only Jewish apostates are truly dangerous.

The Talmud goes on to discuss the instruments used in kosher slaughter. The key concern is that the trachea and esophagus must be cleanly severed. If they are ripped or compressed, the animal would technically die of strangulation, rendering it forbidden. For this reason, the slaughterer's blade should be smooth, without notches or indentations that could grip and tear the flesh. Usually a knife is used, but "one may slaughter with any item" that meets this standard, including a sharpened flint or a reed. But one may not use "a harvest sickle, a saw, teeth, and a fingernail," which tear instead of cutting (15b).

Yehuda HaNasi says that the slaughterer must hold the knife in his hand, following the example of Abraham, who "stretched forth his hand and took the knife to slaughter his son." But Rabbi Hiyya challenges him in aggressive terms, comparing his words to "a vav that is written on a tree trunk"—that is, a fissure on a tree's bark that looks like a letter but is actually meaningless. The rabbis agree that the cutting instrument doesn't need to be held in the slaughterer's hand; it can also be embedded in a wall or attached to a rotating water wheel. But it must be "detached and then reattached"—that is, it has to be a tool made for the purpose of slaughter, rather than natural growth like a sharp flint emerging from a wall.

The Talmud takes for granted that slaughter involves slitting an animal's neck, but this isn't stated explicitly in the Torah. Rav Kahana finds a verbal basis for the idea in the Hebrew word for slaughter, shechita, which resembles the word for bends, shach, suggesting that an animal should be slaughtered at a place where its body bends (27a). But as the Gemara points out, the neck isn't the only body part that bends. Why not slaughter animals by severing their tails or their ears? Ultimately, the rabbis say that slaughtering at the neck is a tradition handed down from Moses on Sinai—the standard Talmudic explanation for rules that have no apparent scriptural basis.

The proper way to cut an animal's throat is to draw the blade back and forth across it. Severing the head with one blow is forbidden, as is dropping a knife onto the neck guillotine-style. Two people can collaborate in slaughtering, either by grasping the same knife or by cutting at different places on the animal's neck. Once the cutting begins, it shouldn't be interrupted; if the slaughterer drops the knife or gets tired, the slaughter is invalid (32a).

Slaughter requires cutting both the trachea and the esophagus, but they don't have to be completely severed. For a large animal like a sheep or bull, it's sufficient to cut most of the way through both tubes, while for a bird, the majority of just one tube is enough. The Talmud finds a basis for this distinction in Leviticus 11:46: "This is the law of the animal, and of the bird, and of every living creature that moves in the waters." The ordering suggests that birds are halfway between land animals and fish. Slaughtering an animal requires cutting two tubes, while fish don't require slaughter at all, since they have neither a gullet nor a windpipe; so it stands to reason that birds require only one tube to be cut. The Gemara supports this taxonomy with an interpretation of the creation story in Genesis: God created animals out of earth and fish out of water, but he created birds out of mud, which is a mixture of earth and water (27b).

Every Torah scholar is supposed to have the skills and knowledge to perform a kosher slaughter (9a), but in practice the job is delegated to professional slaughterers. However, all Jews have to know the rules about kosher cooking, in particular the prohibition on mixing meat and milk. The Talmud states that "It is prohibited to cook any meat in milk" and "It is prohibited to place any meat together with cheese on one table" as part of the same meal (103b).

This rule is much broader than the commandment in Exodus 23:19: "You shall not cook a kid in its mother's milk." Read literally, this prohibition involves just one species of animal, a baby goat; it only forbids the milk of the kid's mother, not milk from another animal; and it only applies to cooking, not to eating meat along with a dairy product. When halakha goes far beyond the Torah in this way, the Gemara will usually notice the difference and ask why. But there's no questioning here. The ban on mixing meat and milk in any form is so fundamental that it's taken for granted.

Instead, the rabbis ask about how to define meat. The Mishna states that fish aren't considered meat for the purposes of kashrut: you can eat milk and fish at the same meal. So why is poultry forbidden? The Gemara explains this according to a rule of Rabbi Akiva's: "Anything about which an agent sent to purchase a given item would inquire, being unsure whether it qualifies as that type of item, is considered its type" (104a). In Nedarim, Akiva applies this principle to a case where a man vows that he will not eat vegetables. Is he allowed to eat gourds? Akiva says no, because gourds are a type of vegetable. But are they, other rabbis ask? Isn't it the case that "a person says to his agent: Purchase vegetables for me, and the agent returns and says: 'I found only gourds.'" Doesn't this show that there's a difference between vegetables and gourds?

But Akiva turns the example around on the questioners: "Does the agent return and say: 'I found only legumes?'" Obviously he doesn't, because the question of whether legumes are vegetables wouldn't arise. If the question about gourds does arise, then, it must be because gourds have a similarity with vegetables as well as a difference. The same rule applies to poultry: if you sent a servant to the market with instructions to buy meat for dinner, he wouldn't come back with fish, but he might come back with chicken.

As for mixing meat and dairy "on one table," the Gemara wonders, "How much time should one wait between eating meat and cheese?" The rule is that if you eat meat, you have to wait before eating dairy, but if you eat dairy, you only have to wash your hands and rinse your mouth before eating meat. This is because meat flavors and particles remain in the mouth after eating, while dairy flavors and particles don't. As for how long to wait, the rule is derived from Mar Ukva, who says that "I am, with regard to this matter, like vinegar, son of wine, with respect to my father"—in other words, his practice is less stringent. "Father, if he were to eat meat at this time, he would not eat cheese until tomorrow at this time. But as for me, only at this meal do I not eat cheese; at a different meal on the same day I will eat cheese," Mar Ukva says (105a). This implies that meat and dairy must be separated by the time between two meals, which later authorities interpreted to mean six hours.

The rabbis also have opinions about the right way to eat that go beyond kashrut. At a meal, if you wash your hands over the ground rather than in a basin, the spilled water attracts evil spirits. If you take food from the table while someone is drinking, it might give him "a spirit in half his head," a migraine. The foam on top of a beverage like beer is especially tricky to handle: drinking it causes catarrh, blowing it away causes headache, and removing it with your hand invites poverty. The best approach, the Gemara says, is to sink the foam into the beverage.

Today, the Yiddish word treyf is used to describe any kind of nonkosher food. But the Hebrew word from which it is derived, tereifa, means "torn" and is used in the Talmud for one particular kind of forbidden food: an animal that is injured or diseased and expected to die within twelve months. There are a number of ways an animal can become a tereifa: a perforated or severed organ, a missing body part, injuries inflicted by another animal, breaking bones by falling. Hiyya bar Rava adds that there are eight internal organs that render an animal a tereifa if they are injured, including the gullet, brain, heart, lung, and intestine (42a).

A qualified rabbi is required to inspect these organs to make sure they're not damaged. This is a heavy responsibility, since disqualifying an animal causes a financial loss to its owner. Naturally, a lenient rabbi would be more popular than a strict one. The Gemara mentions a case where Rav inspected an animal and ruled that the majority of its windpipe was severed, rendering it a tereifa, but when his judgment was challenged he sent the animal to Rabba bar bar Chana for a second opinion, who ruled that only a minority of the windpipe was severed, rendering the animal permitted. To emphasize his ruling, Rabba bar bar Chana bought some of the meat for himself.

To avoid this kind of second-guessing, rabbis are supposed to respect one another's judgments: "If a halakhic authority deemed an item impure, another authority is not allowed to deem it pure; if he prohibited, another is not allowed to permit it." In this particular case, the rule wasn't technically broken, because Rav intended to judge the animal a tereifa but hadn't yet officially done so. But Rabba bar bar Chana is open to another criticism: a rabbi is discouraged from buying meat from an animal he has judged kosher, since this creates the appearance of a conflict of interest. According to Rav Hisda, the ultimate test of a sage's honesty is being willing to disqualify his own animal: "Who is a Torah scholar? One who sees his own tereifa" (44b).

Hullin is concerned with how animals are born as well as how they die. The first offspring of every female animal must be given to the priests; as God says in Exodus 13:2, "Consecrate to me every firstborn, that which opens the womb." But what exactly does it mean to open the womb? Does it require physical contact between the newborn and the walls of the birth canal? To test this idea, the Talmud offers up a series of hypotheticals. What if a fetus is wrapped in palm fibers while in the womb? What if a midwife reaches into the womb and pulls the newborn animal out with her hands?

The strangest thought experiment of all involves a case where a weasel enters a cow's womb, swallows the fetus, and then comes out again (70a). In this case, the fetus emerges from the womb without touching its opening, since it's concealed inside the weasel's stomach. The Talmud rules that in this case it doesn't open its mother's womb, so the cow's next offspring would count as its firstborn.

What if the weasel swallows the fetus and leaves the womb, but then reenters and vomits out the fetus so that it can be born normally? In that case, the newborn exits its mother's womb twice, once inside the weasel and once in the normal way. Or what if "one pressed together the openings of two wombs of two animals giving birth to firstborns, and a fetus exited from the womb of this animal and entered the womb of that animal, and then emerged from the womb of the second animal, after which the second animal gave birth to its fetus"? Is the second fetus to emerge considered a firstborn child, or do we say that the womb of the second animal had already been opened by the fetus that crawled into it from the first animal?

This sounds preposterous, and the Gemara leaves the problem unresolved. But it's a good example of how the Talmud's speculations can end up being useful in ways the rabbis themselves could not have anticipated. Today, surrogacy and in vitro fertilization mean that it's actually possible for a child to be conceived in one uterus and born from another.

The duty to sacrifice a firstborn animal takes center stage in tractate Bechorot, whose name means "firstborn." In Numbers 3:13, God's claim on the firstborn is connected with his slaying of the firstborn Egyptians on the night of the Exodus: "On the day I struck down every firstborn in the land of Egypt, I consecrated to myself all the firstborn in Israel, both man and beast."

All firstborn kosher animals must be given to a priest for sacrifice, and one nonkosher species as well—donkeys. Since donkeys can't be sacrificed, the owner is supposed to redeem a firstborn donkey by sacrificing a lamb in its place. Failing this, he must kill the donkey by breaking its neck.

The Gemara asks why donkeys are singled out for special treatment: "In what way are donkeys different from firstborn horses and camels," which are not consecrated? Rabbi Eliezer replies that no explanation is necessary: "It is a Torah edict," and that's that. But he proceeds to give an explanation anyway. Donkeys are unique because when the Israelites fled Egypt, they used them to carry goods seized from the Egyptians as reparations. "There was not one member of the Jewish people that did not have ninety Nubian donkeys with him, laden with the silver and gold of the Egyptians," Eliezer says (5b).

It's possible to get around this obligation by selling a firstborn donkey to a gentile while it is still in the womb. Even if the Jew only sells the donkey's ear, it will be born unconsecrated, because the gentile's part ownership means that it doesn't count as a "firstborn in Israel." But the Talmud frowns on depriving God of his rights by a technicality, and warns that it won't work anyway. A sage named Rav Mari bar Rachel tried this trick, and his firstborn animals died (3b).

In Hullin the rabbis discussed the prohibition on mixing meat and milk, but in Bechorot they raise a more fundamental question. How do we know that it's permitted to drink milk at all? There might not seem to be a reason to doubt it, except that according to Talmudic biology, milk is actually a byproduct of blood. This is the rabbis' explanation for why nursing mothers don't menstruate: "the blood is spoiled and becomes milk." But consuming blood is a sin punishable by karet, so why is it permitted to drink milk, which is blood in another form?

The Torah never explicitly states that milk is permitted, but the Gemara finds a number of Bible verses that seem to take it for granted. In the book of Samuel, the young David comes to the battlefield where he will slay Goliath to bring cheeses to his brothers, who are soldiers in the army. The Gemara suggests that maybe the cheeses weren't for eating—perhaps David was supposed to sell them and give the money to his brothers. But this idea is rejected as implausible. "Is it the norm during war to engage in commerce?" the rabbis ask.

The clincher is Exodus 33:3, where God describes the land of Israel to Moses as "a land flowing with milk and honey." "If milk was not permitted, would the verse praise the land with an item that is not suitable for consumption?" the Gemara asks (6b). This verse not only proves that milk is permitted; it does the same thing for honey, which is made by bees, which like all insects aren't kosher. The Talmud explains that honey is permitted because it's not produced in the body of the bee. Rather, it's made from the nectar of flowers, and the bee merely stores it.

The obligation to sacrifice a firstborn animal means that Jews must keep track of which animals in the flock have already given birth. Gentile breeders have no such obligation, which can create difficulties when a Jew purchases a female animal from a gentile. When the animal gives birth for the first time in his possession, how can the owner tell if the offspring is a firstborn? The Talmud offers a rule of thumb: If a goat is younger than one year old, a ewe younger than two, or a cow younger than three, the assumption is that it hasn't given birth before. If the animal is older than that, the offspring's status is uncertain (19b).

However, one can't err on the side of safety and simply give the "uncertain" animal to the priests, because this might result in the sacrifice of an ineligible animal, a serious transgression. In these cases, Rabbi Akiva says that the offspring should be left to graze until it develops a physical blemish. That disqualifies it from sacrifice in any case, so it is safe for the owner to slaughter it. Until the animal becomes blemished, it can't be used for labor, because if it actually is a firstborn then one can't derive any kind of benefit from it.

The Talmud's assumptions about when animals give birth leads to a more detailed discussion of fetal development, which has implications for human beings as well. As Rabbi Akiva observes, an animal that is too young to have given birth isn't necessarily too young to have had a miscarriage. Since a miscarriage "opens the womb" of an animal, a live birth following a miscarriage is not considered a firstborn for the purposes of sacrifice. But how can you tell if an animal has had a miscarriage? According to Rava, the sign to look for is "murky discharge," while Shmuel says it is "bubbles of blood" (21a). To be certain, however, one must consult an experienced herder.

Turning to human reproduction, the Talmud says that "the formation of a fetus in a woman takes forty days." Before that time, it is "like water," without a recognizable form. This timing squares with the fact that a fetal heartbeat is first detected around the sixth week of pregnancy. For halakhic purposes, however, fetal development is measured not by the calendar but by size. Contact with a corpse imparts ritual impurity, but if a woman has a miscarriage, she doesn't become ritually impure unless "the head of the fetus is round like the size of a skein of yarn." The rabbis go on to debate exactly how big a skein of yarn is meant—is it a ball of warp threads or of the thicker woof threads?—but the principle is clear: A fetus isn't considered to be a human being until it has reached a certain stage of development.

Most of Bechorot deals with animals, but God's claim on the firstborn extends to humans as well. Unlike animals, firstborn sons don't have to be handed over to a priest; instead, Numbers 18:15 says that they must be redeemed by paying a priest five shekels. This leads the Talmud to note that the Torah establishes two categories of firstborn sons, with different rights and obligations. The firstborn son of a mother, who "opens her womb," must be bought back from the priests, while the firstborn son of a father receives a double inheritance, because "he is the first of his strength" (Deuteronomy 21:17). Usually the same child will be the firstborn of each parent, but not always: "There is a son who is a firstborn with regard to inheritance but is not a firstborn with regard to redemption from a priest," and vice versa (46a). The most common way for this to happen is if either parent has children from an earlier marriage.

It's even possible for a woman to give birth to a living child without having her womb opened, if she delivers by caesarean section. This can lead to paradoxical results. Say a first-time mother gives birth to a son by caesarean section, and then has another son who is born vaginally. The first son doesn't count as the mother's firstborn because he didn't open her womb, and the second doesn't count as the father's firstborn, because he isn't "the first of his strength." Oddly, then, it's possible for a woman to have two sons and no firstborn (47b).

In the Talmudic era and long after, this would have sounded like a purely hypothetical discussion, since before modern medicine it was basically impossible for a woman to survive a caesarean section. The operation was performed only to remove a child from a mother who had died or was about to die. Today, when a third of babies in the U.S. are delivered by caesarean, it's become a practical halakhic problem.

Arachin, Temura, and Karetot
On the value of a life, switching sacrifices, and a punishment worse than death.

Tithes and sacrifices were the main ways Jews contributed to the upkeep of the priesthood, but not the only ones. Tractate Arachin, "valuations," deals with a special kind of donation to the Temple—a monetary contribution tied to the value of a person's life. For instance, someone who survived a dangerous illness might express gratitude by donating his own value to the Temple.

This sum can be measured in two ways. In an "assessment," the donor promises to pay the market value of the dedicated item—with a person, this means the price he would command if sold as a slave. In a "valuation," by contrast, the value of a life follows a scale laid down in Leviticus 27, which assigns monetary equivalents based on age and sex. In the prime of adulthood, aged twenty to sixty, a man is worth fifty shekels and a woman thirty. Over the age of sixty, a man is worth fifteen shekels and a woman ten. From age five to twenty, males are worth twenty shekels and females ten shekels; and from one month to five years, a boy is worth five shekels and a girl three shekels. You couldn't ask for a clearer demonstration of the meaning of patriarchy than this literal devaluation of women's lives.

Vows of valuation can be taken by almost everyone—men and women, free people and slaves, priests and Israelites. The Talmud makes its usual exception for deaf-mutes, imbeciles, and minors, who are considered halakhically incompetent because they're presumed not to understand the meaning of their actions. However, they can be the object of vows of valuation, so a parent could make a valuation of a child.

Conversely, there are people who can take vows of valuation but not be their object. A hermaphrodite, who has both male and female genitalia, and a tumtum, the Talmudic term for someone with concealed genitalia, can't be valuated—not because their lives are valueless, but because the scale of valuation depends on a clear division between male and female (2a).

The term used in the Torah to describe valuation of a person is nefesh, a soul, which implies that only a living person can be the object of a valuation. If you promise to pay the Temple the value of a dead person or one who is about to be executed, the promise is legally meaningless. This distinction leads the Talmud once again to questions about when a fetus becomes a legally independent person. If a pregnant woman is sentenced to death, should the execution be delayed until after she gives birth?

This problem would rarely have arisen in practice, since as tractate Sanhedrin says, Jewish courts almost never issued death sentences. But in principle, a pregnant woman can be executed, which suggests that the law doesn't consider the fetus an independent being. Not until labor has begun and the woman "sat on the travailing chair," the seat used during childbirth, must the execution be postponed, since "once the fetus uproots, it is an independent body" (7a).

This principle turns out to have important implications for inheritance law. In the ancient world, if a mother and child both died in childbirth it would usually have been impossible to determine which died first. If the mother died first, even by a few minutes, her son would inherit her property, so after his death the estate would go to his paternal relatives. But if the boy died first, the mother's property would go to her own relatives. To avoid this uncertainty, the Talmud says that in such cases the child is always considered to have died first. "Since the fetus's vitality is minimal, the Angel of Death's drop of poison enters his body and cuts the two organs that must be severed in ritual slaughter," the trachea and the esophagus.

In addition to pledges based on the value of a life, one can make pledges tied to other aspects of one's person, as in "it is incumbent upon me to donate my weight." This ordinarily involves specifying what material you are measuring your weight in, silver or gold. But "if he did not specify the means of payment, he may exempt himself with any material," the Talmud says, so long as it has some monetary value. "In a place where merchants weigh pitch when selling it," you could get away with donating your body weight in pitch—a much cheaper alternative to gold. But a man should always pay "in keeping with his status": if he's rich enough to pay in gold, he shouldn't try to get away with paying in pitch (19a).

In addition to your weight, you can also pledge to donate your height, which is calculated using a "thick rod that cannot be bent" made of silver or gold. Things get more complicated if someone promises to donate "the weight of my forearm" or "the weight of my leg," which are hard to measure. But the Talmud suggests a method based on the principle of displacement. Fill a barrel with water and put your arm or leg into it, which will cause an equivalent volume of water to overflow, and then add donkey flesh to the barrel until the water level is full again. The weight of the donkey flesh will equal the weight of the limb. Of course, as Rabbi Yosei points out, this assumes that donkey flesh has the same density as human flesh, which may not be correct: "Is it possible to match flesh with flesh, sinews with sinews, and bones with bones"? But Rabbi Yehuda replies that it's close enough.

A pledge to donate the weight of a limb is valid, but a formal vow of valuation can't be made on a limb, because the Torah's scale of value only applies to whole human beings. Likewise, if you vow to donate "half of my valuation," you simply divide your Torah-assigned valuation in half. But if you say you're going to donate "the value of half of myself," you must pay the full amount, because it's impossible for half a person to survive.

Tractate Temura, whose name means "substitution," deals with the question of whether an animal consecrated for sacrifice can be substituted for a different one. The question is more complicated than it might seem, because the Torah apparently contradicts itself on this point. According to Leviticus 27:9–10, "an animal given to the Lord becomes holy. They must not exchange it or substitute a good one for a bad one, or a bad one for a good one; if they should substitute one animal for another, both it and the substitute become holy." In other words, the Torah first prohibits substitution and then implies that it is still effective.

The Mishna in Temura 2a shares this ambiguity: "Everyone substitutes, both men and women; not that it is permitted for a person to effect substitution; rather, if one substituted, the substitution takes effect," though the person receives lashes. As the Gemara points out, this is "difficult." How can the act of substitution have legal force if it is forbidden? Rava and Abaye, one of the Talmud's most important pairs of antagonists, disagree on this point. According to Rava, a forbidden action is ritually meaningless: "If one performed it, it is not effective at all" (4a). On this view, if you consecrated a sheep and then tried to substitute a different sheep for it, the first sheep would remain consecrated and the second sheep would be unconsecrated.

But Abaye argues that even forbidden actions have a real ritual effect: "With regard to any matter that the Merciful One states in the Torah not to perform, if one performed it, his action is effective, but the violator is flogged." He makes the point that if substitution had no effect at all, it wouldn't be punishable by lashes, since there would be nothing to punish—the offender would just have uttered meaningless syllables. Rava counters that this doesn't necessarily follow. Perhaps the punishment isn't for the action itself but for the defiant intention behind it, "because he transgressed the statement of the Merciful One."

The Gemara supports Abaye's position by showing that there are a number of forbidden acts that are nonetheless valid. A high priest is forbidden to marry a widow, but if he does they are legally married. When tithing produce, you're not supposed to pick the worst-quality crops to give to the priests, but if you do, it is still a valid tithe. And as Bava Kamma says, in certain circumstances a thief becomes the legal owner of the items he steals, even though theft is against the law.

The Talmud rarely acknowledges that the animal sacrifices it discusses in such detail are no longer performed. But there is an exception in Temura, when the rabbis discuss whether it's permitted to use "artifice" to get around the obligation of sacrificing every firstborn animal. The problem is that while the absence of the Temple makes sacrifices impossible, firstborn animals are still born consecrated to God, which means they can't be eaten or used for labor. Instead, as we saw in Bechorot, they are supposed to be left to graze until they develop a blemish that renders them unfit for sacrifice.

Rav Yehuda offers a way to get around this: "It is permitted to inflict a blemish upon a firstborn before it left the womb and entered into the air of the world" (24b). If you reach into the womb and clip the animal's ear, it will be born with a blemish that renders it unfit for sacrifice, making it unnecesssary to wait for a blemish to develop. The Gemara acknowledges that this technique would be forbidden "when the Temple is standing," but "today, when offerings are not able to be sacrificed," it is permitted. God isn't really being deprived of anything when you deliberately blemish a firstborn animal, since it couldn't have been sacrificed anyway.

The most fearful penalty in Jewish law isn't flogging or even stoning, but karet. Tractate Karetot begins its discussion of the laws of karet by listing thirty-six sins that earn this punishment, including Shabbat violation, breaking the Yom Kippur fast, profaning the Temple, idol worship, and various sexual transgressions. Missing, however, is what might seem like the most important information of all: What is karet? If you receive this punishment, what actually happens to you?

In the Torah, a version of the word karet appears in the recurring formula "his soul shall be cut off from among his people," which sounds like a form of excommunication. Jewish tradition, however, interprets karet as a punishment inflicted by God, variously defined as early death, childlessness, or the extinction of the soul after death. The sins that earn karet are committed against God rather than human beings, so it makes sense that they are left up to God to punish.

The reason why tractate Karetot belongs in Seder Kodashim is that if someone unwittingly commits a sin punishable by karet, he can atone by bringing a sin offering. The most effective atonement for sins is Yom Kippur: "Once Yom Kippur passed, there is no remaining sin, as Yom Kippur atoned for him," Reish Lakish says (7a). As the Gemara notes, however, atonement is supposed to depend on repentance. What happens to a person who refuses to repent, insisting that "Yom Kippur does not atone" for his sins? Reish Lakish believes that the power of Yom Kippur is so great that it even atones for one who rejects atonement, but the rabbis conclude that "Yom Kippur only atones for those who repent."

Sacrifices can only atone for unwitting sins, leading the Talmud to ask what it means to sin without knowing you're sinning. If you unwittingly violate Shabbat by performing several of the thirty-nine forbidden categories of labor, how many sacrifices do you need to bring—just one for violating Shabbat, or a separate sacrifice for each type of labor you performed? The answer depends on which part of the sin involved lack of awareness. If you knew it was Shabbat but did work unintentionally, you need to bring a sacrifice for each category of work. If you didn't know it was Shabbat in the first place, the sin lies in your forgetfulness of the day, so you only need to bring one sacrifice no matter how many kinds of work you did (3a).

Idol worship, too, might involve several types of forbidden actions; slaughtering an animal, burning incense, pouring a libation, and bowing down to an idol are all prohibited. But here the rule for atonement is somewhat different than for Shabbat violation. If you bowed down in a temple of Venus or Baal because you thought you were in a synagogue, you haven't sinned at all, since what matters is whether "your heart is directed toward Heaven." If you bow to an idol deliberately but only "out of love or out of fear"—to curry favor or avoid persecution—you are guilty of unintentional idol worship, which requires a sacrifice for atonement. Only someone who worships an idol out of genuine religious conviction receives karet.

Theoretically, there's another way to commit unintentional idol worship—if you don't know that it's forbidden. But how could you ever find such a Jew, Rav Pappa wonders? The only person who could be so ignorant is "a child who was taken captive among the gentiles" and raised in ignorance of Judaism.

Meila, Tamid, Middot, and Kinnim
On stealing from God, a day in the life of the Temple, and avian brainteasers.

Once an animal has been consecrated to God, it's forbidden to derive any personal benefit from it. The misuse of consecrated items is the sin of meila, and according to Leviticus 5:15, atoning for it requires paying back the value of the item plus an extra one-fifth, as well as offering a sacrificial ram. Meila comes up in various connections throughout the Talmud. In tractate Pesachim, for instance, there is a discussion of whether Rabbi Yochanan ben Zakkai committed meila when he sat in the shade of the Temple's walls to teach Torah, since this was a way of deriving personal benefit from the building. (The conclusion is that he didn't, because only the inside of the Temple is sacred.)

Tractate Meila focuses specifically on the misuse of sacrificial animals. The Talmud explains that an animal is only subject to misuse when it is an "offering of the most sacred order," belonging entirely to God. If at any point it has "a period of fitness to the priests," when it can be eaten by human beings, it's no longer subject to meila. One consequence of this rule is that if slaughter isn't carried out properly—for instance, the animal is killed in the southern half of the Temple courtyard, rather than in the northern half as required—it can never be eaten. It became a "most sacred" offering when it was consecrated, and since it can't ascend to the altar, it can never reach the stage of being fit for consumption by the priests.

The same principle applies to other types of consecrated items: "Anything whose mitzva has been performed" is no longer subject to meila. Thus consecrated wine belongs to God until it's poured on the altar as a libation, but once it flows away into the drainpipes it is no longer subject to meila. That's the theory, anyway, but according to Rabbi Elazar bar Rabbi Tzadok, the priests did treat wine as sacred even after it was poured. Every seventy years, he says, the drainpipes would be cleaned and the congealed wine would come out in a state resembling "dried cakes of pressed figs."

To dispose of them, the priests "would burn them in sanctity," suggesting that the refuse was still sacred long after its mitzva was performed (11b).

The Gemara resolves the contradiction by saying that this wasn't required by Torah law. Rather, the wine dregs were burned by rabbinic edict, because if they were eaten or sold people might think the same could be done with consecrated wine itself. Similarly, ash from the altar wasn't sold for fertilizer and priests' linen garments weren't reused.

The Talmud wonders whether the consecration of an animal extends to its secretions. If a consecrated ewe gives birth to a lamb, is she allowed to nurse it, or would this constitute meila because her milk is also consecrated? This was apparently a matter of dispute, with some authorities allowing nursing and others forbidding it. Rav's view is that since an animal "cannot exist without blood," its blood is considered part of its body and so is subject to meila. But an animal can exist without the milk it produces, which means that its milk is a separate substance, not subject to misuse. Rav Mesharshiyya asks how this rule applies to an animal's dung, which is like blood in the sense that "the animal cannot exist without dung"—everything living has to excrete. The Gemara responds that there's a difference, since dung "comes to the animal from an external source." Food that passes through an animal and emerges in the form of dung isn't part of its body (12b).

In the case of animal flesh or dung, using it means using it up, depriving the Temple of a potentially valuable resource. But if you drink out of a consecrated cup or wear a consecrated ring, they can still be used afterward. Do these nondestructive acts also constitute meila? The Talmud decides that meila is only committed when "the individual both damages and derives benefit from sacred items," but damage can be construed broadly. Gold isn't used up immediately, like wood or meat, but over a long period of time it does sustain wear and tear, so drinking out of a gold cup or wearing a gold ring is a form of meila.

In addition to offerings brought by individuals, the priests sacrificed two lambs in the Temple every day, one in the morning and one in the afternoon. This olat tamid or perpetual offering is the nominal subject of tractate Tamid. But the Talmud uses that as an occasion to discuss the daily workings of the Temple in general, including where the priests slept and how their tasks were assigned. In the Daf Yomi cycle, Tamid is followed by

Middot, a tractate of the Mishna that has no Gemara. It offers a detailed verbal blueprint of the Temple's various rooms and their functions—such as the wood chamber, where priests would pick worms out of the logs meant for burning on the altar, and the chamber of the nazirites, where a nazirite completing a vow would cut off the hair he had allowed to grow.

The rabbis' curiosity about such details is limitless, since they knew the Temple only as an abandoned ruin. Reconstructing its workings on the basis of oral traditions and Biblical references was a way of restoring it in virtual form, in anticipation of the actual rebuilding that will be accomplished by the Messiah.

Tamid and Middot explain that the Temple was never unoccupied. At night, three priests and twenty-one Levites kept watch at specified locations. The Temple Mount was also patrolled by a guard, who would check on the watchmen to make sure they didn't fall asleep. If the guard found someone asleep on the job he "used to beat him with his rod. And he had permission to burn his clothes. And the others would say: What is the noise in the courtyard? It is the cry of a Levite who is being beaten and whose clothes are being burned, because he was asleep at his watch" (Middot 1:2).

The priests designated for the next day's service would sleep in the Temple the night before, to be ready to begin the ceremonies at daybreak. They slept in a large hall called the Chamber of the Hearth, where there was a fire to keep them warm. There were no beds, however, since as Abaye explains, "It is not proper conduct to bring beds into the Temple" (26b). Instead, the older priests slept on stone benches and the younger ones slept on the floor, using their ritual vestments as a pillow.

The Gemara in Tamid is doubtful about this detail, however, for two reasons. Using priestly vestments as a pillow seems to constitute meila, since it means deriving personal benefit from a sacred object. To make matters worse, the vestments included a belt made of mixed linen and wool fibers, a combination that is strictly prohibited for every purpose except priestly service. According to Rabbi Shimon, "Even if there are ten mattresses piled one atop the other and a garment of diverse kinds is placed beneath all of them, it is prohibited to sleep upon them."

The rabbis propose a few ways to meet these objections. Maybe the priests didn't sleep with the vestments under their heads but next to them; or maybe it's only the belt of the High Priest that contains wool and linen, while the belts of regular priests were all linen. But the clinching argument is that the priests were allowed to wear vestments inside the Temple even when they weren't actively carrying out a ritual. Since this was a kind of personal benefit, it follows that it's permitted to derive benefit from the vestments so long as the priest is inside the Temple.

Wearing them outside the Temple grounds is strictly prohibited. This only happened once in history, in the fourth century BCE, when the high priest Shimon HaTzaddik, "the Righteous," put on his white Yom Kippur vestments to plead with Alexander the Great not to destroy the Temple. This emergency justified the sacrilege, as the Talmud explains by quoting Psalms 119:126: "It is time to act for the Lord, they have nullified your Torah." The Gemara goes on to relate a series of ten riddles that Alexander posed to the Jewish sages of his day. Which was created first, the heavens or the earth? Is it better to live on dry land or at sea? And so on. Of course, the sages knew all the answers. Even when Alexander posed the dangerous question of why the Jews resisted him despite his record of military success, they weren't afraid to respond, "Sometimes even Satan is victorious." The emperor was furious and threatened to have the sages killed, but they dissuaded him and ended up giving him useful advice about how to conquer Africa (32a).

These legends are presented alongside the most matter-of-fact details about the Temple: how many sacred implements were stored in the Chamber of Vessels (ninety-three in all), what kind of wood was used for the pyre on the altar (fig, nut, and pine were preferred, while olive was forbidden on account of its knots). The altar itself was made of uncut stone; no iron tool could be used to shape the stones, since iron is used for weapons of war. When the altar was whitewashed every Friday, the plaster couldn't even be applied with an iron trowel, so a cloth was used instead (Middot 3:4).

Regular whitewashing was needed because the altar was splashed with blood from animal sacrifices several times a day. Slaughter took place in the courtyard near the altar, according to a strict protocol. As soon as the eastern sky was lit up as far as Hebron, a lamb was selected from the Chamber of Lambs and given a final inspection for blemishes. Then it was bound, with the two legs on each side tied together, and its neck was secured in one of the twenty-four rings affixed to the Temple courtyard for this purpose. For the morning sacrifice, the second ring at the northwest corner of the altar was used, and for the evening sacrifice the second ring at the northeast corner. The lamb's head was positioned facing south, while its face was turned west (30b). After its throat was cut and its blood collected for the altar, the carcass would be flayed and dismembered.

Dealing with the ashes of the previous day's sacrifices was the priests' first task in the morning. The ash was swept into a pile on the altar until it became so big that it had to be removed. According to the Mishna in Tamid 28b, the pile sometimes reached three hundred kor, equivalent to about eighteen thousand gallons. The Gemara is skeptical of this fantastic figure, however, and Rabbi Ami admits that sometimes the sages speak about the Temple using exaggerated language. Another example is the description of the curtain at the entrance to the Holy of Holies, which is said to have cost 820,000 gold dinars and taken three hundred men to lift. Once the Temple was no longer a real place but a concept in the minds of Torah scholars, there was no limit to how splendid it could become.

Most of Seder Kodashim is concerned with sacrificing large animals like lambs and bulls, but some offerings call for birds instead. In particular, a woman who has given birth but can't afford to sacrifice a lamb can bring a pair of pigeons or doves, known collectively as a nest. That's why Kinnim, "nests," is the only tractate to use female pronouns for the person bringing the sacrifice. Kinnim is just three pages long, but it includes such complicated math problems that it's considered one of the most challenging sections of the Mishna. Like Middot, it's included in the Daf Yomi cycle even though it has no Gemara.

When a woman offers a nest, one bird is sacrificed as a burnt offering and the other as a sin offering. The woman can either designate which bird is for which purpose or she can leave it to the priest to decide. The problem that generates all the discussion in Kinnim is that unlike sheep, which generally stay in a pen when you put them there, pigeons can fly. That makes it easy for different pairs to get mixed up with each other, creating a problem for the priest. How does he know which bird is intended for which sacrifice? The Talmud says he can't run even a tiny risk of sacrificing a sin offering as a burnt offering or vice versa: "Even if only one fledgling became intermingled with ten thousand fledglings of another type of offering, they all shall be placed in isolation until they die" (1:2).

This problem may have arisen sometimes in real life, but in Kinnim, it seems to have been used by some mathematically inclined rabbis as an excuse for inventing logic problems. If you have a certain number of birds but don't know which bird is a sin offering and which a burnt offering, how can you maximize the number of acceptable pairs while ensuring that no bird is sacrificed for the wrong purpose?

Say that two women—the Talmud doesn't use names, but for convenience we can call them Rachel and Leah—each bring three pairs of birds to sacrifice, and they get mixed up. Now there are twelve birds, and there's no way to tell which belonged to which woman or were designated for which sacrifice. You might think that the priest could simply call six of them burnt offerings and six of them sin offerings. But if he did, he would run the risk that both members of one of the original pairs would end up being offered in the same category, which would mean that one of them was definitely invalid. To avoid this, the priest can sacrifice only six birds, three as sin offerings and three as burnt offerings, while the other six must be left to die of natural causes.

Next, imagine that one bird from a pair brought by Leah flies away and joins a group of three pairs belonging to Rachel. Now Leah has one bird and Rachel has seven. The priest can sacrifice six of Rachel's birds, since that group originally contained three burnt offerings and three sin offerings. The problem is that there's no way of knowing whether the seventh bird originally belonged to Rachel or to Leah. As a result, not only can Rachel's seventh bird not be sacrificed, neither can the one remaining bird from Leah's original pair. That's because Leah's second bird might have been among the six birds sacrificed. If it was killed as a burnt offering, Leah's remaining bird would have to go for a sin offering, and vice versa; but since there's no way to know for sure, the solo bird can't be sacrificed at all.

Finally, Kinnim imagines a situation involving seven women, each with an increasing number of pairs: the first woman has one pair, the second two pairs, and so on. Imagine that one bird from the first woman's pair flew to join the second woman's two pairs, giving her five birds; and then one of those birds flew to join the third woman's three pairs, giving her seven birds; and so on, until the last woman ends up with fifteen birds. How many birds can each woman safely sacrifice? Now say that the process was reversed, so that one of the seventh woman's fifteen birds joined the sixth woman's group, and so on, until the first woman had two birds again—but none of the women can be sure that the birds they ended up with are the same ones they started with. How many birds could each sacrifice now?

Obviously, this dilemma could never have arisen in real life. It's a pure math problem, a way of thinking about probabilities long before the invention of probability theory. But Kinnim is just as worthy of study as every other area of the law. In the Talmud, any kind of thinking is sacred if it's applied to solving Jewish problems.

Nidda On menstruation, ejaculation, and why girls are wiser than boys.

The sixth order of the Mishna, Seder Tahorot, deals with ritual purity—a complicated system of taboos that governed many aspects of ancient Jewish life, including food preparation and burial practices. The concepts of pure and impure, tahor and tamei, are discussed throughout the Talmud, but they were mainly of concern to priests, who had to be ritually pure in order to enter the Temple.

After the Temple was destroyed, that issue was moot. In addition, it became impossible to offer the sacrifices that restored ritual purity after certain kinds of contamination. Eventually the rabbis decided that all Jews are presumptively impure. But one type of ritual purity is still practiced today: the prohibition on sexual intercourse between a man and a menstruating woman, who is referred to in Hebrew as a nidda, from the word for "separate." Of the twelve tractates in Seder Tahorot, only Nidda has Gemara in the Babylonian Talmud.

The basic rule is stated in Leviticus 15:19: "When a woman has a discharge, her discharge being blood from her body, she shall remain in her impurity seven days; whoever touches her shall be unclean until evening." Violating this rule is a serious sin, punishable by karet. The problem is that menstrual cycles can be unpredictable. Tractate Nidda begins with a practical question: If a woman examines herself and finds menstrual blood, can she assume that her period just started, or is it possible that it started earlier and she didn't notice?

This question is a subject of dispute between Hillel and Shammai. Usually Shammai takes a stricter line, but this time he is the more lenient one, saying that "For all women, their time is sufficient." In other words, a woman's impurity begins from the moment she finds menstrual blood, and she doesn't have to worry about having missed the signs earlier. Hillel, on the other hand, says that purity is reckoned "from examination to examination" (2a).

Since a woman's period might have begun at any time since her last "clean" self-examination, she is considered retroactively impure for that whole time.

Hillel's view assumes that a woman can begin menstruating without realizing it, since she might mistake the flow of blood for "the sensation of her flow of urine." The Gemara agrees that menstruation feels like urination, arguing that a woman wouldn't sleep through the beginning of her period because "due to her discomfort she would awaken, just as it is with the sensation of the need to urinate" (3a). Of course, the rabbis could have clarified this point by asking a woman what menstruation feels like, but there's no indication that they did. Occasionally in the Talmud a sage will quote his mother or wife, but not here.

The law usually follows Hillel's opinion, but in this case there is a compromise: A woman only has to be concerned about the twenty-four hours before she discovered blood, on the assumption that she wouldn't have missed the signs of menstruation for longer than that. If she examined herself within the past twenty-four hours, she only has to be concerned about the time since the examination. These rules, however, only apply to women who don't have a fixed menstrual cycle, meaning that they can't predict the date of their period. Women whose cycle is predictable don't have to worry about retroactive impurity at all.

If a woman has a vaginal discharge but isn't sure whether it's menstrual blood, it's up to her rabbi to inspect the stain. The Talmud finds an allusion to this duty in Deuteronomy 17:8, which refers to judging "between blood and blood"; Rabbi Oshaya interprets this as meaning "between pure blood and impure blood" for the purposes of nidda. The Mishna in Nidda 19a says that vaginal discharge can come in many colors, including red, black, "like the bright crocus," "like diluted wine," like water in which fenugreek has been soaked, and green.

The Gemara carefully analyzes each of these shades to determine when they are a sign of impurity. Is the red of menstrual blood best compared to the blood of an ox, a bird, or a louse? If a woman kills a louse in her clothes and later finds a blood stain, can she assume it's from the bug or might it be menstrual blood? A black stain is a sign of impurity if it's the color of ink or a grape, but not if it's like tar or an olive. As for the crocus, the Gemara explains that this refers to the crimson center of the flower, which is used to make saffron. Shmuel adds that all discharges should be examined on a white cloth, so the color stands out clearly (20a).

Menstruation is the main subject of Nidda, but there is also a way for men to become ritually impure. According to Leviticus 15:16, "When a man has an emission of semen, he shall bathe his whole body in water and remain unclean until evening." The parallel between menstruation and ejaculation makes a kind of sense, but the Talmud views the two types of emission very differently. Menstruation takes place automatically, and while it's obviously related to reproduction, it's not part of the sexual act or accompanied by sexual pleasure. Accordingly, there's no shame associated with menstruation; the Talmud treats it as a fact of life that must be regulated by Jewish law.

Ejaculation, however, is seen a dangerous temptation for men, since it can be brought about deliberately. As the story of Onan warns, semen is supposed to be used for procreative sex, and wasting it is a serious sin. To prevent masturbation, the Talmud establishes strict rules about how a man should handle his penis. For women, inspecting their genitals for signs of an emission is "praiseworthy," but if a man does the same thing, his hand "should be severed." That's because women "are not susceptible to arousal" when they touch themselves, but men are (13a).

Even if a woman does masturbate, it's not as serious a sin as it is for a man, since the consequences of wasting semen are literally cosmic. According to Rabbi Yosei, "the son of David will not come until all the souls of the body have been finished." God created a finite supply of human souls, and the world can't come to an end until they are all born. Wasting semen means throwing away an opportunity to bring one of these souls to earth, thus delaying the arrival of the Messiah.

This idea, which is elaborated in later kabbalistic tradition, helps to explain rabbinic Judaism's contradictory attitudes toward sex. Sex within marriage is warmly encouraged in the Talmud: all sexual practices are permitted and husbands owe sexual gratification to their wives. At the same time, Rabbi Yochanan says that "anyone who emits semen for naught"—which includes any sex act that couldn't lead to conception—"is liable to receive death at the hand of Heaven."

To avoid the temptation to masturbate, the Talmud prohibits men from touching their penises for any reason. To check for a seminal emission, a man should use "a rock or a piece of earthenware" to scrape off any fluid. Rabbi Eliezer says that touching one's penis is even forbidden while urinating: "anyone who holds his penis and urinates, it is considered as though he is bringing a flood into the world." Rabbi Ami explains that erections are a gateway sin: once you start "arousing the evil inclination," you'll end up worshiping idols.

As for the statement that a man who touches his penis should have his hand severed, the Gemara wonders whether it is meant to be taken literally or as a hyperbolic "curse." According to Rabbi Tarfon, it means just what it says: "If one's hand goes to his penis, his hand should be severed upon his navel." Even if a man has a thorn stuck in his belly and will die unless he removes it, Tarfon forbids him to move his hand in the direction of his genitals: "It is preferable that his belly be split open, and he should not descend into the pit of destruction" (13b).

In addition to its implications for ritual purity, the onset of menstruation is also important as a sign of puberty, which in Jewish law marks the transition to legal adulthood. For both sexes, becoming an adult involves biology as well as chronology: a boy must be thirteen years old and have grown two pubic hairs, while a girl must be twelve years old with two pubic hairs. The hair is significant not in itself but as as a marker of puberty, which is supposed to bring greater mental and emotional maturity. That's why the ages are different for boys and girls; according to Yehuda HaNasi, "the Holy One, Blessed be He, granted a woman a greater understanding than a man," so she attains maturity sooner (45b).

For the purpose of taking vows, the Talmud also recognizes a transitional phase that begins one year before legal adulthood, starting at eleven for girls and twelve for boys. The vow of a child has no legal validity: "Even if they said: We know in Whose name we vowed . . . their vow is not a vow." The vow of an adult, on the other hand, is always binding: "Even if they said: We do not know in Whose name we vowed . . . their vow is a vow." But during the transitional year, a young person's vows are examined by a rabbi to determine if they were made with sufficient understanding to be valid.

Puberty is defined by what the Talmud calls "the signs below," the growth of pubic hair. For girls, this involves an inspection carried out by a woman, and some sages would entrust the task to their own female relatives: "Rabbi Eliezer would give the girls to his wife to examine, and Rabbi Yishmael would give the girls to his mother to examine" (48b). But as the Gemara observes, for women puberty also involves "the signs above," the development of breasts. Different sages define this as when "a fold appears below the breast" or when "the areola darkens." If a girl develops the upper signs before the lower signs, is that sufficient for her to be considered a legal adult?

After some debate, the rabbis decide that problem can never arise, because it's impossible for a girl to develop breasts before she grows pubic hair. If that appears to be the case, it can only be because the hairs "appeared but later they fell out." Again, this is a question the rabbis could have resolved by asking a woman—maybe one of those wives and mothers—but there's no sign that they did. More than any other tractate, Nidda raises the question of how different Jewish law might be if women had been able to take part in shaping it.

Conclusion

"The school of Elijah taught: Anyone who studies the laws every day is guaranteed that he is destined for the World to Come." With these words—the last sentence on the last page of tractate Nidda—I concluded my Daf Yomi journey on January 4, 2020, after almost seven and a half years.

A few days earlier, on January 1, I had attended the Siyum HaShas at MetLife Stadium, fulfilling the goal that had led me to Daf Yomi in 2012. The venue seemed almost deliberately chosen to illustrate the words of the Hadran, the prayer that Talmud students say when they complete a tractate. It draws a pointed distinction between those who study Talmud and idlers "who sit on street corners": "We run, and they run. We run toward eternal life, and they run to a pit of desolation." Just so, instead of cheering for running backs, the crowd of eighty thousand—almost all ultra-Orthodox Jews, almost all men—applauded the heads of rabbinic academies who gave speeches in praise of Talmud study.

Yet the event also showed, in large ways and small, how fluently Orthodox Judaism speaks the American idiom. As at a football game, the press gallery was full of reporters, and the luxury suites had been rented out to families and groups. On the stadium's video crawl, instead of statistics about touchdowns, there were statistics about Talmud—which is the shortest chapter and which the longest, or how many times a particular rabbinic sage is mentioned in the text. In between speeches, the Jumbotrons showed expertly produced videos including "Heroes of the Daf," an inspirational montage featuring people who overcame obstacles to learn their page of Talmud every day. Among them was a Brooklyn man suffering from advanced ALS, who managed to study with the help of a computer that responds to his eye movements.

The culmination of the day-long event came when those who were completing the Daf Yomi cycle were invited to stand and recite the Hadran. Few of the attendees, it turned out, were actually "making a siyum"; as at a football game, the players were far outnumbered by those who had come to cheer them on. After some internal debate, I decided not to stand. I looked conspicuously secular compared to the Hasidim in my section, and I knew that my Talmud study was done in a different spirit than theirs. Maybe I was being too self-conscious. After all, one person attended the Siyum dressed as Waldo from the *Where's Waldo* books, which made for an excellent visual joke—a red-and-white-striped jersey among the sea of black hats and coats. A photo of the prank went viral on Jewish Twitter.

During the years I was writing about my Daf Yomi experience, I was sometimes asked whether it had made me a better Jew. My answer—a good Talmudic answer—was "No, but . . . " For pious Jews like those at the Siyum, Torah study is a devotional exercise. The student learns how to live in this world while earning spiritual reward in the next world. These weren't my reasons for learning Talmud, and at the end of seven and a half years I was no more observant than I was when I began. In fact, the gulf between the way I understand the world and the way rabbinic tradition understands it only widened as I came to know more about the Talmud's moral and metaphysical assumptions.

At the same time, doing Daf Yomi was by far the most important Jewish experience of my adult life. It made me more knowledgeable about what Judaism is, more thoughtful about the meaning of Jewish law, more connected to the Jewish past. It also helped me understand more about Orthodox Jewish experience today—something most non-Orthodox Jews know so little about that we don't even know what we don't know.

This was brought home to me early in the Daf Yomi cycle when I wrote in *Tablet* about the Talmud's rule for how to put on shoes in the morning. According to Shabbat 61a, there are two teachings on this subject: Rabbi Yochanan says you should put on your left shoe first, while a baraita says you should start with the right shoe. These rules appear irreconcilable, leading Rav Yosef to conclude that either way is acceptable. But Mar, the son of Rabbana, found a way of satisfying both. First he would put on his right shoe without tying the laces, then he would put on his left shoe, then tie the left shoe, and finally tie the right shoe. In this way, each shoe could be first.

As I would come to recognize, this is a very Talmudic approach to problem-solving. The rabbis often maximize the opportunity to perform mitzvot by creatively redefining the terms of the problem. It is also a very Talmudic way of thinking about what matters to God, which is absolutely everything, down to something as trivial as which shoe you put on first in the morning. In my *Tablet* column, I wrote about how I found this way of thinking about God unfamiliar and challenging. The most enlightening response I got was from an Orthodox reader who said—more or less in these words—"Why should I read anything you say about the Talmud if you don't even know something as basic as how to put on your shoes?" In an Orthodox home, children are taught the Talmudic rule as soon as they start to wear shoes. The fact that I could consider myself somewhat knowledgeable about Judaism while not knowing something so basic illustrates the depth of the divisions between Orthodox and non-Orthodox Jews.

For traditional Judaism, the rigors of halakha are justified because they bring the Jew into contact with God. The strictness of the Talmud lies not so much in its attitude toward punishment, which is often surprisingly lenient, but in its demanding choreography of everyday life. Joseph Soloveitchik, the Rav of modern Orthodoxy, extolled this strictness in his book *Halakhic Man*: "When halakhic man approaches reality, he comes with his Torah, given to him from Sinai, in hand. He orients himself to the world by means of fixed statutes and firm principles."

In addition to obeying those statutes, rabbinic Judaism insists that we study and understand them, and Talmud study offered many generations of Jews a rigorous education. Mastering the Talmud requires logical reasoning, textual interpretation, memory training, and mastery of two ancient languages. Certain tractates involve specialized knowledge of mathematics, astronomy, and anatomy. And then there are the practical skills the Talmud teaches, from inspecting slaughtered animals to examining leprous sores. No wonder the greatest sages are given the title gaon, meaning genius.

The modern Jewish world was born when many Jews began to feel that Talmud study was no longer a stimulus to intellectual creativity, but a waste of their mental powers on trivia and superstition. Solomon Maimon, born in Lithuania in 1753, was an illui, a child prodigy, who came to see the Talmud as a symbol of everything that was backward in Jewish life. As he records in his classic autobiography, he left his family to move to Berlin, the center of the Enlightenment, where he could apply his gifts to secular philosophy— work that really mattered.

Isaac D'Israeli, an English man of letters, expressed a similar feeling in his 1833 book *The Genius of Judaism*, where he describes the Talmud as "a system of barbarous learning," "a mass of ritual ordinances, casuistical glosses, and arbitrary decisions." "I would implore the Jews," he writes, "to begin to educate their youth as the youth of Europe, and not of Palestine; let their Talmud be removed to an elevated shelf, to be consulted as a curiosity of antiquity, and not as a manual of education." D'Israeli followed this principle in bringing up his own son, Benjamin Disraeli, who vindicated it by becoming prime minister of England.

Most of the Jews who came to America from Eastern Europe treated the Talmud the same way. The hero of Abraham Cahan's 1917 novel *The Rise of David Levinsky* begins life as a Talmud student in Eastern Europe, but quickly forgets his learning once he moves to America. There's no need for it, any more than there is for sidelocks, which a barber cuts off the day he lands in New York. David becomes a successful garment manufacturer, but he secretly wishes he was an educated man—not educated in Talmud, the way his ancestors were, but in some secular field such as medicine. Whenever he passed City College, David "felt like a convert Jew passing a synagogue." Cahan suggests that American Jews translated the ancient Jewish reverence for intellectual study into secular fields—which surely helps to explain why modern Jews have made such disproportionate contributions in science and the arts.

The result of American Judaism's abandonment of the Talmud is that non-Orthodox Jews generally take their ideas about halakha from hostile non-Jewish sources. One of the most famous Christian sayings is the apostle Paul's from 2 Corinthians 3:6: "the letter kills, but the spirit gives life." The idea that Judaism is obsessed with the letter of the law while Christianity transcends it can be found in European literature from Shakespeare to Hegel. In this view, the Talmud is synonymous with arid legalism. Indeed, in English the word "Talmudic" is pejorative, used to suggest perverse hairsplitting.

One reason why I wanted to study Talmud is that, as I read more deeply in modern Jewish literature, I came to realize the cost of this estrangement from Judaism's central texts and ideas. For most of the great twentieth-century American Jewish writers, the Talmud simply doesn't exist. Saul Bellow, with his profound spiritual gifts and cravings, never thinks of exploring Jewish tradition, though he has time for all kinds of eccentric gurus. Philip

Roth, a secularist through and through, rebels against Judaism without quite knowing what he's rebelling against.

European Jewish writers had a greater sense of what they had lost. In Franz Kafka's story "Before the Law," a spiritual seeker spends his entire life waiting for permission to pass through the door to "the Law," only to learn in his dying moments that the door was intended for him all along. There's nothing explicitly Jewish about this parable, but the idea that there is a divine law waiting for us to approach, which we fail to do out of sheer timidity, perfectly describes the relationship of most modern Jews to Torah and Talmud.

In the twenty-first century, however, non-Orthodox and even non-religious Jews are making a new effort to reclaim their textual heritage. In ways that I didn't anticipate in 2012 when I started the Daf Yomi cycle, my experience was part of a growing trend. Talmud study is increasingly popular in Conservative synagogues, Jewish community centers, and campus Hillels; I've had the opportunity to teach in some of these places, and seen how eager people are to explore the ancient text. In such settings, and even in some modern Orthodox schools, women are studying Talmud in greater numbers than ever before in Jewish history. In January 2020, the first international Siyum HaShas for Women drew 3,300 attendees. It was sponsored by Hadran, an Israeli nonprofit dedicated to advancing Talmud study for women, which offers its own Daf Yomi resources online.

This book is the product of my "return" to the Talmud, and I hope it will be useful to others who are curious about making their own journey. Even students like me who don't approach the Talmud with the traditional tools, or in the traditional spirit, can find meaning in the words of the Hadran: "We will return to you, Talmud Bavli, and you will return to us; our mind is on you and your mind is on us; we will not forget you and you will not forget us—not in this world and not in the next world."

ACKNOWLEDGMENTS

In August 2012, I was in Amherst, Massachusetts, for an event at the National Yiddish Book Center, when I had the idea of joining the Daf Yomi cycle that had just started. I sent an email to Alana Newhouse, the editor-in-chief of *Tablet*, to ask if she would be interested in a regular column about my Daf Yomi study. Her only question was whether I could start immediately—after all, the new cycle was already underway, and we wouldn't want to miss a week. Journalism is a business with short horizons, and at the time I had no idea whether I would actually be able to keep writing the column until the next Siyum HaShas, seven and a half years later. But Alana's commitment didn't waver for the entire 2,711 days, making it possible for me to complete the longest project of my professional life. I doubt any other editor would have done the same, and I will always be grateful to Alana for her support—this book wouldn't exist without it.

From 2012 to 2020, I worked on every one of the 288 columns with Matthew Fishbane, *Tablet*'s features editor, who helped me find the right form and tone for writing about my Talmud study. Along the way I often relied on the advice of Menachem Butler, a contributing editor at *Tablet* who is both extraordinarily knowledgeable about the world of Jewish studies and extraordinarily generous in sharing his knowledge. Menachem was my guide at the Siyum HaShas in 2020 and helped me see the whole event with the eyes of an insider.

Writing about the Talmud brought me into contact with the Orthodox Jewish world in a new way, and this turned out to be one of the most gratifying parts of the experience. From Agudath Israel, the ultra-Orthodox organization that sponsors the Siyum HaShas, to Yeshiva University, the leading modern Orthodox academic institution, and beyond, the rabbis and laypeople I met and corresponded with were always encouraging of my Talmud study and patient with my limitations, even though they knew my beliefs and assumptions were different from theirs. I'm particularly indebted to Matthew Miller of Koren Publishers Jerusalem, which publishes the English version of the Steinsaltz Talmud. Not long after I started my Talmud study, he reached out to me and offered to send me each volume of the Koren edition as it was published, an invaluable gift.

Studying the Talmud and sharing my reflections in *Tablet* was an experience of *klal Yisrael*, Jewish community, that I wish more American Jews could have—which is one of the reasons why I wanted to write this book. So I'm especially grateful that Sylvia Fried and Sue Ramin of Brandeis University Press welcomed my proposal for *Come and Hear* and helped shape the book to serve that purpose. Finally, I owe thanks to Erez DeGolan, doctoral candidate in the department of religion at Columbia University, who reviewed the manuscript and gave me the benefit of his knowledge of the Talmud and academic Talmudic scholarship. The errors and limitations that remain are, of course, my own.

INDEX

ABOUT THE AUTHOR

Adam Kirsch is a poet, literary critic, and journalist. He is the author of three collections of poems and five books of criticism and biography, including a study of Lionel Trilling, *Why Trilling Matters* (Yale University Press, 2011). His essays and reviews appear regularly in *The New Yorker*, the *New York Review of Books*, and other publications. A former book critic for the *New York Sun* and *The New Republic*, he is currently a contributing editor of the online magazine *Tablet* and an editor at the *Wall Street Journal*'s weekend reviews section. He is the author most recently of *The People and the Books: 18 Classics of Jewish Literature* (Norton, 2016) and *The Blessing and the Curse: The Jewish People and Their Books in the Twentieth Century* (Norton, 2020).